CORPORATE VALUATION
Tools for Effective Appraisal and Decision Making

Bradford Cornell

IRWIN
Professional Publishing
Burr Ridge, Illinois
New York, New York

Senior editor: Amy Hollands
Project editor: Jess Ann Ramirez
Production manager: Mary Jo Parke
Jacket designer: Randy Scott
Art coordinator: Heather Burbridge
Compositor: BookMasters
Typeface: 11/13 Palatino
Printer: Book Press, Inc.

Library of Congress Cataloging-in-Publication Data

Cornell, Bradford.
  Corporate valuation : tools for effective appraisal and decision making / Bradford Cornell.
    p.   cm.
  Includes index.
  ISBN 1-55623-730-8
  1. Corporations—Valuation.   2. Business enterprises—Valuation.
I. Title.
HG4028.V3C68   1993
658.15—dc20   92–42519

Printed in the United States of America
3 4 5 6 7 8 9 0   BP   0 9 8 7 6 5

Preface and Acknowledgments

This book is designed to be a bridge between the rarefied world of academic finance and the "what do we do today" world of managers, appraisers, regulators, and attorneys who have to value real companies. My realization of the need for such a book grew out of personal experience. First, as a professor of finance at UCLA for the past 15 years, I have come to appreciate the importance of new models developed by financial economists for the valuation of businesses. However, as founder of FinEcon, a consulting firm faced with the task of valuing actual companies, I have also learned that financial economic models are only one ingredient that goes into a successful appraisal. The problem is that despite all their mathematical complexity, financial models are at best crude approximations of real companies. In addition, the data available to an appraiser are typically far rougher than the information required to apply an academic model without alteration. As a result, appraisals of real companies involve a combination of academic theory, business judgment, knowledge of rules of thumb that work in practice, and experience.

Given the diverse nature of the information required to value a company, this book is neither an academic text nor an appraisal manual. Instead, it is best seen as an appraisal tool kit that demonstrates how all the tools of the trade can be used together. The book is designed to explain how academic models can be put to work, not how they are derived. This means going beyond the mathematical statement of the models and mixing them with approximations, business judgments, and tricks of the trade applied by practicing appraisers. However, appraisal practices and rules of thumb are not accepted as gospel. Their relation to underlying finance principles is explored to elucidate when such practical devices are likely to break down and produce misleading valuations.

As a result of the combination of theory and practice, the book may seem like a hodgepodge to some readers; however, the mixture of techniques reflects the current state of appraisal practice. Valuing a company is neither an art nor a science but an odd combination of both. There is enough science that appraisers are not left to rely solely on experience, but there is enough art that without experience and judgment, failure is assured.

As regards the preparation of this book, I want to thank my colleagues at FinEcon. John Hirshleifer, Grant Sugimoto, and Simon Cheng all spent innumerable hours discussing valuation with me, not only with respect to the book but also regarding the wide variety of companies we were asked to evaluate. My greatest debt, however, is to Lisa Grassi, who worked on the book with me from its inception, proofing every chapter, confirming every reference, and checking every calculation. Without her diligent effort, the project would never have been completed. Finally, I want to thank my wife and family who accepted the fact that I was undertaking another task that would occupy almost every evening for the better part of a year.

Bradford Cornell

Contents

Chapter One

Introduction

The idea that a critical goal of corporate management is to maximize value has remained a constant throughout the debate regarding the proper role of management. Too frequently, however, this goal is misunderstood. Value maximization is seen as conflicting with other corporate goals, such as winning market share or treating employees and customers fairly. The conflict is more imagined than real. Companies that do not pay sufficient attention to market share or fail to treat their customers and employees fairly will find that they are worth less than competing firms.

Value maximization has been the linchpin of financial management as it has been taught at virtually every American business school for the last 50 years. Despite this widespread acceptance in the academic community, however, the role of value maximization in corporate management received little public attention until the takeover wave of the 1980s began. The situation changed dramatically when competing management teams began fighting for control of corporations worth billions of dollars, raising the obvious question "who ought to win?" The answer provided by the court was that the victor, in most circumstances, should be the management team that could maximize value. Though the courts also expressed concern over the plight of noninvestor stakeholders, such as customers and employees, the courts recognized that companies that did not treat their customers and employees fairly would tend to be worth less, so judicial modification of the "maximize value" rule was unnecessary except in special situations.

The fight between Time, Inc., and Paramount Communications, Inc., for control of Warner Communications illustrates the the issue. Time and Warner were in the process of completing a merger when Paramount suddenly made a cash offer for Time in excess of the consideration Time shareholders would receive in the merger. To block Paramount, Time put in place a "poison pill," which imposed dire legal consequences on Paramount if it acquired more than a minimal fraction of Time's shares. In response, Paramount sued, asking the court for an injunction to invalidate the poison pill. In the suit, Paramount claimed that the poison pill was not in the interest of Time's shareholders and was simply a device designed to entrench Time's management by preventing a hostile takeover. The Time and Warner attorneys retorted that the pill was put in place to protect Time shareholders from an unfair offer. They argued, furthermore, that long-run shareholder value would be maximized by a combination of Time and Warner as originally planned, rather than a sale to Paramount. Paramount attorneys rejected Time-Warner's argument out of hand. How, they asked, could the unrealized long-run plan be worth more than Paramount's cash offer?

Despite their opposing stands, the attorneys for Paramount, Time, and Warner did agree that control of Time ought to go to the party that could maximize the "long-run" value of Time's shares. Time-Warner attorneys claimed value maximization would result from a Time-Warner merger, which would allow the long-run plan already in place to be realized. Paramount attorneys argued that Time shareholders could do no better than accept their cash offer. It was up to the court to decide.

The court ultimately sided with Time-Warner. An injunction to block the poison pill was not granted. Paramount's offer, which was contingent on removal of the pill, expired, and Time acquired Warner. From a valuation standpoint, the key element of the decision was not that Time-Warner won but that the court, in a trendsetting opinion, affirmed the view that the goal of corporate management is to maximize value. Value maximization was a key standard applied to evaluate the management plans.

The takeover battle of the 1980s also produced changes in the law that have more dire implications for managers and directors with respect to their duty to maximize value. In *Smith* v. *Van Gorkum*, the Delaware Supreme Court held that the directors breached their fiduciary duty in approving a merger without becoming adequately informed about its valuation consequences.

The litigation involved a class action suit brought by the shareholders of Trans Union Corporation challenging a merger of Trans Union into Marmon Group, Inc. The terms of the merger appeared generous. Shareholders of Trans Union were to receive $55 in cash for their shares, which were previously trading in the mid-$30s. This attractive premium caused shareholders to vote overwhelmingly in support of the merger. Following the shareholder vote, Trans Union directors approved the merger in a brief two-hour meeting without consulting an investment banker or other finance expert regarding the adequacy of the offer. Although the Delaware Court of Chancery, relying on the business judgment rule, dismissed the class action, the decision was reversed by the Delaware Supreme Court, which found the directors negligent. Among the factors cited by the Delaware Supreme Court for its decision was the lack of involvement of the directors and the absence of relevant valuation information possessed by the directors when approving the merger. The court concluded that the directors could not be attempting to maximize value if they were not in possession of the information necessary to measure value and found the directors personally liable for any resulting damages to shareholders.

The *Smith* v. *Van Gorkum* case was not unique. The directors of Walt Disney, Inc., were sued by Disney shareholders who argued that the board's decision to repurchase Disney shares from Saul Steinberg's Reliance, Inc., reduced the value of the remaining Disney shares. Attorneys for the Disney directors responded that the repurchase was necessary to maximize the long-run value of the shares. Nonetheless, the directors decided to settle the case for $50 million. Similarly, the directors of MGM/UA were sued by the firm's shareholders for failing to adequately investigate whether Kirk Kiekorian paid a fair price when he repurchased part of the company in a leveraged buyout in 1986. The directors settled for $20 million in 1990.

The message conveyed by these cases is unambiguous. Owners of a company's securities will hold managers and directors responsible for failing to maximize firm value. This raises an obvious practical question. How can managers be expected to maximize firm value unless managers understand what the value of a company depends on and how the value is to be measured. It is here that valuation theory and appraisal practice enter the picture. Whereas these may have been treated as arcane academic subjects in the past, they are now of central importance to managers. Executives must understand what determines value so that they can convince security holders and the courts that their actions are consistent with value maximization.

While it is true that managers can turn to appraisers and investment bankers to perform the valuation calculations, there are limitations to the reliance that can be put on outside advice. Management and the board are ultimately responsible for selecting the appraisers and investment bankers. Consequently, they must have sufficient grasp of valuation principles to make reasonable choices and to evaluate the work produced by appraisers and investment bankers. More importantly, managers need an intuitive understanding of what factors are most likely to affect firm value in order to make effective operating decisions. Value-maximizing decisions cannot be made without some knowledge of how value is determined in the marketplace.

Takeover-related issues are not the only reasons that companies need to be concerned with valuation theory. Every year, hundreds of thousands of American firms, from small privately held companies to giant corporations like AT&T, have to be appraised for a host of practical reasons. For instance, every state in the union requires that railroads and utilities operating within the state be appraised each year for the purpose of assessing property taxes. Appraisals are commonly required for estate tax purposes and in divorce proceedings. Initial public offerings require accurate appraisals in order to properly price the new securities. If the offering price is too high, the offer will fail; if the offering price is set too low, the issuing company will not receive full value for the securities sold. Regulatory policy is also related to valuation. One way to interpret public utility regulation, for example, is to say that regulators attempt to set rate of return on equity so that the value of a utility's shares equals the value of the assets financed by sale of equity. Recently, the growing popularity of employee stock option plans, or ESOPs, has greatly increased the need for annual appraisals. The ESOP association states that

The stock of a private company with an ESOP should generally be appraised at least every year. An appraisal is also usually needed before a company decides whether to set up an ESOP and is recommended for any significant transactions involving the ESOP.[1]

In short, understanding how to estimate the value of a business is no longer something that can be left to finance professionals. It is a practical problem of immediate concern to the managers, jurists, and regulators who determine the operating policies of America's corporations.

Despite the growing importance of appraisals for the management of American corporations, appraisal practice and its relation to finance theory is rarely covered in finance texts.[2] Corporate valuation is typically included only as an example to illustrate application of discounted cash flow analysis. Alternative approaches to valuation commonly used by appraisers, such as the adjusted book value approach and the direct comparison approach, typically are not covered at all. Discussion of actual appraisal practice and examples of how appraisals are performed, including analysis of the rules of thumb appraisers often employ, is nonexistent.

Conversely, books on appraisal practice suffer from the reverse problem in that they generally cover finance theory in an incomplete fashion. While the equations and models of modern finance may be presented, the theories on which the equations are based and the intuition underlying the theories are omitted. Such omission reduces appraisal practice to the application of a series of ad hoc rules of thumb with little underlying conceptual structure.

This book is designed to bridge the gap between finance theory and appraisal practice. As such, it is not another finance textbook nor an appraisal manual. The central topics of leading finance textbooks, including the time value of money, the derivation of

---

[1]Robert W. Smiley and Ronald J. Gilbert, *Employee Stock Ownership Plans* (New York: Prentice Hall, 1989), p. 15–1.

[2]Two exceptions to this rule are T. C. Copeland, T. Koller, and J. Murrin, *Valuation: Measuring and Managing the Value of Companies* (New York: John Wiley & Sons, 1990); and A. Rappaport, *Creating Shareholder Value* (New York: Free Press, 1986). However, in both of these books, the coverage of appraisal practice is limited to the discounted cash flow approach.

the capital asset pricing model, and the derivation of the Miller-Modigliani theorems on capital structure, are covered only tangentially. Instead, the book focuses on providing an intuitive understanding of finance theory as it applies to appraisal practice. A related goal of the book is to demonstrate how rules of thumb employed by appraisers are related to finance theory. For readers interested in the theoretical details, references are provided to finance articles and leading textbooks.[3]

In the same vein, the book is not a "how to" appraisal manual.[4] Topics such as what to do on a visit to the company being appraised and how to write an appraisal report are not included. In addition, appraisal problems that are unrelated to finance theory, such as how to conduct interviews with management so as to develop reliable forecasts of future cash flow, are omitted. This is not to imply that such subjects are unimportant. They are excluded to sharpen the focus on the relation between finance theory and appraisal practice.

In short, the book attempts to walk a fine line between appraisal practice and the finance theory on which it is based. This is difficult because appraisal is half art and half science. It builds off valuation models developed by financial theorists, but it does not stop there because estimating the value of a real business requires the application of judgment that can only be developed through experience. The key to successful appraisal is blending the art and the science. Too often, finance theorists dismiss the work of practical appraisers as ad hoc applications of rules of thumb, while practicing appraisers and managers dismiss the work of finance theorists as esoteric and irrelevant. The fairest assessment is that both views are wrong. Financial models have not developed to the point where they can be applied without prac-

---

[3]Four leading finance texts were relied on in the preparation of this book: R. A. Brealey and S. C. Myers, *Principles of Corporate Finance*, 4th ed. (New York: McGraw-Hill, 1991); T. C. Copeland and J. F. Weston, *Finance Theory and Corporate Policy*, 3rd ed. (Reading, Mass: Addison Wesley Publishing, 1988); S. A. Ross, R. W. Westerfield, and J. F. Jaffe, *Corporate Finance*, 2nd ed. (Homewood, Ill.: Richard D. Irwin 1990); and A. C. Shapiro, *Modern Corporate Finance* (New York: Macmillan, 1989).

[4]A detailed description of the appraisal process is contained in S. Pratt, *Valuing a Business*, 2nd ed. (Homewood, Ill.: Business One Irwin, 1989).

tical experience and judgment. On the other hand, appraisers who attempt to proceed without any understanding of finance theory are sure to go astray.

WHAT ARE WE TRYING TO APPRAISE?

It seems self-evident that the goal of an appraisal is to approximate the fair market value of a company. But there are two ambiguities in the phrase "fair market value of a company." What is meant by "fair market value" and what is meant by "a company"? The most quoted, if not the most succinct, definition of fair market value was that laid down by the Internal Revenue Service in March 1959. Revenue ruling 65-193 defines fair market value as

> the price at which the property would change hands between a willing buyer and a willing seller when the former is not under any compulsion to buy and the later is not under any compulsion to sell, both parties having reasonable knowledge of relevant facts. Court decisions frequently state, in addition, that the hypothetical buyer and seller are assumed to be able, as well as willing, to trade and be well informed about the property and concerning the market for such property.

The IRS's rational buyer, rational seller rule has become the standard in the appraisal profession.

It should be noted at the outset that several words are used interchangeably throughout this book. In particular, *valuation* and *appraisal* both refer to the process of estimating the price at which a property would change hands between a willing buyer and a willing seller as stated in the IRS definition. Similarly, *value, market value,* and *fair market value* all refer to the estimated price except in special circumstances, which are noted explicitly.

When the asset being appraised is a corporation, the property the hypothetical rational buyer and seller are trading consists of the claims of *all* the company's security holders. This includes the value of outstanding common stock, preferred stock, bonds, and privately held debt such as bank loans. Confusion can arise because there are numerous corporate "acquisitions" in which all the securities do not change hands. For example, a company may have a fair market value of $300 million, of which $200 million represents the market value of the common stock and $100 million represents the market value of a bank loan. In one possible transaction, a buyer may purchase the stock for $200 million and "assume" the bank debt. Thus, the company appears to change hands for a price of $200 million. However, this does not mean that the value of the company is $200 million because only the common stock was purchased for that price. The bank retains a claim on a portion of the company's cash flow that has a market value of $100 million, so that the total value of the company remains $300 million.

What corporate valuation models are trying to approximate, therefore, is the aggregate fair market value of all a company's securities, not just the equity. This seems to suggest an appraisal procedure in which the values of the company's debt, preferred stock, and common stock are estimated and summed to arrive at the value of the firm. While this is an ideal approach when it is applicable, it is often not feasible because some of the company's securities are not traded in a public market. Under such circumstances, the best approach is generally to estimate the entire value of the firm in one step rather than estimating the value of each class of security separately and summing.

Of course, there are situations in which the appraiser is interested exclusively in valuing one class of securities issued by the firm, such as the common stock. Even in this case, however, it is often better to value the total firm and then to allocate the total value among the various classes of securities rather than attempting to value the equity directly. Valuing the entire firm as a unit makes it easier to deal with issues such as control premiums, minority discounts, and discounts for nonmarketability in a consistent fashion.

THE ORGANIZATION OF THE BOOK

Though coming to grips with valuation theory may be important, it is not necessarily easy or fun. In this book, a number of steps have been taken to make the process as painless as possible. Nonetheless, the reader should be forewarned that a working knowledge of how to value a company cannot be achieved without delving into some of the technical details. Proper handling of the details not only leads to more accurate appraisals, it also provides insight into the concepts that underlie appraisal practice.

To help reduce the pain of dealing with technical details, every attempt is made to avoid the "computer manual" problem that is common to many finance books. Computer manuals frequently provide general instructions printed in various combinations of plain, **bold**, and *italic* type accompanied by square brackets [ ], round brackets ( ), and braces { }. From these general instructions, the reader is supposed to discern how to give the computer specific commands. Unfortunately, the computer often responds to such commands with statements such as "Error, illegal statement." The problem is that something is almost invariably lost when translating the general theory in the manual into specific commands. In such situations, the only hope, short of calling the support line and being put on hold for an hour, is to search through the manual for an example that is similar to the problem you are trying to solve. The mathematical models presented in finance books have a similar drawback. Theories that seem clear in the pages of a finance text suddenly become murky when it comes time to apply them to a specific problem. Even after 20 years in the profession, I still find myself hunting through finance books for examples that are similar to the problem I am trying to solve.

To help overcome the computer manual problem, this book contains numerous intuitive examples designed to elucidate the financial concepts on which appraisal practice is based. Furthermore, one detailed example involving Forms Engineering Company (FEC) is developed throughout the book to illustrate each of the valuation approaches. Forms Engineering is selected for two reasons. First, the problems that arise appraising FEC are typical of the problems that arise in most appraisal situations. Second, FEC is a small company that has not issued complicated securities such as convertible debt or warrants, nor does it have multiple divisions or international operations. These simplifications help to highlight the main appraisal issues.

Two other aspects of the book are designed to make life easier for the reader. First, consistent with the choice of FEC as an example, the focus is on the major appraisal issues, with limited time spent on more complicated but less central topics such as option pricing. Second, as noted at the outset, the book is oriented toward understanding and applying financial models, not deriving them. Instead of derivations and proofs, intuitive discussions, analogies, and examples are provided.

The Appraisal Approaches

The book covers all four appraisal approaches that are used widely in practice. The first approach, which is presented in Chapter 2, is to make use of the balance sheet. The simplest balance sheet valuation procedure is to sum the book values of the company's outstanding securities. The problem with this procedure is that it equates the historical values of assets and liabilities, as recorded by accountants, with their market values. Because book and market values frequently diverge, appraisers typically adjust the balance sheet entries with the goal of more accurately approximating market values. The procedures that are used to adjust the data, and their theoretical underpinnings, are also discussed in Chapter 2.

The second approach, presented in Chapter 3, is to estimate the value of a company by summing the market values of its outstanding securities. This approach, dubbed the stock and debt approach by state property tax appraisers, is by definition applicable only to publicly traded companies. Its theoretical foundation is the efficient market hypothesis, which states that the prices of publicly traded securities accurately reflect the true underlying value of a company. Although the stock and debt approach can be applied directly only to a limited number of companies whose securities are publicly traded, it serves as an input into appraisals based on direct comparisons.

The third approach is to appraise a company on the basis of comparisons with comparable companies whose value is known, either because the comparable company was recently sold or because it can be valued using the stock and debt approach. The direct comparison approach, which is sometimes referred to as the direct capitalization approach, consists of calculating ratios such as market value to earnings for the comparable companies and then multiplying the ratios by the appraisal target's earnings. The term *direct comparison* is preferred over *direct capitalization* because capitalization is often confused with discounting. In this book, the name direct comparison is used because the approach involves comparing selected companies to the appraisal target; discounting is not involved. As shown in Chapter 4, this seemingly straightforward procedure, which is widely used in practice, masks a host of thorny valuation issues.

The fourth and final approach to appraisal is to project the future cash flows that a company will earn for its security holders and then to discount those cash flows to present value. This approach, called the discounted cash flow approach, is based on the assumption that no matter what product a company produces, investors hold its securities because they expect those securities to produce future cash payouts for them. The more cash that is expected to be received, and the sooner the cash is expected to be received, the more highly investors will value the company's securities. There are three parts to estimating the discounted cash flow value of a company. First, year-by-year cash flows must be forecast into the future. The procedure for forecasting cash flow is presented in Chapter 5. Because corporations have indefinite lives, cash flows cannot be forecast for the life of the company. Thus, a terminal date must be selected at which time the cash flow forecasts stop and the continuing value of the company is estimated. Chapter 6 analyzes how the terminal date is selected and how the continuing value is estimated. In order to calculate the present value of the future cash flows and of the continuing value, a discount rate must be selected. Procedures for selecting the appropriate discount rate, which is referred to as the firm's cost of capital, are presented in Chapter 7.

With four fundamental approaches, and several variations of each approach, the appraiser often ends up with a group of different value indicators. Chapter 8 analyzes how the value indicators produced by the various approaches should be aggregated into a final estimate. In addition, questions regarding possible adjustments of the appraised value are addressed. Appraisers frequently adjust value indicators to take into account two factors:

marketability and control. Nonmarketable positions are usually discounted, while premiums are added for control. The theoretical justifications for these discounts and premiums also are analyzed in Chapter 8.

Finally, Chapter 9 discusses three extensions of the basic approaches. The first addresses the problem of valuing multibusiness firms. The second examines the problem of estimating the cost of capital for derivative securities such as warrants and convertible bonds. The final extension deals with the problem of valuing managerial flexibility. Managers have options such as the ability to cut back operations in bad times and expand them in good times. Such flexibility is difficult to account for in the context of some traditional appraisal models.

THE INTENDED AUDIENCE

The book is written with three groups of readers in mind. First, for managers, attorneys, bankers, fiduciaries, and other consumers of appraisal reports, the book is designed to provide a primer on business valuation and the financial economic concepts on which it is based. For those who feel that modern finance is too theoretical to be practical, I hope to convince you that this is not the case. Nonetheless, the theory cannot be ignored. Without an intuitive feel for the finance principles on which appraisal practice is based, it is impossible to tell a careful appraisal report from a piece of propaganda, and a diligent appraiser from a salesperson. Furthermore, practitioners who apply rules of thumb when valuing a company without understanding the theory on which those rules are based do so at their own peril. The situation is analogous to driving in a foreign land with a detailed set of instructions. As long as the instructions are followed perfectly, you will get to your destination. But if you happen to make a wrong turn, it is almost impossible to find your way back. Similarly, if the rules of thumb apply perfectly to the company being appraised, a reasonable value indicator will result. But if the rules are not applicable directly, an appraiser without an understanding of finance theory will be lost.

Second, for students of finance, the book is designed to demonstrate how the theoretical concepts learned in introductory finance courses are related to appraisal practice. The book is also designed to introduce finance students to valuation techniques such as the direct comparison approach that are employed by professional appraisers but are typically omitted from finance courses. Though these techniques are not as thoroughly grounded in finance theory as the discounted cash flow approach, in some circumstance they can produce more accurate estimates of value. Students of finance need to understand why this occurs and why practical rules of thumb are often superior to detailed mathematical models.

Finally, for professional appraisers, the book has two uses. First, it provides a review of finance theory as it applies to appraisal practice. Second, it explores the strengths and weaknesses of competing appraisal procedures from the standpoint of financial economics.

A DETAILED EXAMPLE: FORMS ENGINEERING COMPANY

As stated earlier, each of the appraisal techniques will be illustrated by applying it to Forms Engineering Company (FEC). This chapter closes, therefore, with a brief description of FEC.

Forms Engineering Company was founded in April of 1967 by Clark Gwaltney. Although FEC began as a business forms printer, it rapidly evolved into a leading printer for the direct mail marketing industry. By 1989, the company's sales were divided between 65 percent direct mail printing and 35 percent commercial printing.

FEC's customers include large financial institutions, oil companies, and political organizations that rely on direct mail for marketing. The company's plant and equipment have been designed, and its employees have been trained, to produce a large volume of high-quality, color, direct mail work product on short notice. Among the major products that FEC produces are brochures, credit applications, statement stuffers, flyers, and letters in up to 12 colors. Because FEC's share of the direct mail market is still small, the company has excellent prospects for future growth.

FEC operates in a highly competitive industry. There are approximately 2,500 printers in Southern California and over 35,000 nationwide. This makes it relatively easy to find companies that are comparable to FEC, although most of the comparables do not have publicly traded securities outstanding.

In July 1989, the chairman of FEC, Mr. Gwaltney, turned 65 and decided that it was time to either take the company public via a small regional offering or sell stock to its employees by starting an employee stock option plan. In either case, Mr. Gwaltney concluded that the company would have to be appraised. ESOP regulations state that an appraisal is required when an ESOP is established. Similarly, the value of the equity would have to be determined if the company were to offer shares to the public.

As of July 1989, FEC was a relatively small company. It had only one production facility, which was located in the Los Angeles area. The firm employed approximately 150 people including management. For the fiscal year ended June 30, 1989, a bad year for FEC, the company earned $48,236 after taxes on sales of $15.24 million.

As of July 1989, FEC was financed by a combination of bank loans (the debt), preferred stock, and common stock. The book value of debt was $2.35 million, the book value of the preferred stock was $1.06 million, and the book value of the common stock was $2.77 million. None of FEC's securities were publicly traded.

Complete financial data on FEC, including internal projections prepared at the end of fiscal year 1989, were provided by Mr. Gwaltney and Edward Bergstrom, his chief financial officer. The projections include not only estimates of futures sales and expenses, but also future capital spending plans and related depreciation schedules. These projections are used extensively in the discounted cash flow appraisal of FEC.

Chapter Two

The Adjusted Book Value Approach

The most straightforward approach to valuing a company is to rely on the information provided by the balance sheet. There are two ways the balance sheet information can be used to appraise a firm. Both rely on the definition of value presented in the first chapter: The value of a company is the sum of the values of all the claims investors have on the firm. (The terms *investor claims* and *securities* are used interchangeably throughout the book. However, it should be noted that from a legal perspective, some investor claims, such as privately placed loans, may not be defined as securities.) First, the book values of investor claims, including debt, preferred stock, and common stock, can be summed directly. Second, the net assets can be summed and liabilities other than investor claims deducted.

The obvious weakness of the balance sheet approach is that the book values of assets and liabilities reported on the balance sheet by accountants may not equal their market values. Because book values are based on historical cost, they fail to take into account factors such as inflation and obsolescence that will cause book value and market value to diverge. In addition, there are valuable assets, such as firm's organization capital, that are not reported on the balance sheet. As defined later in the chapter, organizational capital represents the value that is created by bringing employees, customers, suppliers, and managers together in a cohesive unit. The most striking evidence of the weakness of an unadjusted balance sheet approach is the sharp divergence between book value per share of common stock and market value per share of common stock for most publicly traded companies. For instance, at year end 1990, Monsanto had a book value per share of $24.93, while the market value of the stock was $48.75. In the case of Microsoft, the market value was over 10 times the book value at the end of 1991. These discrepancies arise because investors take account of factors such as inflation, obsolescence, and organizational capital when pricing a company's stock, despite the fact that these factors are not accounted for on the balance sheet.

In spite of factors such as inflation and obsolescence, it is not always necessary to abandon the book value approach. In some situations, book values can be adjusted so that they approximate market values more accurately. The two most common adjustments are to replace the book values of a company's assets by estimates of the replacement cost or liquidation value of those assets. As will become clear, such adjustments have two drawbacks. First, it is often difficult to determine whether adjusted book values are accurate estimates of market value. Second, the adjustment process typically fails to take proper account of assets such as organizational capital that do not appear on the balance sheet.

APPRAISALS BASED ON BOOK VALUES

Appraising a company based on unadjusted book value literally amounts to reading a balance sheet. For example, Table 2–1 presents Forms Engineering's balance sheet for the fiscal year ended June 30, 1989. The balance sheet shows that FEC had three classes of investors: owners of the notes, preferred stockholders, and common stockholders. In FEC's case, the notes represent bank loans.

From the balance sheet, the value of the firm can be calculated directly, by summing the book value of the investor claims, or indirectly, by summing net assets and subtracting current liabilities (other than debts owed to investors) and deferred taxes. Both methods, the investor claims approach and the asset-liabilities approach, are illustrated in Table 2–2. The claims of investors include FEC's short-term notes, long-term notes, preferred stock,

TABLE 2–1
Forms Engineering Balance Sheet for the Fiscal Year Ending June 30, 1989

Cash	$ 383,168	Accounts payable	$ 510,258
Accounts and notes receivable	2,885,742	Accrued commissions	78,934
Inventories	933,087	Accrued payroll	101,475
Tax claim receivable	117,318	Accrued vacation pay	157,838
Prepaid income taxes	80,386	Employee benefit plan	20,330
Prepaid expenses	6,961	Notes payable	581,146
Deposits	43,244	Other liabilities	35,496
Deferred income taxes	47,136		
Current Assets	$4,497,042	Current Liabilities	$1,485,477
		Notes due after one year	$1,768,929
Leasehold improvements	$ 169,015	Deferred income taxes	227,682
Machinery and equipment	6,166,997	Total	$1,996,611
Office equipment	141,868		
Automotive	162,683	Total Liabilities	$3,482,088
Computer equipment	201,807		
		Preferred stock	$1,055,580
Total	$6,842,370	Common stock/paid in capital	58,000
		Retained earnings	2,714,243
Accumulated depreciation	4,029,501		
Net property and equipment	$2,812,869	Total shareholders' equity	$3,827,823
		Total liabilities and	
Total assets	$7,309,911	shareholders' equity	$7,309,911

and common stock.[1] Summing these items gives an estimated value of $6,177,898. Remember that only the claims of investors are included in the valuation. Claims of trade creditors and employees, such as accounts payable, accrued payroll, and accrued commissions, reflect accrued costs of operation, not investments in the firm.

Deferred income taxes are also excluded because they are not investor claims. Deferred taxes arise because the Internal Revenue Service allows companies to use accelerated depreciation for

---

[1]In some situations, leases may also be capitalized and included as debt. Doing so will increase the total book value of investor claims but not the book value of equity.

TABLE 2–2
Balance Sheet Valuation

Investor Claims Approach		*Asset-Liabilities Approach*	
Notes payable	$ 581,146	Total assets	$7,309,911
Notes (due after one year)	1,768,929	Less: Current liabilities	
		– notes payable	904,331
Preferred stock	1,055,580	Less: Deferred income taxes	227,682
Common stock and			
retained earnings	2,772,243		
Total	$6,177,898	Total	$6,177,898

tax purposes, while reported earnings are based on straight-line depreciation. A simple example illustrates how this leads to a "deferred tax." Assume that a company with earnings before depreciation and taxes of $500,000 buys a new machine that costs $1 million and has a 10-year life. Though the straight-line depreciation is $100,000 per year, the company employs accelerated depreciation for tax purposes and writes off $200,000 in the first year. If the tax rate is 40 percent, the company will owe $120,000 in taxes the first year. (The tax due equals the earnings of $500,000 minus the depreciation of $200,000 times 40 percent.) However, if the firm reports earnings based on straight-line depreciation of $100,000, the apparent tax due will be $160,000 ($500,000 minus $100,000 times 40 percent). The company accounts for this discrepancy by showing $120,000 as the tax paid and by adding $40,000 to deferred income taxes. Deferred tax is an appropriate name because as the asset ages, accelerated depreciation falls below straight-line depreciation and taxes paid rise relative to apparent taxes due, so that tax deferrals eventually become negative and the deferred tax account for that asset falls. By the end of the asset's life, the deferred tax account for that asset is back to zero. Of course, total deferred taxes for a company may continue to rise if the firm is buying other new assets, but the contribution of the older asset to deferred taxes must eventually turn negative. Thus, the benefit of accelerated depreciation is not that it reduces taxes but that it postpones them. Assuming that tax rates remain constant, the same total tax is paid over the life of an asset, but less is paid at the beginning and more is paid at the end. To the extent that this deferral is valuable, it will cause the market value of equity to rise above the book value because benefits of the deferral are not included on the balance sheet.

The deficiencies of the book value approach are most easily seen by looking at the indirect calculation of value. Because current liabilities have short maturities, their book value will be close to their market value. This makes it clear that the accuracy of a book value appraisal depends on how well the net book values of the assets approximate their market values. There are three reasons why the book value of a company's assets commonly diverge from their market value. First, inflation drives a wedge between the current value of an asset and its historical cost, less depreciation. Second, technological change renders some assets obsolete before their depreciable life ends. Third, assets may be combined in such a way that their value as part of a going concern exceeds the sum of their values as individual entities. Each of these points is fundamental to understanding valuation theory and is worth exploring in some detail.

Inflation

Because inflation is measured by the rate of increase in a price index such as the consumer price index (CPI), the producer price index (PPI), or the GNP deflator, people naturally associate inflation with widespread increases in the cost of goods and services. But this is the wrong way to think about inflation. Instead, inflation represents a decline in the value of one good: the U.S. dollar. When the value of the dollar declines, prices of all other goods and services rise, because those prices are measured in terms of dollars.

To see how this works, suppose that for some bizarre reason the inch, the unit used to measure distance, began to shrink. For instance, suppose that in 1990, the inch shrank by 10 percent. Because the inch is the unit of measurement, everything else would appear to be 10 percent bigger in 1991. A 6-foot man in 1990 would be over 6'7" in 1991. But he would not be a better basketball player because the rim would be 11 feet off the floor rather than 10 feet as it was in 1990. As the shrinking continued, familiar measures would pass into history. A two by four would become a three by six and then a four by eight. Eventually, the 17-mile drive in Carmel would be 100 miles long.

The shrinking inch would cause endless headaches for architects and engineers. Plans and drawings would have to be dated because the stated dimensions of a building would grow each year even though the building was not actually getting any bigger. If the inch were shrinking fast enough, and unpredictably enough, architects and engineers would be forced to invent a "constant inch" based on, say, the 1980 inch, to reduce the confusion. Plans could then be drawn in terms of the 1980 inch and converted to "current inches" by multiplying by a ratio of the 1980 inch to the current inch.

Seem ridiculous? That is exactly what is happening in the case of the dollar. The value of the dollar has declined in virtually every year since the end of World War II, in some years losing more than 10 percent of its purchasing power. As a result, the 1992 dollar is worth less than 12 cents measured in terms of the 1945 dollar. This shrinkage in purchasing power has forced economists to invent a constant dollar. The most popular choice for the constant dollar is the 1980 dollar. Prices stated in terms of these constant dollars, which are called *real* prices, are translated into prices stated in terms of current dollars, called *nominal* prices, by multiplying by the ratio of the CPI in 1980 to the current CPI. It should be noted that there is nothing magical about the CPI. Real and nominal amounts can also be calculated using the PPI or the GNP deflator. However, the CPI is the best known and most widely used index.

One weakness of historical cost accounting and, therefore, of valuation techniques based on historical cost, is that it ignores the impact of changes in the purchasing power of a dollar. The value of the assets on the balance sheet is presented in terms of nominal dollars for the year in which the assets were purchased. For instance, a press FEC bought in 1982 is valued in terms of 1982 dollars, while a folder purchased in 1985 is valued in terms of 1985 dollars. Because the depreciation schedule for each asset is based on its historical cost, depreciation schedules are also stated in terms of historical dollars.

The impact of the failure to adjust for inflation is illustrated by a simple example. Suppose that FEC purchases a press in 1985 for

$1 million and that the press is depreciated straight line over its 10-year life span. (To avoid added complications, assume that 10 years represents the true economic life of the asset and that straight-line depreciation fairly approximates true economic depreciation. In general, neither of these assumptions will necessarily be true, but that is an issue unrelated to the inflation problem.) By 1990, the book value of the press reported on the balance sheet will be $500,000. (This equals the purchase price minus five years of depreciation at $100,000 per year.) Between 1985 and 1990, the average rate of inflation was approximately 4.5 percent per year, so that a 1985 dollar was worth approximately $1.25 in 1990. Assuming that the increase in the price of the press matches the rate of inflation, a new press would cost $1.25 million in 1990. If the press were depreciated straight line for five years based on a cost of $1.25 million, the adjusted book value in 1990 would be $625,000, $125,000 greater than the reported book value.

In the case of FEC, the value of each of the assets shown on the balance sheet, particularly those with longer lives, is affected by inflation. Because a dollar today has less purchasing power than dollars on the days the assets were acquired, the net book value is *almost* certain to understate the market value of FEC's assets. (The word *almost* is added because factors other than inflation affect the relation between book value and market value.) Clearly, an adjustment to book value is required to estimate market value during a period of inflation.

It is important to note that the impact of inflation extends beyond the adjusted book value approach to valuation. For instance, the discounted cash flow approach is based on forecasts of cash flows to be earned in future years. Cash flows received in future years will be stated in different dollars, so account must be taken of inflation. In addition, inflation affects interest rates on debt and required returns on equity and thereby alters the cost of capital. These issues will be discussed in depth later in the book.

Obsolescence

Because of technological change, some assets become obsolete before the end of their depreciable lives. AT&T carries on its books phone lines and switching equipment whose book value exceeds its market value because copper phone lines were made obsolete by optical fiber lines and because analog switches were made obsolete by digital switches.

The most direct way to measure obsolescence is to observe the difference between the market value of an asset and its net book value. Unfortunately, this is not possible in many cases because there is not an active market for the company's assets. For instance, AT&T's copper phone lines are not traded in the marketplace, so it is difficult to know what anyone would pay for them. In contrast, there are active secondary markets for used diesel trucks. Therefore, a trucking firm can estimate easily the obsolescence of its trucks by comparing their book value with their value in the secondary market.

Another way to measure obsolescence is to estimate the value of the asset based on its projected earning power. In this framework, saying that an asset is obsolete is equivalent to saying that the company's earnings would be increased if the net book value of the asset were invested in state-of-the-art equipment. In this context, obsolescence equals the difference between the value of an asset estimated on the basis of its earning power and the book value of the asset.

Estimating obsolescence on the basis of the earning power of the assets can lead to circularity in an appraisal whereby the discounted cash flow approach is counted twice. That is, the appraiser first uses the discounted cash flow (DCF) method to calculate the value of the firm. The DCF estimate of value is then used again to measure obsolescence, where obsolescence is defined as the difference between the book value of the assets and the DCF value of the assets. For instance, in an appraisal of a major railroad, a well-known appraiser estimated the DCF value of the company to be approximately $300 million compared to an historical book value of about $1 billion. The appraiser calculated obsolescence as the difference between the DCF value and the historical book value, or $700 million. He then deducted this estimate of obsolescence from the historical book value to reach an adjusted book value of $300 million. By construction, this "book" estimate of value equals the DCF value indicator.

Such circular reasoning reduces the adjusted book value approach to the DCF approach. In this situation, the adjusted book value approach does not add new information about the value of the company and should not be considered an independent approach. If adjusted book value is to provide new information, the adjustments to book value to account for obsolescence must depend on something other than the DCF estimate of value.

Finally, the fact that obsolescence and inflation have a significant impact may not be evident by examining book values because the two forces tend to offset each other. Whereas inflation causes book value to understate market value, obsolescence causes book value to overstate market value. It is possible on net that book and market values will be approximately equal even though both obsolescence and inflation are important.

Organizational Capital

In accord with common sense, modern finance teaches that corporate investment decisions should be based on a simple rule: Buy an asset if the value of that asset to the company exceeds its cost. For example, if FEC determines that a press that costs $1 million will produce benefits to the company with a present value of $1.5 million, FEC should buy the press. This decision rule begs the question of how the $500,000 in added value is created.

For a corporation to create value for security holders, the *value of the assets as part of an ongoing organization* must exceed the value of the assets in isolation. Cornell and Shapiro call the "stuff" that creates this added value *organizational capital*.[2] Organizational capital, which includes intangible assets and goodwill, takes a variety of forms. Some key components of organizational capital include:

- Long-term relationships between managers and employees that allow them to work together effectively and do their jobs efficiently. For example, over the years, people develop the ability to communicate intuitively and learn how to take on tasks without lengthy instructions.

---

[2] B. Cornell and A. Shapiro, "Corporate Stakeholders and Corporate Finance," *Financial Management* 16 (Spring 1987), pp. 5–14.

- The company's reputation with customers and suppliers, including any brand names, that makes it easier to sell products and negotiate terms. For instance, people pay a premium for Campbell soup because the name has come to signify quality.

- The company's opportunities for profitable investment that grow out of the specialized skills of its management and its work force and relationship with its customers. These opportunities, which are sometimes referred to as investment options or growth options, can account for a significant fraction of a company's value. For example, the value of many high-technology companies is based on new products that the company is expected to develop, not products the company is currently producing.

- A network of suppliers, distributors, and repairmen that know the company's products and are willing to support and enhance them. For instance, Apple Computer profits from all the software developers who support the company's Macintosh machines.

An important attribute of the firm's organizational capital is that it is difficult to separate from the firm as a going concern. For instance, the value Campbell derives from its brand name cannot be separated easily from the company and sold like a printing press.[3] For this reason, the value of a brand name typically is not reflected in the replacement cost or liquidation value of the fixed assets. The value of the brand name, like the value of most other forms of organizational capital, can be estimated only by examining the earning power of the company.

By focusing on the balance sheet entries as individual items, the adjusted book value approach ignores organizational capital. In some cases, the resulting error can be huge. For instance, following Genentech's initial public offering, the market value of its stock was over $500 million, while the net book value of the fixed

---

[3]There are some situations in which intangible assets can be separated from a going concern and sold. For example, Miller Brewing purchased the trade name "Lite" from Peter Hand Brewing Company without purchasing any other assets. However, in most circumstances, it is difficult to realize the full value of intangible assets without purchasing the going concern to which they are attached.

assets was less than $20 million. The difference, more than 25 times the book value, was due to Genentech's organizational capital, particularly the company's investment opportunities.

WHEN IT IS REASONABLE TO USE BOOK VALUE APPRAISALS

Despite the drawbacks associated with inflation, obsolescence, and organizational capital, there are situations in which an appraisal based on the book value approach will produce a useful value indicator. For example, regulatory authorities typically attempt to ensure that utilities, including gas and electric companies, earn approximately a fair rate of return on their rate base, where the rate base is defined to be the net book value of the company's assets.[4] Under such circumstances, the historical cost approach may produce a valid value indicator because, due to regulation, the future earning power of the company is tied to the net book value of the assets. However, even in the case of utilities, net book value and market value may diverge. Regulations are not perfect nor are they completely binding, so that utilities often earn more or less than their true cost of capital. In addition, investors may believe that regulation will change in the future or that the utility has opportunities for future growth.

The question of whether net book value is a valid indicator of market value for a utility cannot be resolved by theoretical debate, necessitating instead an empirical analysis. To determine whether book value and market value are closely related for utilities, it is necessary to collect data for a sample of pure utility companies and to compare their book values with their market values. Of course, this requires an objective measure of market value. As described in the next chapter, such an objective measure for publicly traded companies is provided by the stock and debt approach, which is based directly on the valuation assessments of investors. An empirical study, therefore, should

---

[4]The fair rate of return is set so that the utilities earn their cost of capital in the long run. Methods for estimating the cost of capital are analyzed in Chapter 7. The rate base is approximately the historical cost of the assets less depreciation and deferred taxes.

compare net book value with the stock and debt value of the pure utilities. This is difficult to do because most utilities are owned by holding companies that have diversified into nonutility businesses. Nonetheless, Table 2–3 provides some illustrative results for a sample of 10 utilities and 10 high-technology companies. The table presents the book value of equity, the market value of equity, and the ratio of market to book value for all 20 firms. (In comparing the book value of equity to the market value of equity, it is assumed that the book values of debt and preferred stock equal their market values.) The results show that in no case is the ratio of market value to book value greater than 1.65 for the utilities, whereas it is never less than 1.95 for the high-technology companies. For Microsoft, the ratio is 13.16.

As the discussion regarding utilities indicates, the key questions that determine whether the book value approach or the adjusted book value approach produces a reasonable estimate of value are, "Is the earning power of the company's assets closely related to the book value of those assets? If not, is there a straightforward adjustment, such as accounting for inflation and obsolescence, that will bring the two into line?" Unfortunately, with the possible exception of regulated utilities, there are few situations in which the historical net cost of an asset and its earning power are likely to be closely related so that the unadjusted book value approach can be applied. Table 2–3 shows that the approach clearly would be misleading in the case of high-technology companies.

In some cases, the divergence between book value and market value can be eliminated, or at least greatly reduced, by adjusting book value to reflect the replacement cost or the liquidation value of a company's assets, thereby taking into account inflation and obsolescence. However, the adjustments are often difficult, and the situations in which they will produce a reliable value indicator are rare. As will be seen, furthermore, these adjustments rarely take into account organizational capital.

ADJUSTING BOOK VALUE TO REFLECT REPLACEMENT COST

Though the earning power of an asset is unlikely to be related to the historical net cost of the asset, particularly if the asset is old, it is more likely to be related to the current replacement cost.

TABLE 2–3
Ratio of Book Value of Equity to Market Value (As of Fourth Quarter 1991)

	Book Value per Share	Market Value per Share	Ratio	Line of Business
Utility Companies				
Baltimore Gas & Electric	$25.60	$ 30.00	*1.17*	Electricity and gas
Consolidated Edison	20.25	24.00	*1.19*	Electric, gas, and steam
Ohio Edison	16.80	20.00	*1.19*	Electricity
American Water Works	18.15	23.00	*1.27*	Water
The Southern Company	21.95	28.00	*1.28*	Electricity
American Electric Power	23.05	30.00	*1.30*	Electricity
California Water	20.75	28.00	*1.35*	Water
Pacific Gas & Electric	18.45	29.00	*1.57*	Electricity and gas
Carolina Power	29.30	48.00	*1.64*	Electricity
Detroit Edison	19.40	32.00	*1.65*	Electricity
High-Technology Companies				
Intel	$22.00	$ 43.00	*1.95*	Manufactures integrated circuits
Sun Microsystems	12.58	25.00	*1.99*	Computing systems
Dell Computer	11.25	27.00	*2.40*	Maker of personal computers
Apple Computer	14.80	53.00	*3.58*	Maker of personal computers
Genentech	8.55	34.00	*3.98*	Biotechnology firm
Abbott Labs	7.80	54.00	*6.92*	Health care products
Borland International	10.00	83.00	*8.30*	Developer of personal computer software
Wang Laboratories	0.31	2.90	*9.35*	Maker of personal computers
Novell Inc.	3.85	45.00	*11.69*	High-performance area networks for PCs
Microsoft	7.75	102.00	*13.16*	Developer of personal computer software

Source: ValueLine Investment Survey, 4th quarter 1991.

Thus, one way to adjust the balance sheet entries is to substitute estimates of replacement cost for the net book value of the assets. Unfortunately, there is disagreement among appraisers and economists regarding how to measure replacement cost. One possibility is to use a price index such as the CPI to convert dollars in the year the asset was purchased to current dollars. In the case of the $1 million press purchased in 1985 discussed earlier, the book value is adjusted upward from $500,000 to $625,000 to reflect the 25 percent decline in purchasing power between 1985 and 1990.

Using a price index in this fashion, however, fails to take into account obsolescence. It also fails to reflect changes in the prices of specific assets. For example, the prices of computer equipment, for a given level of processing power, fell dramatically during the years from 1985 to 1990 despite increases in the CPI. A better approach, therefore, is to adjust each asset separately to reflect its own replacement cost today. If done properly, such an adjustment would take into account both inflation and obsolescence because both factors would influence the cost of replacing assets today. Unfortunately, defining what is meant by a "replacement" is no easy task. Even for relatively stable goods, such as railroad cars and steel, new products incorporate enhancements and improvements that differentiate them from earlier vintages. Thus, substituting a new asset for an old one represents an upgrade as well as a replacement. Put differently, the substitution includes both an element of replacement and an element of new investment. For more rapidly evolving goods such as computers, distinguishing replacement from new investment requires a good deal of judgment because new products typically offer features not available on earlier models.

The greatest deficiency of the replacement cost approach is that it ignores organizational capital. As noted earlier, corporations exist because they make it possible to combine assets and people in such a fashion that the value of the whole exceeds the sum of the parts. Appraisals based on replacement cost, even when replacement cost is measured perfectly, ignore this value-creating synergy. Therefore, they fail to account for that element of value that leads to the formation of a corporation in the first place.

ADJUSTING BOOK VALUE TO REFLECT LIQUIDATION VALUE

The most direct approach for approximating the market value of the assets on a company's balance sheet is to determine what they would sell for if the company were liquidated today. If the assets trade on an active secondary market—for example, diesel trucks—liquidation prices equal secondary market prices. As noted earlier, however, secondary markets do not exist for many corporate assets such as AT&T's copper phone lines or Union Pacific's rail system. Consequently, the appraiser must attempt to estimate the *hypothetical* price at which such assets could be sold. Although trade publications may be of aid when estimating a hypothetical price in some situations, the appraiser most often will be forced to rely on management's estimates of liquidation value. Appraising the liquidation value of the assets will be difficult even for senior managers because they focus on the value the assets produce as part of a going concern. Only in rare circumstances, such as bankruptcy, will managers pay attention to the liquidation value of assets. In most cases, therefore, it is not worth the time and expense to independently estimate the liquidation value of all of a company's assets, unless the appraisers are convinced that liquidation value will provide a valid indicator of market value. Exceptions are situations in which a company has a few large assets, such as a large office building, so that estimating liquidation value is not overly time-consuming.

One of the situations in which the liquidation approach is most applicable is the appraisal of natural resources firms. If the main holdings of a company are natural resource properties, then the value of the company should be approximately equal to the liquidation value of the properties, because organizational capital rarely adds much value to such companies. However, this is not always the case if extraction of natural resources requires a unique technology or if the company is also active in exploration.

In the case of FEC, estimating the replacement cost and the liquidation value of the assets is straightforward. Because there are thousands of printing companies in the United States, a relatively liquid market for used printing equipment has developed. When there is an active secondary market, the best estimate of the replacement cost and of the liquidation value of an asset is simply its price in the secondary market.

Based on his knowledge of the secondary market for printing equipment, the chief financial officer of FEC was able to estimate the secondary market value of the company's equipment. (Because the plant is rented, it is not an asset of the company.) These

TABLE 2-4

Estimates of Secondary Market Value of FEC's Assets Compared to Book Value (July 1, 1989)

Item	Net Book Value	Secondary Market Value
Computer equipment	$ 33,398	50,000
14-inch press	29,818	140,000
17-inch press	0	50,000
22A press	0	80,000
23P press	208,981	300,000
Acti "V" Line Camera, equip	0	2,000
Dupont processor/blender	0	1,500
Trimmer/light vac	0	2,000
Plough folder	12,121	35,000
Refrigerated dryer, compressor	0	7,000
Hyster forklift	7,583	7,000
Compressor-125 HP	7,162	7,000
Bunch 1000 series press folder	9,602	5,000
HBO T-79-6 folding machine	40,181	30,000
Schriber Collator	0	6,000
Bunch 600 folder	0	4,000
Stahl folder	3,599	6,000
Stahl Buckle folder	4,314	6,000
Lawson paper cutter	8,200	10,000
Burgess Consolux Proofing Sy	1,657	1,500
22C press	176,373	200,000
22D press and insert	1,053,907	2,000,000
Videojet printer	10,693	5,000
22C2 press	310,795	280,000
Total	$1,918,384	$3,235,000

Secondary market value − net book value = $1,316,616

estimates, along with the reported book values, are shown in Table 2–4. The table shows that in most cases, but not all, the secondary market value of the assets significantly exceeds the net book value. In the aggregate, the secondary market value is $1,316,616 greater than the net book value.

The excess of the market value over the book value of the assets can be used to adjust the historical cost appraisal to reflect the replacement cost (and the liquidation value) of the firm's assets. For Forms Engineering, the calculation proceeds as follows.

- Book value of the firm = $7,309,911 (from Table 2–1).
- Excess of secondary market value of assets over book value = $1,316,616 (from Table 2–4).
- Replacement cost and liquidation value of the firm = $8,626,527.

The key deficiency of the liquidation value approach is that, like the replacement cost approach, it ignores organizational capital. Rather than valuing the firm as a going concern, it values the firm as a collection of assets to be sold piecemeal. Whether or not the approach is reasonable for FEC depends on whether FEC has developed specialized skills, name recognition, customer relationships, and the like, so that its value as a going concern exceeds the value of its assets. To reiterate, the management of FEC felt strongly that the company has significant organizational capital. In holding this view, of course, management may be reflecting its own unwarranted optimism. Substantiating management's beliefs regarding organizational capital requires an analysis of the earning power, or cash flow generating capacity, of the company. If FEC has considerable organization capital, then the value of the assets based on their earning power will exceed the liquidation value of the firm. Unfortunately, it is not possible to determine whether FEC has significant organizational capital in the context of a book value approach to valuation. The earning power of the company must be appraised directly, using an alternative approach, and the resulting value indicator compared with the adjusted book value of the assets.

It is worth noting that there are situations in which the liquidation approach can be combined successfully with other appraisal methods. Consider, for example, a conglomerate firm consisting of a variety of loosely related subsidiaries. If each of the individual subsidiaries has significant organizational capital, then an approach that takes account of a subsidiary's earning power will be required to appraise each of them. It is possible, however, that the corporate headquarters adds little organizational capital. In that case, the value of the firm can be calculated by estimating the value of each of the subsidiaries and summing as if the subsidiaries are individual assets that can be liquidated.

As an interesting sidelight, Shleifer and Vishny argue that such an approach was utilized by corporate raiders during the takeover wave of the 1980s.[5] Shleifer and Vishny contend that for situations in which raiders concluded that the sum of the value of the subsidiaries, if sold as individual entities, exceeded the value of a conglomerate firm, they made a bid for the conglomerate with the intent of "busting it up." The raider's profit in such a bust-up takeover arises from the negative organizational capital of the conglomerate firm. By eliminating the corporate bureaucracy and selling the subsidiaries to companies in the same lines of business, overhead costs are reduced and economic efficiency is improved. The value created by breaking up the bureaucracy flows to the raider as profits from the transaction.

THE BOTTOM LINE

The bottom line is that only in rare situations, such as the appraisal of regulated utilities, is unadjusted book value likely to be a reasonable value indicator. The conclusion is not so stark with respect to adjusted book values. If replacement cost or liquidation value can be estimated, and if there is reason to believe that the earning power of the company's assets is tied to their replacement cost or liquidation value, then adjusted book value will be approximately equal to market value. This is the case if most of the firm's value is attributable to its holdings of natural resources. Unfortunately, such situations are rare because organizational capital, which the book value approach ignores, is an important source of value for most going concerns. Book value approaches to appraisal are particularly inappropriate for high-technology or service firms that derive much of their value from organizational capital. The only way to assess the impact of or-

---

[5]A. Shleifer and R. Vishney, "The Takeover Wave of the 1980s" (unpublished working paper, Graduate School of Business, University of Chicago, 1990).

ganizational capital is to determine how effectively a company's assets work together as part of a going concern by examining the earning power of the company or by comparing the performance of the company with comparable firms in the same line of business. But in each case, that requires an altogether different approach to valuation. Thus, in most practical situations, the book value approach to valuation should be given little weight by the appraiser.

Chapter Three

The Stock and Debt Approach

When the securities of a company being appraised are publicly traded, there is a straightforward valuation procedure: Sum the market values of all the outstanding securities. This simple procedure has been dubbed the stock and debt approach by property tax appraisers. It is also occasionally referred to as the market approach because it is based on observation of the market prices of the firm's securities.

The valuation of Monsanto, a diversified chemical company, provides an example of the stock and debt approach. On December 30, 1990, Monsanto had short-term outstanding debt with a market value of $582 million and long-term debt outstanding with a market value of $1,652 million. The company also had 164,394,194 shares of common stock outstanding. At the closing price of 48¼ on December 30, these shares had a market value of $7,932 million. Adding the market value of the debt to the market value of the equity gives a total value of $10,166 million for Monsanto. (The value of the preferred shares is also added if the company has preferred stock outstanding.)

Though the stock and debt approach is straightforward, debate has arisen over what prices to use when valuing the securities, particularly the equity. Because of the volatility of stock prices, some appraisers advocate using an average of recent stock prices, rather than the price of the stock on the lien date. (The lien date is the day on which the appraiser is attempting to estimate value.) Depending on the length of the average employed, this can have a marked impact on the calculated value. (Averaging is often used by state ad valorem tax appraisers. In some cases, security prices may be averaged over a period extending backward in time a year or more from the lien date.) The rationale for averaging is that an

34

average of past prices is a more reliable indicator of a company's "true underlying value" than the current stock price. Determining whether averaging is a reasonable procedure requires an understanding of the relation between the information possessed by investors and stock prices. That relation is the subject of the efficient market hypothesis. As the next section demonstrates, one implication of the efficient market hypothesis is that appraisals should always be based on current market prices, not averages of past prices. The efficient market hypothesis also implies that the stock and debt approach, where it can be applied, provides the most accurate estimate of a company's true value.

THE EFFICIENT MARKET HYPOTHESIS

The efficient market hypothesis (EMH) is one of the foundations of modern finance. Because of the central role it plays, understanding the EMH is helpful not only in applying the stock and debt approach, but in grasping the general principles on which valuation theory is based. It is worthwhile, therefore, to spend a little time explaining and illustrating the efficient market hypothesis.

Often, the most difficult step in learning a new idea is setting aside previous preconceptions. With the possible exceptions of religion and politics, there are few subjects about which businesspeople have stronger opinions than the operation of investment markets. To prevent possible preconceptions about the behavior of investment markets from impeding the present discussion, the efficient market hypothesis is presented in the context of the football betting market rather than the stock market. Though this may seem like a peculiar choice, a little reflection reveals that the football betting market and the stock market are fundamentally alike. In both markets, investors put their money at risk today in hopes of having more tomorrow.[1]

---

[1]Several studies by financial scholars have examined the efficiency of the football betting market. For a relatively recent and complete analysis, see J. Golec and M. Tamarkin, "The Degree of Inefficiency in the Football Betting Market," *Journal of Financial Economics* 30 (December 1991), pp. 311–24.

Although it is not relevant to the discussion of market efficiency, there is one basic difference between the football betting market and the stock market that should be noted at the outset. Football betting is a pure redistributive activity, or what is sometimes called a zero sum game. What one party wins, another loses. Holding stock, on the other hand, allows an investor to participate in the growth of the American economy. Profits for one investor need not be associated with losses for another. As long as there are no short sellers, it is possible for every investor to win in the long run in the stock market.[2]

In the football betting market, the analog to a security price is the point spread. Point spreads determine how much you must "pay" to bet on the team of your choice. For example, the point spread prior to the 1991 Super Bowl was "Buffalo plus seven." This spread means that a bet on the Buffalo Bills pays off only if the Bills win by eight points or more. If the Bills win by seven points, the bet is a tie and all moneys are returned. If the Bills win by six points or less, or if they lose the game, the bet is lost.

To see how the point spread is analogous to the price of a security, imagine an investor who has decided that the Bills are a better team and thinks that the Bills should win by 10 points. At spreads of Buffalo plus seven or Buffalo plus eight, this hypothetical investor will bet on the Bills. However, at a spread of Buffalo plus eleven, the cost of betting on the Bills is so high that the hypothetical investor will switch sides and bet on the New York Giants. In a market made up of thousands of such investors, the number betting on the Bills falls as the point spread rises in the same fashion that the number of investors willing to buy IBM stock falls as the stock price rises.

Like stock prices, point spreads are determined by the law of supply and demand operating through a network of brokers

---

[2]There is another more subtle difference between the football betting market and the stock market. Whereas the risk of betting on football games can be eliminated, even for society as a whole, by simply not betting, the risk of holding stock cannot be eliminated. To the extent that corporations issue shares, someone must hold the stock and bear the risk. This has important implications for the relationship between risk and return in the stock market as compared to the football betting marketing, as described in Chapter 7.

(called bookmakers) with whom investors place their bets. The bookmakers earn their money by charging a small commission on every bet. The commission, commonly referred to as *vigorish*, is typically 5 percent. It is collected by requiring the loser to pay $110 for every $100 bet while the winner collects only $100. As long as equal amounts are bet on each team, the bookmakers earn their commission no matter who wins and thus bear no risk.[3] To ensure that equal amounts are bet on each team, the bookmakers adjust the point spread. If more money is being bet on the Bills than on the Giants at Buffalo plus six, the spread is raised to Buffalo plus seven. By adjusting the point spread, the bookmakers balance the amount bet on each team in the same fashion that the specialist on the floor of the New York Stock Exchange balances buy and sell orders for IBM stock by adjusting the price. When supply equals demand—that is, when equal amounts are being bet on each team—the market is in equilibrium.

The extent to which bettors influence the market price (point spread) depends on the amount they are willing to bet. The more confident bettors are in their selections, the more they will bet and the greater their impact on the point spread. In equating supply and demand, the market aggregates the opinions of all investors, weighted by the amount they are willing to bet, to arrive at an average "opinion." This average, or market, opinion is represented by the equilibrium point spread. Prior to the 1991 Super Bowl, the market opinion was that Buffalo was seven points better than New York.

Though the equilibrium point spread reflects the average opinion, the average is not a consensus. In fact, if everyone agreed that the appropriate point spread was Buffalo plus seven, no one would bet on the game. Clearly, those betting on Buffalo feel the equilibrium point spread is too low, while those betting on New York think the equilibrium spread is too high.

Because the equilibrium point spread is an average of the opinions of all the investors who bet on a game, weighted by the

---

[3]Active football gamblers may recognize that bookmakers typically bear some risk even when equal amounts are bet on each team because not all bets are placed at the same point spread.

amount they are willing to bet, anything that alters investor opinions will affect the point spread. Suppose, for instance, that two days prior to the 1991 Super Bowl, the Bills' star quarterback, Jim Kelly, is injured. As soon as this information is released, investor estimates of the outcome of the game will change. At Buffalo plus seven, some people who had originally planned to bet on the Bills would now bet on the Giants instead. As a result, supply no longer equals demand at the plus seven point spread. Consequently, bookmakers would adjust the point spread until equal amounts are being bet on each team once again. To continue the illustration, assume that the new equilibrium point spread is Buffalo plus three.

The change in the point spread from seven to three demonstrates the sense in which market prices can be said to incorporate, or reflect, new information. Prior to Mr. Kelly's injury, the equilibrium point spread was Buffalo plus seven. Following his injury, the equilibrium spread was Buffalo plus three. Thus, the information regarding Mr. Kelly's injury was worth four points. The spread moves from seven to three to reflect the new information.

In the case of IBM stock, the analog to betting on the Giants or the Bills is deciding whether to buy or sell the stock. Whereas the point spread averages opinions about football teams, the stock price averages opinions about IBM. For IBM to sell at $100 per share, the number of shares of IBM that investors want to hold at that price must equal the number of IBM shares outstanding. Furthermore, stock prices respond to new information in the same fashion that the point spread does. If IBM announces an unexpected drop in earnings, supply and demand will no longer be equal at the previous market price. To bring the market back into equilibrium, the price must fall.

The football betting analogy makes it easy to understand the concept of an efficient market. According to the most widely accepted definition, *an efficient market is a market in which the price of a security reflects all publicly available information.* Despite the widespread use of the standard definition, there are three forms of the efficient market hypothesis. The weak form says that all past trading information, including price and volume data, is reflected in the current market price of a security. The semistrong form says that all publicly available information is reflected in the market price. Such public information includes all information released by the company, including financial statements. The strong form says that all information is reflected in the market price. It is worth noting that the profits earned by inside traders such as Ivan Boesky indicate that the strong form of the efficient market hypothesis is too strong. Mr. Boesky made spectacular profits because the market price did not reflect the inside information he possessed.

In the context of the football betting market, the EMH says that the point spread reflects all publicly available information about the relative abilities of the two teams. In the case of the stock market, the EMH says that the market price of a security reflects publicly available information regarding the value of the security. It is thus the best possible estimate, on the basis of public information, of the security's true value.

It is important to distinguish market efficiency from market clairvoyance. The EMH maintains that the market processes publicly available information as well as any professional investor; it does not say that the market processes information perfectly or that it can predict the future without error. This is clear in the context of the football betting market. Buffalo was a seven-point favorite in the 1991 Super Bowl, but the Giants won the game. It is also clear in the case of the stock market. Highly valued companies on occasion have performed hideously, to the surprise of many. (IBM is a good example.) The EMH recognizes that both markets and well-informed investors will make mistakes, but it predicts that, on average, market forecasts and market valuations will be at least as accurate as those produced by individual investors and appraisers, no matter how expert.

Empirical Tests of the Efficient Market Hypothesis

The literature on tests of the efficient market hypothesis has become so voluminous that a fair review is beyond the scope of this book.[4] Nonetheless, it is worth illustrating the concepts on which the tests are based, presenting a few of the major findings, and

---

[4]The best summaries of tests of the efficient market hypothesis are contained in two review papers by Eugene Fama. E. F. Fama, "Efficient Capital Markets: A Review of Theory and Empirical Work," *Journal of Finance* 25 (May 1970), pp. 383–417; and Fama, "Efficient Capital Markets: II," *Journal of Finance* 46 (December 1991), pp. 1,025–75.

discussing the major criticisms of the EMH. All of these issues have a bearing on the stock and debt approach to valuation.

The most important implication of the efficient market hypothesis follows directly from the discussion of the football betting market. If the point spread reflects all publicly available information, then even the most informed gamblers should not be able to win more than half of their bets. For example, suppose that a respected football coach is provided with detailed information about competing teams and asked to predict the outcome of each week's games. If the market is efficient, the coach's predictions should be no more accurate than the point spread because the point spread already reflects all the information available to the coach. Therefore, if the coach used his predictions to bet on games at the point spread, over the long run he would not win more than 50 percent of his bets. Pete Rose provides a striking example of the efficiency of the sports gambling market. Despite his detailed knowledge of baseball, he was unable to win more than half of his bets. Because he bet so frequently and in such large amounts, most of his money went to pay commission charges and Mr. Rose had to declare personal bankruptcy.

In the context of investment markets, the analog to winning more than half of the bets is earning rates of return greater than those earned by naive investors who buy and hold securities of equal risk. Because stock prices have an upward drift, trading strategies involving holding long positions in common stock all tend to make a profit. As a benchmark, therefore, strategies are compared with buying and holding securities of similar risk. In the football betting market, no such benchmark is necessary because football gambling is a zero sum game with no analog to the upward drift in stock prices.

If security prices reflect all publicly available information, then even the most astute investors cannot discern, on the basis of public information, which securities are underpriced and are, therefore, "better" investments. Accordingly, the EMH predicts that over the long-run, professional investors will earn rates of return equal to those earned by naive investors who buy and hold securities of equal risk. This prediction of the efficient market hypothesis has been studied extensively. The results are strongly supportive of the EMH. Neither technical investors, who rely on mechanical trading rules, nor professional money managers, as a group, are able consistently to earn rates of return greater than those earned by a simple buy and hold strategy.[5] Of course, there are exceptions. Men like Warren Buffet and Peter Lynch have outperformed the market year after year. But it is easy to make too much of this fact. First, both Mr. Buffet and Mr. Lynch are extraordinary individuals who devoted much of their lives to studying investments. Second, even if professional investors on average fail to beat a buy and hold strategy, given the great number of professional investors and the volatile nature of stock prices, some investors are bound to evidence superior performance, if only by the luck of the draw. To illustrate this fact, consider a simple thought experiment. Start with 10,000 people and tell each of them to flip a coin. Once the coins are flipped, declare those with heads to be superior performers and those with tails to be losers. Tell the losers to go home and ask the superior performers to flip again. After 10 to 15 flips, the original group of 10,000 will be reduced to a few consistent winners. In the real world, these few winners, not recognizing the random nature of their victories, would no doubt be giving television interviews and writing books explaining how they beat the market!

A second key prediction of the efficient market hypothesis focuses on stock price changes. Because the current stock price reflects all currently available information, the EMH predicts that *changes* in stock prices are caused by the arrival of *new* information.[6] By definition, the arrival of new information must be random. Any information whose arrival could be predicted on the basis of current data would not be new. On this score, Martin Feldstein noted, when he was head of the Council of Economic

---

[5] A classic study of the performance of professional investors is M. C. Jensen, "The Performance of Mutual Funds in the Period 1945–1964," *Journal of Finance* 23 (May 1968), pp. 389–416. Similar results have been reported in numerous follow-up studies.

[6] The change in the stock price referred to in the text is the change net of the expected return. As shown in Chapter 7, stocks must offer a positive expected return or investors would not be willing to hold them. This positive expected return accounts for the upward drift in stock prices. For most stocks, the magnitude of this expected return is on the order of 10 percent per year or .04 percent per trading day. That means that for a $40 stock, the expected price change is approximately one tenth of a cent per day. Clearly, most of the day-to-day variation in stock returns is unexpected.

Advisers, that "bond prices would not move sharply unless something unexpected happened and *I don't expect anything unexpected.*" Professor Feldstein's observation is tautological—you never expect the unexpected. The key is defining clearly what is new information. For instance, news that soft drink consumption rose in July is not likely to be new information, because such an increase is predictable. On the other hand, news that a major soft drink manufacturer had a fire at its largest production facility is new information.

If stock prices respond only to new information, as the EMH predicts, then by definition stock price changes must be random. Neither the most astute technical investors nor the most sophisticated statistical packages should be able to uncover a pattern in stock returns.[7] This prediction of the EMH has also stood up remarkably well to over 25 years of careful testing.[8]

Finally, the EMH predicts that stock prices must respond immediately and without bias to the response of new information. For example, suppose that IBM announces unexpectedly lower earnings, and as a result, the stock drops from $100 to $95. According to the EMH, the decline should occur immediately following the announcement. The drop should not be lagged so that the price declines slowly to $95 over several days, nor should the market "overreact" with the price falling below $95 and then recovering. These predictions of the EMH have been tested in hundreds of event studies that examine the response of stock prices to announcements regarding earnings, dividends, stock splits, takeover bids, and a host of other news releases.[9] The results are almost uniformly supportive of the EMH. In study after study, prices are found to respond immediately and without bias to new information. Taken as a whole, these event studies provide perhaps the strongest support for the EMH.

---

[7]More precisely, returns net of expected returns should be random. Patterns in expected returns can induce minor patterns in total returns. For a detailed analysis of the behavior of expected and unexpected returns and references to other papers on the subject, see E. F. Fama and K. R. French, "Business Conditions and Stock Prices," *Journal of Financial Economics* 25 (November 1989), pp. 23–49.

[8]See Fama, "Efficient Capital Markets: A Review"; and Fama, "Efficient Capital Markets: II."

[9]Ibid.

Evidence of Market Inefficiency

Though the great bulk of the evidence supports the efficient market hypothesis, a number of inconsistencies have been found. It is difficult to interpret these inconsistencies because no historical data can be perfectly random. Even a set of random numbers generated by a computer will appear to have some pattern after the fact. Those patterns, however, are spurious and will not be replicated in another generation of random numbers. Many scholars feel that the same is true of stock prices. Given the thousands of studies that have been conducted using historical stock price information, the data have been so well mined that it is inevitable that some patterns would be found. According to this interpretation, the observed patterns are historical quirks that will not be repeated in the future and are not actual inefficiencies. While it cannot be determined whether a particular inefficiency is the result of data mining without waiting to see if history repeats itself, this possibility should be kept in mind when evaluating evidence on stock market anomalies.

The inefficiencies that have been most widely documented fall into three general categories: patterns in stock prices, mispricing of securities, and excess volatility in stock returns. With respect to patterns in stock prices, the strongest evidence against market efficiency is provided by the seasonal effects, including the "turn of the year" effect and the "day of the week" effect. The turn of the year effect is the tendency of stock returns to be larger from the last trading day of December through the end of January than during the rest of the year. The day of the week effect is the tendency of stock returns to be lower on Mondays than during the rest of the week.[10]

The most important mispricing that has been discovered is related to firm size. Banz was the first to uncover evidence that investors in small firms (measured in terms of market capitalization) earned significantly greater returns than investors who

---

[10]For a summary of the literature on seasonal patterns in stock prices, see D. Keim, "Stock Market Regularities: A Synthesis of the Evidence and Explanations," in *Stock Market Anomalies*, ed. Elroy Dimson (Cambridge: Cambridge University Press, 1988).

purchased the stock of large companies.[11] Further research revealed that the firm size effect was too large to be explained by standard asset pricing models. Although small firms should offer slightly higher returns than large firms because investing in small firms is riskier, the gap reported by Banz is still too large. It should be added that some scholars feel that the small firm effect is evidence not of market inefficiency but of the inability of current models to accurately measure the risk of investing in small firms. In addition, a bizarre twist was added. Most of the difference in returns for small and large firms was found to be attributed to January, leading to the suspicion that the firm size effect and the turn of the year effect were somehow intertwined.[12]

Apparent anomalies such as the small firm effect led Lawrence Summers to make an important observation about tests of the efficient market hypothesis.[13] Summers notes that most tests of the efficient market hypothesis, such as the event study tests referred to above, are based on the short-run behavior of stock prices. Consequently, it is possible that the tests will not uncover long-term mispricing. That is, the tests may indicate that the market is efficient for stocks whose market prices diverge from their true values by a significant amount, as long as the divergence between price and true value remains relatively constant in the short term. Furthermore, active traders have no incentive to attempt to exploit this divergence because they cannot make a profit in the short run. (On this score, Michael Milken complained in a seminar at UCLA that one of the problems with investing in stock is that even if you are smart enough to find an undervalued issue, you will not make a profit until the rest of the market realizes the issue is underpriced and the price rises. In high-yield bonds, on the other hand, an astute investor who chooses bonds that do not default is assured a superior return because of the high interest payments.) Although such divergences may be ignored by

---

[11]R. F. Banz, "The Relationship between Return and Market Value," *Journal of Financial Economics* 9 (January 1981), pp. 3–18.

[12]See Keim, "Stock Market Regularities."

[13]L. H. Summers, "Does the Stock Market Rationally Reflect Fundamental Values?" *Journal of Finance* 41 (July 1986), pp. 591–601.

short-run traders, they are important to appraisers because the goal of an appraisal is to estimate the true value of a company.

Finally, Shiller's path-breaking work ignited a debate regarding the volatility of stock prices.[14] Shiller presents evidence that stock prices jump around more than one would expect on the basis of variation in corporate dividends and cash flow. As explained in Chapters 6 and 7, a company's stock price should equal the discounted present value of the future dividends or future free cash flow. Therefore, variation in stock prices should be closely tied to variation in dividends and variation in cash flow. If Shiller's findings are correct, then the market cannot be properly valuing securities, at least not all the time. Perhaps the most dramatic evidence in support of Shiller's hypothesis is the stock market crash of October 1987. In just two days, without any major news announcement, the market dropped approximately 30 percent. Under such circumstances, it is hard to understand how stock prices could have properly reflected all publicly available information both before and after the crash.

MARKET INEFFICIENCY AND APPRAISAL PRACTICE

Though market inefficiency remains an active area of academic research, its implications for appraisal practice are limited. To be useful to appraisers, there would have to be documented and predictable inefficiencies that appraisers could incorporate in their valuation analysis. For example, an appraiser might observe that the market price of the stock is $50, but conclude that taking well-known inefficiencies into account, the true value is closer to $55 per share. The fact is that no scientific body of evidence supports such adjustments. It is one thing to say that the market may be inefficient; it is another to say that an appraiser can assess the inefficiency and respond with a more accurate valuation of a

---

[14]R. J. Shiller, "Do Stock Prices Move Too Much to Be Justified by Subsequent Changes in Dividends?" *American Economic Review* 71 (June 1981), pp. 421–36.

company's securities. For example, although Summers argues that market prices may diverge from true value, he does not suggest an alternative procedure for estimating the true value that is more accurate than relying on the market price. A market that is not perfectly efficient may still value securities more accurately than appraisers who are forced to work with limited information and whose judgments by nature reflect their own views and biases.

There is another reason for suspecting that appraisers cannot value securities more accurately than markets, even possibly inefficient markets. Suppose that by adjusting the market price, an appraiser could arrive at a more accurate assessment of a company's true value. Such an individual would be well advised to leave the appraisal business and enter money management. Presumably, the market price would tend to move toward the companys' true value over the long run, allowing the appraiser (money manager) to make a speculative profit. Similarly, if averaging produced a more reliable value indicator than the current market price, the appraiser (money manager) could profit by buying a stock whenever the current price was significantly below the average and selling when the current price rose above the average. Such moving average investment rules have been tested extensively without uncovering evidence that they are consistently profitable.[15]

The market appraisal also has the benefit of objectivity. Appraisals are often solicited in hostile situations such as tax disputes, damage litigation, and battles for corporate control. The market valuation process is free of influence from the parties who have requested the appraisal. Appraisers, on the other hand, usually have an incentive to arrive at a valuation that satisfies their clients.

The bottom line is that although the market may not be perfectly efficient, there is no evidence that any other pricing mechanism works consistently better. As Winston Churchill once said of democracy, "No one pretends that democracy is perfect or all wise. Indeed, it has been said that democracy is the worst form of government except all those other forms that have been tried from

---

[15]See Fama, "Efficient Capital Markets: A Review."

time to time." The same is true of markets. It is one thing for an appraiser to point to market anomalies; it is quite another for this appraiser to suggest his or her judgment should be substituted for that of the market. Though doubts can be raised about whether market prices perfectly measure true value, the uncertainty surrounding any other approach to appraisal is greater still.

Implications of the EMH for Appraisal Practice

The efficient market hypothesis has two important implications for appraisal practice. First, and most importantly, it implies that in situations where the stock and debt approach can be employed, it will produce the most reliable indictor of value. This does not mean everyone agrees that the sum of the market values of a company's securities represents the fair value of the firm. Some investors no doubt believe the market price is too high, while others believe it is too low—that is why there is trading. (Remember that prior to the Super Bowl, some investors believed that the Bills were more than seven points better than the Giants, and some believed that the Bills were less than seven points better.) However, the EMH states that the market assessment of value is more accurate, on average, than that of any individual, including an appraiser. For this reason, appraisers should not substitute their own judgment for that of the market. Though this may seem obvious, it is not uncommon for appraisers to reject the market's opinion when it conflicts with their own views.

For instance, an appraisal report prepared by a leading utility company states that: "Certain conditions in the financial market during the past year have severely limited application of the stock and debt approach. These market conditions have resulted in unusually high stock prices . . . " In the context of the EMH, stock prices cannot be "unusually" high because they always reflect current information. What the appraisal report is really saying is that the appraiser believes that stock prices are too high and, therefore, rejects the stock and debt approach.

Second, the EMH implies that the firm's securities should be valued at the market prices prevailing on the lien date. Despite this implication, some appraisers, when calculating a stock and debt value, average security prices over periods ranging from a month to a year preceding the lien date of the appraisal. For example, one appraisal report prepared for a major telephone company reads as follows:

> On average, interest rates in 1992 were below their respective 1991 levels by about 1.5 to 2.0 percent. Despite the downward trend in capital costs, interest rates continue to be quite volatile. Therefore, a short-term perspective could be misleading and, as always—whether interest rates have increased or decreased—should be avoided and average annual rates should be used.

The efficient market hypothesis states that such averaging is incorrect. Security price fluctuations, including movements in interest rates, are a result of the arrival of new information. When information is arriving rapidly, bond prices (and hence interest rates) will be volatile. Nonetheless, the correct price, or rate, to use in an appraisal is the price that reflects all available information on the lien date. According to EMH, that price is given by the market price, or market rate, on the lien date. Averaging earlier prices, which are based on past information, reduces the accuracy of the appraisal. Furthermore, the more volatile security prices are, the *less* appropriate it is to average them because the high volatility indicates rapid arrival of new information so that historical prices are significantly out-of-date. This is illustrated clearly by the football betting market. On the day of the game, the point spread that correctly reflects the relative abilities of the two teams is the current point spread. Averaging past point spreads that may have prevailed before key players were injured is clearly misleading.

Dealing with Nonpublicly Traded Debt and Preferred Stock

It is not uncommon for a company's common stock to be publicly traded, while its debt or preferred stock are not. Because equity, in most circumstances, is more difficult to value than debt or preferred stock, it would be a shame to forgo use of the stock and debt approach simply because the company's preferred stock and debt were not marketable. Fortunately, the stock and debt approach does not have to be discarded when debt and preferred stock are nonmarketable. Because debt and preferred stock offer fixed payouts, they can be valued by discounting the promised payments to present value at the yields prevailing on marketable securities of equivalent risk. The details of this procedure are presented in Chapter 4 and, therefore, are not repeated here. At this juncture, it is worth noting that in many cases, a shortcut can be employed. If the average rate on the outstanding debt and preferred stock are similar to average yields prevailing in the market, then the book value of the securities will be approximately equal to the market value. Accordingly, the book value can be used as an estimate of the market value.

As a note of caution, the shortcut should not be utilized until the appraiser has carefully investigated all the features of the debt and preferred stock. Sometimes, issues of debt and preferred have imbedded options, such as call options or convertibility options. When such options exist, valuation of the securities requires more sophisticated techniques than simple discounting, so that the principle on which the shortcut is based is not applicable.[16]

If the shortcut is applicable, the estimated values of the debt and preferred are added to the market value of the equity to give the total value of the firm.

Taking into Account Possible Control Premiums

The value indicator calculated using the stock and debt approach is based on the prices at which minority positions trade in the market. Therefore, it will not take into account a "control premium." If the appraiser believes that a controlling block of securities would trade for a premium price, that premium must be estimated separately. The question of whether a control premium should be added and, if so, how large that premium should be is addressed in Chapter 8.

---

[16]J. Hull, *Options, Futures and Other Derivative Securities*, (Englewood Cliffs, N.J.: Prentice Hall, 1989), provides a detailed explanation of the valuation of the options embedded in debt and equity securities.

INDIRECT APPLICATIONS OF THE STOCK AND DEBT APPROACH

Because the stock and debt approach is directly applicable only to companies with publicly traded equity, its usefulness may appear limited. However, stock and debt valuations also play a key role as an input in other appraisal procedures. Specifically, the stock and debt approach is used to develop the ratios that are the basis for direct comparison appraisals. As described extensively in the next chapter, a commonly employed method for valuing companies whose equity is not publicly traded, as well as divisions and subsidiaries of publicly traded companies, is to calculate ratios such as price to earnings for comparable firms and then to apply those ratios to the appraisal target. However this procedure only pushes the appraisal problem back one step. To calculate the ratios, it is necessary to value the comparable firms. The preferred solution to this problem is to find comparable companies that have publicly traded securities so that the stock and debt approach can be applied. For example, investment bankers commonly utilize direct comparisons when setting prices for new offerings of common stock. Ratios such as price per share to earnings per share are calculated for companies that have already gone public. These ratios are then applied to the earnings of the target firm as a means of setting the offering price.

The stock and debt approach also provides a useful benchmark for testing other appraisal procedures. As illustrated in Chapter 2, the question of whether the market value of a utility equals its rate base was tested by applying the stock and debt approach to a sample of utility companies. Similarly, the stock and debt approach can be used to test the accuracy of other appraisal models. For instance, the state of California commissioned a study to determine whether the value indicators produced by the state's proprietary valuation model were consistent with stock and debt value indicators.

The stock and debt approach can also be applied when the appraiser is asked to value a company's assets rather than the firm itself. Though this distinction may seem semantic, it plays an important role in property tax appraisal. Each year, every state in the union appraises all the railroads and public utilities that op-

FIGURE 3–1
Market Value of Assets and Liabilities

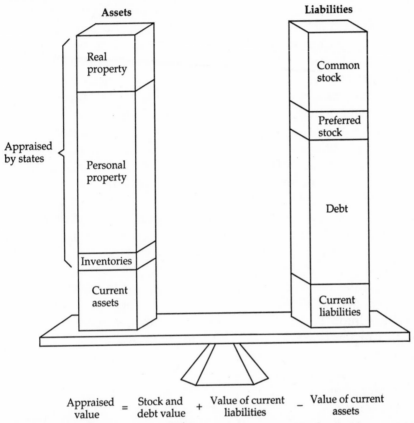

$$\underset{\text{value}}{\text{Appraised}} = \underset{\text{debt value}}{\text{Stock and}} + \underset{\text{liabilities}}{\text{Value of current}} - \underset{\text{assets}}{\text{Value of current}}$$

erate within its borders. Although the specific property tax rules vary from state to state, the general charge is that the tax be based on the market value of the company's "operating property." The operating property, in this context, typically is interpreted to be the total assets of the firm net of short-term working capital.

By employing the balance sheet identity that total assets must equal total liabilities stated in terms of market value, the stock and debt approach can be used to value a company's assets for property tax purposes. To illustrate, Figure 3–1 presents a schematic of the balance sheet. The schematic shows that the value of the property subject to taxation (real property, personal property, and inventories) equals the stock and debt value of the firm plus the value of the current liabilities minus the value of the current assets.

From the standpoint of property tax appraisal, the stock and debt approach has several beneficial attributes. First, the stock and debt approach is straightforward, so that the probability of errors arising from incorrect application is reduced. Second, the stock and debt approach requires little information other than the market prices of securities, so that the cost of gathering and processing information is minimized. Finally, and most importantly, the stock and debt approach is based on the judgment of the market, not the individual appraiser. This avoids potential biases that may creep in when judgment is required. Furthermore, the efficient market hypothesis implies that the stock and debt approach should produce the most accurate value indicator.

The stock and debt approach to value can also play a role in the appraisal of subsidiaries of diversified corporations. For example, Union Pacific Railroad, which is subject to a unitary property tax, is a subsidiary of Union Pacific Corporation. However, only the parent corporation has publicly traded securities outstanding. In this situation, a two-step procedure is required to make use of a stock and debt analysis. First, the stock and debt approach is applied to Union Pacific Corporation. Second, the value of Union Pacific Corporation is allocated among the subsidiaries, including Union Pacific Railroad. The allocation is typically based on observable accounting variables.

Popular choices of accounting variables used to allocate value among the subsidiaries of a parent corporation are net income, operating income, free cash flow, gross revenue, total assets, and net assets. No matter which variable is chosen, the value of the subsidiary is computed by multiplying the value of the parent by the ratio of the parent's accounting variable to the subsidiary's. The appraisal of AT&T Communications by the state of California provides an example. AT&T Communications, which provides long-distance telephone service, is subject to a unitary property tax, but the remainder of the company is not. In 1991, the stock and debt value of AT&T was $48.96 billion. To allocate a fraction of that total value to AT&T Communications, California state appraisers proceeded as shown in Table 3–1.

TABLE 3–1
Allocation of Value for AT&T Communications Based on the 1991
Stock and Debt Appraisal of AT&T

Total stock and debt value of AT&T as of March 1, 1991: $48,960,000

Allocation Factors	AT&T Communications	AT&T Parent	Percent due to AT&T Com	Implied Value of AT&T Com
Operating income	$ 1,587,599	$ 2,922,790	54.3%	$26,594,058
Gross revenue	20,717,909	45,382,350	45.7	22,351,174
Net assets	23,843,598	52,601,250	45.3	22,193,057
Gross assets	34,556,393	74,115,470	46.6	22,827,637
Average			48.0%	$23,491,482

The allocation was based on four accounting variables: operating income, gross revenues, net assets, and total assets. For each accounting variable, the ratio of AT&T Communications to AT&T was calculated. For example, AT&T Communications operating income was found to be 54.3 percent of the total operating income of AT&T. Using 54.3 percent as an allocation factor gives an estimated value of $23,491,482 for AT&T Communications. As shown in the table, the allocations based on gross revenue, net assets, and gross assets are 45.7 percent, 45.3 percent, and 46.6 percent, respectively.

When calculating ratios of accounting variables to serve as allocation factors, there are two important points to bear in mind. First, the data used to compute the ratios must be comparable for both the subsidiary company (in the numerator) and the parent company (in the denominator). For example, if net income is measured before extraordinary items (which is generally a good idea), then it must be so defined for both the parent and the subsidiary. Second, the appraiser should recognize that in some cases, ratios of accounting variables may not represent relative value. For instance, one subsidiary may earn more on its assets than the parent. In that case, an allocation ratio based on either total assets or net assets will understate the value of the subsidiary. This problem will be mitigated by developing ratios based on earnings rather than assets. However, it is also possible that the subsidiary has greater potential for growth than the parent. In that case, ratios based on current earnings will still understate the relative value of the subsidiary.

In dealing with situations in which ratios of some of the accounting variables may not properly reflect relative value, the appraiser has a number of choices. First, it is possible to pick and choose among the accounting variables. As noted above, there are situations in which ratios based on earnings may reflect relative value, while ratios based on assets do not. Second, it may be possible to adjust the accounting variables so that they more accurately reflect relative value, as discussed below. Finally, in some situations the appraiser may choose to ignore the accounting variables and allocate value using alternate valuation models. In this final case, however, it is probably best to avoid the allocation problem altogether by appraising the subsidiary directly. Valuing the subsidiary of interest directly is easier than valuing the conglomerate firm and then subtracting the estimated values of all the other subsidiaries.

One way to adjust allocation ratios based on earnings in order to bring them into line with relative values is to use a variant of the direct comparison approach. Though a detailed discussion of the direct comparison approach is postponed until the next chapter, a simple example using earnings illustrates the basic idea. Suppose that the parent company, which has been valued at $1 billion, consists of a railroad and an oil exploration company. Assume, furthermore, that an analysis of railroad companies, reveals that the average price per share of common stock is 5 times earnings, and an analysis of oil exploration companies reveals that they trade at 15 times earnings. (As discussed in Chapter 4, The Direct Comparison Approach, ratios should be computed using properly normalized earnings that do not necessarily equal reported earnings.) Finally, assume that the total earnings of the parent company are $100 million, and that these earnings are divided equally between the two subsidiaries. An unadjusted earnings allocation would divide the $1 billion in total value equally between the subsidiaries. But such an allocation fails to take into account the fact that the market is willing to pay more for a dollar of oil exploration earnings than for a dollar of railroad earnings. To adjust for this fact, it is necessary to solve a system of equations that includes the value/earnings (or price/earnings) ratios. The system of equations reflects the fact that the value of one dollar of earnings depends on which subsidiary earns the dollar.

$$\text{Value}_{\text{railroad}} + \text{Value}_{\text{oil exploration}} = \$1 \text{ billion}$$

$$\text{Earnings}_{\text{railroad}} = \text{Earnings}_{\text{oil exploration}}$$

$$\text{Value}_{\text{railroad}} / \text{Earnings}_{\text{railroad}} = 5$$

$$\text{Value}_{\text{oil exploration}} / \text{Earnings}_{\text{oil exploration}} = 15$$

Solving the system of equations yields an estimated value of $250 million for the railroad and $750 million for the oil exploration company.

CONCLUDING OBSERVATIONS

When a company's securities are publicly traded, a firm can be appraised simply by adding the market values of its outstanding securities. This stock and debt approach to appraisal is based on the efficient market hypothesis, which states that the market prices reflect all publicly available information regarding the value of securities. The efficient market hypothesis implies that the stock and debt approach will produce the most accurate appraisals on average. In addition, the EMH implies that the appraiser should make use of current market prices, not averages of past prices, because it is current prices that reflect current value.

Though the efficient market hypothesis is consistent with the bulk of empirical evidence on the behavior of securities markets, there is also some contradictory evidence. However, the implications of possible inefficiency for appraisal practice should not be exaggerated. The key question is not whether the market values companies perfectly in *every* case, but whether it is possible to identify situations in which another appraisal approach will produce a more accurate valuation than the market. There is no reliable evidence supporting the view that the valuation errors on the part of the market can be identified by an alternate appraisal procedure. Any appraiser who could consistently spot such valuation errors could make a vast fortune as an investor.

Chapter Four

The Direct Comparison Approach

Economic theory and common sense agree on the basic principle that similar assets should sell at similar prices. Based on this principle, a straightforward way to value an asset is to find an identical, or at least closely comparable, asset that has changed hands between a reasonably informed buyer and seller. The principle implies that the value of the asset being appraised equals the sale price of the comparable. This approach works well in real estate. If there are five similar houses on a block and one sells, the appraised values of the other four equal the sale price.

Even in real estate, differences in scale make it difficult to find properties that are directly comparable. If the house next door to yours sold for $200,000 but is only half the size of yours, it would be a mistake to appraise your house for $200,000. The solution to the scale problem is to make the comparison on a per unit basis in terms of ratios. For instance, if the house next door is 2,000 square feet, the selling price comes to $100 per square foot. If your house if 4,000 square feet, and if square footage is closely related to value, then your house should be appraised at $400,000.

As the example illustrates, the direct comparison approach, adjusted for differences in scale, involves two quantities, a value indicator and an observable variable that is related to value. For direct comparisons to be possible, data on both the value indicator and the observable variable must be available for the comparable asset, and data on the observable variable must be available for the appraisal target. In the real estate example, the value indicator is the price of the house and the observable variable is the number of square feet. The ratio of the price of the house to the number of square feet is calculated for the comparable houses that sold recently and multiplied by the number of square feet in the house being appraised.

Expressing the direct comparison approach in mathematical terms yields further insight into how it works and the assumptions on which it depends. Define the value indicator to be V and the observable variable to be x. The critical assumption on which the direct comparison approach depends is that the ratio of V to x for the appraisal target equals (at least approximately) the ratio of V to x for the comparable firms, as shown in Equation (4-1).

$$V_{target}/x_{target} = V_{comparables}/x_{comparables} \qquad (4-1)$$

If Equation (4-1) holds, the appraisal procedure is trivial. Solving Equation (4-1) for the one unknown variable, the value indicator for the appraisal target, gives:

$$V_{target} = x_{target} \cdot V_{comparables}/x_{comparables} \qquad (4-2)$$

Equation (4-2) works for any observable variable x, as long as the ratio of V to x is constant across firms, as shown in Equation (4-1). For instance, x could be the number of paintings in a house. If the relation between the price of a house and the amount of artwork it contains is relatively constant across houses, the direct comparison approach based on art will produce an accurate appraisal. The problem is that there are people who live in expensive homes and do not like art. For these homes, Equation (4-1) breaks down and the direct comparison approach will not produce a reasonable appraisal. For this reason, a critical step in applying the direct comparison approach is choosing observable variables, x, that have a consistent relation to value, V. In general, the best way to do this is to find x variables that economic theory indicates will be causally related to value. In the case of a house, square footage is a good candidate because larger houses tend to sell for higher prices. In the case of a company, variables such as cash flows and earnings are good choices because the ultimate sources of value are the net benefits received by investors.

DIRECT COMPARISON VERSUS DIRECT CAPITALIZATION

In some cases, appraisers choose to divide by a capitalization rate rather than multiplying by a ratio. For instance, one way to apply the direct comparison approach is to calculate the average price-earnings, or P/E, ratio for a sample of comparable firms and multiply it by the earnings of the appraisal target. An equivalent procedure is to divide the appraisal target's earnings by the average E/P ratio for the comparable firms. In the second case, the E/P ratio is referred to as a capitalization rate, and the appraisal process is often described as direct capitalization. Nonetheless, the alternative procedure is conceptually identical to the direct comparison approach based on multiples. The only difference is that in direct capitalization, the inverse of the ratio is divided into the observable variable instead of multiplying the ratio by the observable variable.

To illustrate, one way the state of Washington appraises companies is by developing capitalization rates based on the ratio of total market value to earnings before interest, depreciation, and taxes, EBIDT. That is, state appraisers compute EBIDT/Market value for a sample of comparable companies. The value of the appraisal target is calculated by dividing the target's EBIDT by the capitalization rate. For instance, if EBIDT for the target is $150 million and the average EBIDT/Market value ratio for the comparable companies is 0.10, the estimated value of the target is $1.5 billion ($150 million/0.10.) This procedure clearly is equivalent to multiplying $150 million by an average Market value/EBIDT of 10.

Despite the fact that direct comparison and direct capitalization are equivalent, confusion has arisen in practice because of misinterpretation of the concept of direct capitalization. As the foregoing makes clear, direct capitalization depends on comparisons. Ratios such as price to earnings or EBIDT to market value are calculated for comparable companies and applied to the appraisal target. The confusion arises when capitalization rates get mixed up with the cost of capital.[1] This confusion is not solely due to the fact that names are similar. Under unique circumstances, it is possible to appraise a firm by dividing a measure of income by the cost of capital as if it were a capitalization rate. For example, the value of a firm that produces a constant cash flow CF into perpetuity equals CF/k, where k is the cost of capital.[2] However, situations in which the cost of capital can be used as a

---

[1] The cost of capital is discussed in detail in Chapter 7.

[2] More generally, if the cash flow stream is growing at a constant rate g, its value is CF/$(k-g)$, as discussed subsequently.

capitalization rate are extraordinarily rare. Nonetheless, some appraisers fall into the trap of employing the cost of capital as a capitalization rate. To avoid such confusion in this book, the term *direct comparison* rather than *direct capitalization* is used. The name *direct comparison* highlights the fact that this approach to appraisal is based on making comparisons and not on discounting cash flows to present value at the cost of capital.

In a similar vein, it should also be recognized that a capitalization rate is not a discount rate. It is just as misleading to discount future cash flows to present value at a capitalization rate as it is to capitalize an income stream by dividing by the cost of capital.

ACCEPTANCE OF THE DIRECT COMPARISON APPROACH BY COURTS OF LAW

Courts of law have recognized the idea that valid value indicators can be derived by making direct comparisons. In two landmark decisions, *Central Trust* and *Bader*, the court ruled that the value of a target company could be estimated by capitalizing the company's dividends and earnings.[3] An income stream such as a dividend stream is "capitalized" by applying the direct comparison approach. Ratios of dividends to market value are computed for comparable companies to arrive at a capitalization rate. The stream is then capitalized by dividing the current dividend paid by the target company by the capitalization rate. This process is analyzed in detail in the remainder of the chapter.

In a review of the *Bader* and *Central Trust* cases, Hickman and Petry observe that in endorsing the direct comparison approach, the court is relying on the "Law of One Price." The law of one price is simply a restatement of the basic principle that similar assets should sell at similar prices.[4] For corporations, the courts

---

[3]*Central Trust*, 59-1 USTC par. 9431; 172 F. Supp. 833 (DC Ill.); and *Bader*, 62-2 USTC par. 12,092; 304 F 2d 923.

[4]K. Hickman and G. H. Petry, "A Comparison of Stock Price Predictions Using Court Accepted Formulas, Dividend Discount and P/E Models, *Financial Management*, Summer 1990, pp. 76–87.

interpret the law of one price in terms of ratios. If a comparable company that earns $10 million is worth $100 million, then a target that earns $20 million should be worth $200 million.

The impact of *Central Trust* and *Bader* has been significant. In a study of the precedent set by *Central Trust* and *Bader*, Englebrecht and Lesson conclude that "Bader and Central Trust have exerted a great deal of influence on subsequent decisions in the Court of Claims and the district courts. Thus, valuation professionals who utilize market comparable formulas may feel they are standing on the firm ground of legal precedent."[5]

SELECTING COMPARABLE COMPANIES

There are two obstacles to overcome when valuing companies by direct comparison. First, unlike single-family homes, sales of corporations are relatively rare. Therefore, it is typically difficult to find sales of comparable companies to serve as the basis for comparisons. Second, and more importantly, the concept of a "comparable" company is nebulous. Corporations are complex entities characterized by a wide variety of traits. Which traits must be similar for two companies to be deemed comparable?

The first problem can be overcome by using data for publicly traded firms. Although entire companies rarely change hands, minority positions in publicly traded companies, as represented by ownership of the firm's stock and debt, are bought and sold daily. These comparable publicly traded firms can be valued by applying the stock and debt approach.

With respect to the second problem, it is important to recognize that from a valuation standpoint, all companies produce the same product—cash. Whether the company is in steel, biotechnology, or computers, its value to potential buyers is determined by the cash flows it is expected to generate. Ideally, therefore, comparability should be defined in terms of the statistical properties

---

[5]T. Englebrecht and C. Lesson, "Valuation of Closely Held Stock," *The Tax Executive*, October 1978, pp. 57–64.

of the anticipated cash flow stream. Applying this definition, two firms are comparable if the correlation between their expected future cash flows is high.

Unfortunately, this definition of comparability requires forecasting future cash flows many years into the future. One of the prime reasons for the popularity of the direct comparison approach is that application of Equation (4–2) does not require cash flow forecasts. If cash flow forecasts are necessary to select comparable companies, this rationale for using the direct comparison approach is undermined. Furthermore, if cash flow forecasts are available for the appraisal target, the value of the firm can be calculated directly by discounting the forecast cash flows to present value, so that it is not necessary to search for comparable companies.

For the direct comparison approach to be useful, there must be a way to identify comparable companies without developing detailed cash flow forecasts for each firm. One common solution is to rely on industry classifications. The assumption behind this approach is that if two companies are in the same industry, their cash flows will react to similar market forces and, therefore, will be highly correlated. In support of the view that comparability can be assessed, at least in part, by relying on industrial classification, the IRS, in its Revenue Ruling 59-60, states:

> In selecting the corporations for comparative purposes, care should be taken to use only comparable companies. Although the restrictive requirement as to comparable corporations specified in the statute is that their lines of business be the same or similar, yet it is obvious that consideration must be given to other relevant factors in order that the most valid comparison possible will be obtained.

Industry classifications are typically defined in terms of standard industrial classification (SIC) codes. Data on SIC codes are published in the U.S. government's *Standard Industrial Classification Manual*. SIC information is also published by Standard & Poor's and Moody's and is available in a variety of on-line computer databases, such as the Compustat database distributed by Standard & Poor's Corporation, the Dow Jones News Service, and Compuserve.

As the IRS quotation makes clear, however, industrial classification alone provides only a rough estimate of comparability. For instance, IBM and AST Research, which are both computer companies, share the same four-digit SIC code, 3573. Nonetheless, the companies are of vastly different size, have different capital structures, make largely different products, have distinct management philosophies, and have markedly disparate corporate histories.

The fact that SIC codes alone cannot be relied on to define comparable companies has been recognized by the courts in decisions subsequent to *Central Trust* and *Bader*. Pratt reports that in *Tallichet* v. *Commissioner* and in *Estate of Victor P. Clarket*, the tax court recognized that in addition to industrial classification, comparability should also be measured, among other things, in terms of:

1. Products.
2. Capital structure.
3. Depth of management.
4. Personnel experience.
5. Nature of competition.
6. Earnings.
7. Book value.
8. Credit status.[6]

Assessing the nature of a company's products, weighing the merits of its personnel, and evaluating the depth of its management involves judgment and experience that are largely independent of finance. Instead of knowledge of finance, making such judgments requires a detailed understanding of the business being appraised, the industry in which it operates, and the competitive and regulatory forces that impact it. Because this book focuses on financial valuation models, suggesting how to make such judgments is beyond its scope. Fortunately, it is usually not necessary for the appraiser to make such difficult judgments in

---

[6]S. Pratt, *Valuing a Business* (Homewood, Ill.: Business One Irwin, 1989).

isolation—there are sources to which an appraiser can turn to help identify comparable companies.

One excellent source of information on comparability is security analyst reports. Reports prepared by leading analysts, in addition to offering a wealth of data about the target company, often contain a detailed list of comparable firms. In some cases, furthermore, the list of comparables is accompanied by a discussion of the economic factors that led the analyst to conclude that the companies were comparable. Analyst reports are available from the firms that employ the analysts and from a variety of public sources. For example, Investext, which is available through Dow Jones News Retrieval, maintains a relatively complete database of both current and historical analyst reports.

Investment research companies such as Standard & Poor's, Moody's, and Valueline also prepare economic reports on a large number of firms. These reports generally identify comparable firms as part of the analysis. The publications of these investment services are available at most major libraries. In addition, investment research firms are beginning to distribute their analyses on floppy and optical disks.

Relying on independent information such as analyst reports and studies produced by investment research companies also adds credibility to an appraisal. Most appraisals are performed for a purpose, and the client typically wants an appraised value that suits specific needs. (For instance, in ad valorem tax proceedings, firms want the appraised value to be as low as possible to reduce property taxes.) If the appraiser relies exclusively on his or her own judgment to make difficult decisions about comparability, independent parties such as courts and taxing authorities are likely to suspect that the judgments are biased in favor of the appraiser's client. Utilizing independent reports that were not prepared as part of the appraisal to select comparables reduces this suspicion. Of course, the appraiser must demonstrate that a representative sample of independent reports was used—a biased list of comparables can be constructed by relying on a hand-chosen series of "independent" reports.

If analyst reports and independent investment studies are not available, the appraiser is well advised to seek the aid of an industry expert in developing the appraisal. An industry expert can provide valuable information not only regarding potential comparable companies but also in developing forecasts regarding the appraisal target's future profitability and cash flow.

In addition, the appraiser has the option of asking the target's managers which firms they see as most comparable to their own and why. The advantage of such direct questioning is that the target's managers, on the basis of firsthand experience, should be excellent judges of comparability. The problem is that target managers may also have an interest in determining the final appraised value, and this may cloud their judgment regarding comparability.

Finally, financial ratio analysis can also be used to assess comparability. Though ratio analysis is typically presented in the context of measuring financial performance, two comparable companies should also be expected to have similar financial ratios. As described by Shapiro, financial ratios are generally divided into four categories.[7]

- *Liquidity ratios* measure the quality and adequacy of current assets to meet current liabilities as they come due. Examples of liquidity ratios are the current ratio (current assets/current liabilities) and the quick ratio [(current assets−inventories) / current liabilities].
- *Activity ratios* measure the efficiency with which the firm is using its resources. Examples of activity ratios include the gross profit margin (gross profit / net sales) and inventory turnover (cost of goods sold / inventories).
- *Leverage ratios* measure a firm's ability to service its debt. Key leverage ratios include times interest earned (EBIT / annual interest expense) and the debt equity ratio (total debt / market value of equity).
- *Profitability ratios* measure management's effectiveness as indicated by the returns on sales, assets, and owner's equity. Commonly used profitability ratios are the gross profit margin (gross profits/net sales) and the operating profit (EBIT/net sales).

---

[7]A. C. Shapiro, *Modern Corporate Finance* (New York: Macmillian, 1989), pp. 731–59.

Analysis of the financial ratios is particularly useful as a check on comparability. Suppose that the appraiser has selected a group of comparable companies based on industry analysis, examination of analyst reports, and discussions with management. Presumably, those comparables should have financial ratios similar to each other and similar to the appraisal target. If one or two comparables are found to have significantly different financial ratios, they can be deleted from the sample. If the comparable firms as a group have widely divergent ratios, the appraiser is well advised to look for other potential comparables with financial ratios more similar to that of the target.

Aside from serving as an aid in choosing comparable companies, financial ratios can also provide insight into the choice of V and x. As discussed later in the chapter, this is particularly true of the debt ratios. Frequently, otherwise comparable companies differ in the degree to which they employ leverage. The extent of this difference can be determined by examination of the leverage ratios. If the differences are significant, care should be taken to choose measures of V and x that are independent of leverage.

Assessing Comparability

The blizzard of criteria for choosing comparable companies can be daunting. What if one potential comparable has the same SIC code as the target but has a different capital structure, while another potential comparable has a similar capital structure but a different SIC code? Does finance theory provide any clues as to which criteria for assessing comparability are the most important? The answer is yes, to an extent.

To see how finance theory can be helpful, consider a staid company in a stable market that is growing at a constant rate, g. If the company's cost of capital is k, it can be shown that the value of the firm and its cash flow are related by the formula:

Market value $=$ Cash flow $/ k - g$

Dividing both sides of the equation by earnings gives:

Market value $/$ Cash flow $= 1 / (k - g)$ (4–3)

Because Equation (4–3) holds only for the case of constant growth, it should not be taken literally as a model for calculating the ratio of market value to cash flow. Despite this drawback, it still provides insight into the factors that will affect the ratio. The equation implies that two companies will be comparable, in the sense of having similar value to cash flow ratios, if $k - g$ is approximately the same for both firms. Consequently, when assessing comparability, the appraiser should pay particular attention to factors that affect the cost of capital or the expected rate of growth in cash flow.

The cash flow growth rate, g, depends on a host of factors. Among them are the size of the market for the firm's current products, the market share of each of the firm's products, the company's potential for expanding into new markets, the likelihood that research and development will produce new products, and the willingness of management to experiment with new ideas. The cost of capital, k, on the other hand is determined primarily by risk. Questions to ask when evaluating risk include: Are the company's earnings sensitive to economic conditions? Is the company highly leveraged so that it may experience financial distress in a recession? Does the company rely on a few key people or specific products to maintain its earnings? The greater the risk exposure, the higher the cost of capital will be.

AN APPLICATION OF DIRECT COMPARISON: THE USE OF P/E RATIOS

One of the most common applications of the direct comparison approach is the valuation of the equity of a firm on the basis of an analysis of price-earnings ratios. Price-earnings valuations are frequently utilized by investment banks when evaluating potential acquisitions, spin-offs, and restructurings. An example of the price-earnings valuation procedure is presented in Table 4–1. The example is based on the spin-off of a transportation company by a conglomerate firm. Because the table is from work papers prepared by an investment bank, the comparable companies are referred to simply as T1 through T9 to protect anonymity.

The comparables chosen by the investment bank in Table 4–1 were selected because they were in the same industry as the appraisal target. Ratios were calculated as of December 1986 using both actual earnings for 1986 and estimated earnings for 1987.

TABLE 4–1
Price Earnings Analysis for a Spin-Off of a Major Transportation Company as of December 1986

Comparable Company	Equity Value/ 1986 Earnings	Equity Value/ Estimated 1987 Earnings
T1	17.8	16.7
T2	12.3	11.8
T3	15.0	14.3
T4	15.8	16.5
T5	28.6	31.0
T6	15.1	14.4
T7	21.5	21.7
T8	53.0	50.5
T9	16.7	16.0
Average excluding T5 and T8	16.3	15.9
Median	16.7	16.5

Implied Values of Appraisal Target's Equity (in millions)

	Estimated Value Using 1986 Earnings of $218 Million (in millions)	Estimated Value Using 1987 (estimated) Earnings of $269 Million (in millions)
Average multiple	$3,557	$4,281
Median multiple	3,641	4,439

(The analysis was performed in early 1987.) Estimated earnings are often used in place of actual earnings because they are less variable. The problem with actual earnings is that they reflect year-to-year fluctuations in profitability that may not be permanent and, therefore, may have little effect on value. Because analysts cannot anticipate such random year-to-year fluctuations, estimated earnings are based more on assessments of long-run trends. As a result, estimated earnings tend to vary less over time and from company to company. For this reason, ratios based on estimated earnings are often considered to be more reliable.

The P/E ratios presented in Table 4–1 reveal that two of the companies, T5 and T8, had price-earnings multiples significantly greater than the others. For this reason, the investment bank chose to drop both companies before calculating the average P/E ratio. (They were not dropped when calculating the median because the median is not significantly affected by their inclusion.) Dropping "outliers" is not uncommon because of the fact that P/E ratios are meaningless for companies with small or negative earnings. If a company's earnings are close to zero, its P/E ratio will be huge, and including it in the average will bias the entire appraisal. An alternative to dropping the companies is to recalculate the ratios for the entire sample using "normalized" earnings. The alternative procedure is analyzed later in this chapter. However, such a procedure does not appear promising in this case because the ratios for T5 and T8 are just as anomalous when calculated using estimated earnings as they are when calculated using actual earnings.

Once the appropriate ratio—in this case, the average or the median—has been selected, the equity value of the target firm is estimated by multiplying the ratio by the actual earnings and estimated earnings of the target firm. For instance, the estimated 1987 earnings for the target company are $269 million. Multiplying this number by the 15.9 average P/E calculated using estimated earnings gives a value of $4,281 million for the equity. More generally, the estimated value of the equity ranges from $3,557 million and $4,439 million depending on whether the average or the median and actual or estimated earnings are employed.

Although the investment bank chose to apply average and median ratios, there is another option. Rather than treat all the companies retained in the sample identically, which is what using the average or median does, comparability can be assessed and the most comparable companies can be given greater weight. As noted above, a more detailed comparability analysis would examine, at a minimum, factors that affect the expected growth and the cost of capital of the target and the potential comparables. The drawback of this approach is that it opens the door to data mining. By employing the average and the median, the investment bank in the example is less likely to be accused of "cherry picking" in order to reach a particular conclusion.

Though the use of P/E multiples provides one illustration of the direct comparison approach, it is not the only, or necessarily the best, way in which direct comparisons can be developed. As the next section demonstrates, in many situations, price per share is not the most appropriate value indicator, and earnings per share is not the most appropriate financial variable.

CHOOSING THE OBSERVABLE FINANCIAL VARIABLE AND THE VALUE INDICATOR

As noted at the outset, for the direct comparison approach to provide an accurate estimate of value, the ratio of the value indicator to the observable variable, V/x, must be approximately the same for the comparable firms and for the appraisal target. Because the variability of V/x depends critically on the choice of V and x, the two variables must be carefully selected.

From a logical standpoint, the financial variables most likely to produce a constant V/x ratio are those that economic theory predicts will be closely associated with the value of the firm. Because the ultimate source of corporate value is cash produced for security holders, financial variables that measure potential payouts, such as earnings and cash flow, are obvious potential choices for x. In addition, variables that indirectly measure the earning power of the firm, such as sales and book value of equity, are also possible choices.

When selecting appropriate financial variables, the appraiser can turn to the data for help. Assuming that a group of comparable companies has been identified, the variability of the V/x ratio across the comparables can be calculated for several choices of x. If the ratio is found to vary substantially for a given x such as cash flow that choice of x is a probably a poor one. How can the appraiser confidently conclude what the V/x ratio will be for the target firm if the comparable firms all have markedly different ratios?

When analyzing variation in V/x as an aid in choosing the proper measure of x, there is an important caveat to keep in mind. In some cases, variability in the V/x ratio may result not from a poor choice of the observable variable but because of short-term aberrations in the data. For instance, suppose that earnings are selected as the observable variable, x. Reported earnings in a given year may be affected by short-term aberrations such as realizations of capital gains or losses, new product introductions, strikes, and foreign exchange fluctuations. In such situations, variation in the V/x ratio often can be mitigated by adjusting the financial data to reduce or eliminate the impact of the aberration. For instance, replacing the current value of x by a five-year average may eliminate most of the variation in the V/x ratio.

Although adjusting the data may reduce variation in the V/x ratio, the adjustment process introduces another source of possible error and bias. For this reason, it is wise to include in the list of financial variables some that do not require adjustment because they are less subject to short-term aberrations, or manipulation by target management. On this score, total sales, which is less volatile and less subject to manipulation, is superior to earnings or cash flow. For instance, partnerships such as law firms and consulting practices are commonly valued as multiples of annual revenues rather than as multiples of earnings or cash flow. Because the "costs" incurred by partnerships are subject to a good deal of discretion, the reported earnings reflect managerial decisions that often vary substantially across otherwise comparable firms. For that reason, appraisers have found that total revenue, which is much less subject to discretionary alterations, is a more reliable indicator of value. Similarly, actors and screenwriters generally ask that their bonuses be tied to a motion picture's gross receipts rather than its "earnings" because studios have a good deal of leeway in defining "costs." As a result, pictures with large gross sales often end up producing virtually no net earnings.

The selection of financial variables also depends on the relation between the comparables and the company being appraised. Suppose the appraisal target and its comparables are similar in all dimensions except for capital structure. Some companies have a great deal of debt, while others have none. In that case, the ratio of earnings to firm value across the comparables will vary substantially because companies with more debt have greater interest expenses and are, therefore, riskier. The impact of increasing risk can be seen by looking back at Equation (4–3). Increasing risk causes a firm's cost of capital to rise and thereby reduces the ratio of value to earnings. On the other hand, earnings before interest, depreciation, and taxes, EBIDT, is independent of the amount of debt and, therefore, should be relatively constant across firms. Thus, EBIDT is typically a more appropriate choice for the financial variable if otherwise comparable firms have different capital structures.

Although the appraiser has some discretion when choosing a financial variable, it must be matched with an appropriate value indicator. If a gross indicator such as EBIDT is selected, then it should be matched with total firm value. On the other hand, if the appraiser decides to use the value of equity (or price per share) in the numerator, then the denominator should measure the earnings or cash flow available to the equity holders, *net* of interest and preferred dividends (or earnings per share). For example, in the P/E analysis presented earlier, the value of the equity was used as the value indicator. Consequently, the result of the analysis is an estimate of the value of equity, not the total value of the firm. The debt and preferred stock must be appraised separately to calculate the total value of the firm.

The view that broader measures of income are more appropriate is supported by the work of Miller and Modigliani.[8] In several classic research papers, Modigliani and Miller present convincing arguments showing that the value of the firm depends little, if at all, on the firm's capital structure. Therefore, the ratio of total firm value to a gross measure of income such as EBIDT should be similar even for firms with different capital structures. This is important because otherwise comparable firms frequently have divergent capital structures. Forms Engineering is a case in point. FEC has a significant amount of debt outstanding, while most comparable printing firms have little. Consequently, applying a P/E ratio observed for the comparable printing companies will result in a misleading appraisal of FEC. Using ratios derived from gross measures such as total firm value and EBIDT (as opposed to net earnings) corrects this mistake.

---

[8]F. Modigliani and M. H. Miller, "The Cost of Capital, Corporation Finance and the Theory of Investment," *American Economic Review*, June 1958, pp. 261–97; and M. H. Miller, "Debt and Taxes," *Journal of Finance*, May 1977, pp. 261–75.

Because the impact of leverage is so pervasive, it is worth illustrating the problem discussed above with a specific example. Consider two identical firms that both produce earnings before interest and taxes, EBIT, of $100. To keep the illustration simple, assume that there are no taxes. The first firm is all equity financed and the equity is worth $800. Because there are no interest payments, both the P/E ratio (on a before-tax basis) and the MV/EBIT ratio are 8.0. The second firm is financed with both equity and debt. Currently, it has $500 in debt outstanding at an interest rate of 10 percent. Consequently, after making annual interest payments of $50, the company will have $50 in net pre-tax earnings available for the equity holders. Assuming that the P/E ratio of 8.0 observed for firm 1 can be applied to firm 2, the value of firm 2's equity is $400 ($50 in pre-tax earnings times 8.0). Adding to this the value of the debt yields a total firm value of $900. Thus, without considering any tax benefits, the use of debt appears to have created value out of thin air.

The illusion is produced by applying the multiplier derived for an all-equity company (firm 1) to a leveraged company (firm 2). This step is incorrect. The equity of the leveraged firm will be riskier and, therefore, each dollar of equity earnings will command a smaller multiplier. In the context of an asset pricing model such as the capital asset pricing model discussed in Chapter 7, it is possible to show that the multiplier will fall to 6.0. Using a multiplier of 6.0, the value of the equity drops to $300, and the total value of the firm remains unchanged at $800.

The problem with adjusting the multiplier, as in the preceding example, is that an asset pricing model is required. Without the guide provided by the model, there is no way to determine how the multiplier should be changed. However, currently there is little consensus on the appropriate model. A safer solution, therefore, is to select a broad measure of income like EBIT, EBIDT, earnings on a debt-free basis, cash flow on a debt-free basis, or sales as the financial variable.[9] In the preceding example, EBIT for both firms is $100, and the total value of both firms is $800. The ratio 8.0 is applicable in both cases as long as it is applied to total value.

---

[9]Earnings on a debt-free basis are defined as the earnings that would have been reported if the firm had no debt.

As noted earlier, when a direct comparison is used to value the equity alone, outstanding debt and preferred stock must be appraised separately. Fortunately, the procedures for appraising both preferred stock and debt are straightforward in most cases.[10] The key again is finding comparables. In the case of preferred stock and debt, however, it is not necessary that the *firms* be comparable, only that the *securities* be comparable. It may seem paradoxical that firms that are not comparable can issue comparable securities, but the paradox has a simple explanation. As long as a company is not so highly leveraged that there is a significant risk of default on its fixed income securities, the prices of those securities depend primarily on the size of the promised payments and on the level of interest rates. Therefore, long-term debt or preferred stock issued by a medical supply company will be comparable to long-term debt or preferred stock issued by a computer company as long as the risk of default is similar.

To apply the procedure suggested above to preferred stock, it is necessary to find publicly traded preferred shares with risk comparable to the appraisal target's preferred. The price of the appraisal target's preferred is estimated by dividing the target's dividend payment by the dividend payout ratio for the comparable security. For instance, suppose that the preferred dividend paid by the target is $1. If publicly traded preferred stock of equal risk pays a dividend of $2 and trades at $20 per share, the appropriate dividend payout rate for valuing the target preferred is 10 percent. Dividing the target's dividend by the dividend payout rate of 10 percent gives an estimated value of $10 for the target's preferred stock. Where possible, more than one comparable security should be selected to estimate the dividend payout rate. Using an average, instead of relying on the payout rate of one comparable, reduces measurement error.

A similar procedure can be applied to debt. The target's debt is valued by discounting the interest and principal that the appraisal target has promised to pay its lenders at the yield to

---

[10]Complications arise when the preferred stock or the debt contain options. For instance, both the preferred and the debt might be convertible and the debt might be callable. In that case, the preferred and the debt can still be appraised independently, but more complicated option pricing approaches, which are beyond the scope of this book, are required. For a detailed analysis of these issues, see J. Hull, *Options, Futures and Other Derivative Securities* (Englewood Cliffs, N.J.: Prentice Hall, 1992).

maturity on comparable bonds. One easy way to select comparable bonds is to rely on credit ratings, because bonds with similar credit ratings tend to trade at similar yields. For example, suppose that the appraisal target has outstanding debt with a coupon rate of 8 percent, a maturity of 20 years, and risk equivalent to an A credit. If 20-year, A credits are currently yielding 9 percent to maturity, each bond issued by the target with a par value of $1,000 has a market value of approximately $908.[11] Information on bond yields classified by rating is readily available. Both Moody's and Standard & Poor's provide detailed monthly data on bond yields and their corresponding credit ratings along with other characteristics of the bonds such as issuer and maturity. Major investment firms compile similar information.

If the debt of the appraisal target is unrated, the rating can be approximated by employing procedures similar to those used by rating agencies. Research has shown that ratings are based primarily on financial ratios such as annual interest due to EBIT and debt to equity. By analyzing the same financial ratios that the ratings agencies examine, it is possible to predict the rating an agency would assign.[12] In fact, computer programs have been developed that mimic the bond-rating process. One of the best, a product called Debt Rater™, is sold by the Alcar group as part of the software package, APT!™.

As a closing word of warning, the flexibility that an appraiser has in choosing the financial variables and value indicators when developing the ratios for comparable companies can open the door to abuse. The fact that there are many financial variables to choose from should not be interpreted as a free hunting license. Computing appraisals for dozens of variables and then selecting the "best" choice is almost certain to introduce bias. Where possible, the list of potential variables should be shortened by sound economic analysis before estimating the value of the appraisal target.

---

[11]The $908 price is calculated by discounting $40 semiannual interest payments and a final principal payment of $1,000 to present value at a semiannual interest rate of 4.5 percent (9 percent/2).

[12]For a discussion of bond-rating procedures and algorithms for mimicking them, see R. S. Kaplan and G. Uritz, "Statistical Models of Bond Ratings: A Methodological Inquiry," *Journal of Business* 52 (April 1979), pp. 211–29.

ADJUSTING THE FINANCIAL DATA

It was observed briefly in the previous section that variation in the V/x ratio can be reduced by careful adjustment of the financial data. A simple example illustrates the potential importance of such adjustments. Suppose that the average price-earnings multiple for a sample of comparable companies is 12. Assume, furthermore, that during the last fiscal year, the company being appraised lost $10 million. Naive application of the direct comparison approach leads to the nonsensical conclusion that the firm has a negative value because the company lost money in the previous year. However, it is unlikely that the $10 million loss represents the company's normal earnings. (If the $10 million loss is normal, then the comparable companies are not truly comparable. Truly comparable companies would also be losing money consistently and, therefore, would also have negative P/E ratios.) The fact is that good companies can have bad years. Ford Motor Company lost money for several years, but the firm was never worthless.

The example demonstrates that for the direct comparison approach to work properly, the ratios and the financial variables to which they are applied must not be based on aberrant data. There are two basic reasons why a firm's financial data may be considered abnormal. First, the company may use accounting practices that are not standard in the industry or may make significant accounting adjustments. Loan write-downs by banks illustrate the extent to which accounting adjustments can affect financial variables. Current regulations give banks a good deal of leeway in deciding when to realize losses on problem loans. As a result, some banks carry questionable loans at book value until the problem becomes so critical that a huge write-down is required. When the write-down is taken, earnings, plunge. For example, Citibank reported losses of nearly $3 billion in one quarter due to a massive write-down of foreign loans. A direct comparison appraisal of Citibank based on that quarter's earnings would clearly be misleading.

Second, short-term economic conditions may be such that current performance does not reflect the firm's underlying earning power. For example, an automaker may lose money during a recession, a computer manufacturer may experience a decline in sales preceding the introduction of a new machine, and a hotel chain's profits may fall while a major building is being renovated. Under such circumstances, direct comparisons based on current financial data will produce erroneous appraisals.

Procedures for adjusting financial data to mitigate the impact of aberrations fall into two general categories. One approach is to apply statistical techniques. For instance, calculating five-year averages is a simple statistical procedure that is commonly employed. The second approach is to study the economics of the firm and make the adjustments directly. For example, a bank's earnings may be recalculated to take into account a large write-down. It is also possible to combine the two approaches.

Statistical Techniques for Adjusting Financial Data

The statistical approach to adjusting financial data is appealing because it is based on mechanical rules that are easy to apply and are, accordingly, less reliant on the appraiser's judgment. Furthermore, analysis of the economic and financial events that caused the aberrations is not required.

The goal of a statistical adjustment is to reduce variation in V/x by smoothing the financial data used to measure x. To see how the adjustment process is supposed to work, consider a hypothetical appraisal of Bank Zero using earnings as the financial variable. Though the example is developed for banks, the points illustrated are not unique to banks. The same considerations apply to most other companies, with appropriate definitions of the variables.

Earnings data for Bank Zero and its four publicly traded comparables, Banks One, Two, Three, and Four, are presented in Table 4–2 for the five years from 1986 to 1990. Because of lending problems in the last three years, all five banks were forced to write off a significant number of loans. Due to divergent management philosophies, however, the timing of the write-offs differed across banks. Bank Two and Bank Four wrote off bad loans at the first sign of trouble, while Bank Zero and Bank Three waited until the last possible moment. Bank One took an intermediate position. The earnings of each bank reflect its decision regarding write-offs. All of the banks report profits in every year except during the year of the write-off.

Table 4–2 also reports the current market value for each of the comparable banks, derived from application of the stock and debt approach, the ratio of market value to current EBIDT, and the ratio of market value to five-year average EBIDT. (For banks, the interest included in EBIDT is interest on bank capital, not interest payable on deposits.) The ratios of market value to EBIDT in 1990 are difficult to interpret because of Bank Three's write-off, which makes its ratio negative. The negative ratio for Bank Three also drags down the average of MV/EBIDT for all the comparable banks. Eliminating Bank Three from the sample fails to solve the problem because the appraisal target, Bank Zero, also reported a loss in 1990 due to loan write-offs. Applying a positive MV/EBIDT ratio to Bank Zero's negative earnings results in a negative estimate of market value.

Replacing current EBIDT with five-year averages solves both problems. First, the ratio of market value to five-year average EBIDT is close to 10 for all the comparable banks. Second, averaging replaces the negative EBIDT for Bank Zero with a positive number. Multiplying the average MV/EBIDT ratio for the comparable banks (calculated using five-year average EBIDT) by Bank Zero's five-year average EBIDT produces a reasonable estimate of market value.

The five-year averages reported in Table 4–2 are simple arithmetic averages. Some appraisers prefer to use weighted averages that place more weight on recent observations. This presents the problem of selecting the weights. One common choice is a "sum of the years' digits" method similar to that employed in depreciation accounting. If five years of data are available, for example, the number 1 through 5 are summed to give 15. The current year is then given a weight of 5/15, the previous year a weight of 4/15, and so forth. It should be noted that weighting is not always appropriate. In the Bank Zero example, for instance, weighting would be a mistake because it places the banks that wrote off bad loans in more recent years at a disadvantage.

In deciding whether to use a weighted average, it should be kept in mind that the goal of the averaging process is to reduce variation in the V/x ratio. However, the appraiser is not free to

TABLE 4–2
Appraisal of Bank Zero

Year	Appraisal Target Bank Zero EBIDT* (000s)	Comparable Banks Bank One EBIDT (000s)	Bank Two EBIDT (000s)	Bank Three EBIDT (000s)	Bank Four EBIDT (000s)	Average of Comparables
1986	$ 1,200	$ 1,600	$ 3,500	$ 1,000	$ 1,800	
1987	1,700	2,500	4,600	1,500	2,700	
1988	1,200	2,000	(4,000)	1,100	(2,500)	
1989	1,500	(2,400)	4,500	1,300	2,800	
1990	(2,000)	1,800	4,000	(1,600)	2,400	
Five-year average	720	1,100	2,520	660	1,440	
Estimated market value (using the stock and debt approach)		$ 11,000	$ 23,184	$ 6,930	$ 15,552	
MV/E (based on current EBIDT)	6.1	6.1	5.8	–4.3	6.5	3.51
MV/E (based on five-year average)	10.0	10.0	9.2	10.5	10.8	10.13

Implied value based on analysis using current year data = 3.51 × (–2,000) = $(7,020)

Implied value based on five-year average data = 10.13 × (720) = $ 7,294

*EBIDT is earnings before interest on debt, depreciation, and taxes.

experiment with dozens of weighted averages to see which leads to the smallest variation in V/x across the comparable firms. Such a procedure reduces variation in V/x by definition, but the reduction is apt to be spurious. The weights should be chosen on the basis of economic analysis, not random experimentation. Only if the appraiser has sound reasons for believing that current information will produce more reliable V/x ratios should current data be given greater weight when calculating the averages.

In the valuation of Bank Zero, using a five-year average improves the accuracy of the appraisal because it distributes the impact of the loan write-off over five years. This distribution is more consistent with economic reality. Although the loan losses are recognized in one fell swoop, the loan problems undoubtedly developed slowly over time. Rather than having four highly profitable years and one year with large losses, each of the banks probably experienced five years of mediocre profitability. In an efficient market, the market value of the banks will reflect this underlying economic reality. Therefore, there is a closer association, across banks, between market value and five-year average earnings than between market value and current earnings.

If the appraiser chooses to use statistical procedures to adjust the comparable firms' financial variable, the same adjustment must be applied to the appraisal target's financial variable before multiplying it by the ratio. For example, if a ratio is developed by dividing market value by five-year average earnings for the comparable firms, the resulting ratio must be multiplied by the five-year average earnings of the target.

When applying statistical techniques, the distinction between smoothing and normalizing must be kept in mind. Some techniques, such as five-year averaging, are designed simply to smooth the data; they are not intended to approximate current levels of the financial variable under normal circumstances. For instance, the five-year averages reported in Table 4–2 are not necessarily good estimates of normalized 1990 earnings for any of the banks. Other techniques, such as regression analysis, can be used to estimate the normalized levels of the financial variables as well as to smooth the data. This distinction between smoothing and normalizing is not critical in the context of the direct comparison approach because the goal of the adjustment is only to make the V/x ratio more consistent across firms. As long as the comparable firms and the appraisal target data are smoothed in the same fashion, a fair appraisal will result even if the smoothed data do represent normalized values.

In other situations, however, the distinction between smoothed values and normalized values is essential. For example, as illustrated in Chapter 5, when applying the discounted cash flow approach, it is necessary to begin with an accurate estimate of normal cash flow for the current year. Using a five-year average to estimate normal cash flow for the current year will be misleading if the cash flows are increasing.

To illustrate this point, the distinction between smoothing and normalizing is explored further in Table 4–3 and Figure 4–1, which present hypothetical five-year earnings data for Stata Corporation. As the table and figure show, Stata's earnings have been growing consistently. However, the huge jump in 1990 suggests an aberration. The figure and the table also demonstrate that a five-year average is unlikely to be a reasonable estimate of normal earnings for 1990. Not only is the five-year average well below 1990 earnings, it is even below 1989 earnings.

One simple but widely employed procedure for normalizing financial data is to fit a trend line. The procedure is illustrated for Stata's earnings in Table 4–3 and Figure 4–1. Trend lines are estimated by regressing the financial variable on time.[13] Spreadsheet packages such as Lotus 1-2-3™ and Excel™ have built-in formulas for estimating trend lines. The rising trend line shown in Figure 4–1 reflects Stata's growing earnings. Table 4–3 shows that the fitted value for Stata's 1990 earnings from the trend line is $3,500, which is above 1989 earnings of $2,600 and above the five-year average of $2,560, but below actual 1990 earnings of $3,900.

The trend line calculates what Stata's earnings would have looked like if they grew constantly over time instead of following

---

[13]If the variable in question is growing exponentially, then it is more appropriate to fit the trend line using a logarithmic scale. However, for all but the most rapidly growing firms, the difference between a logarithmic trend and a linear trend, over five years, is minimal.

FIGURE 4–1
Earnings Data for Stata Corp

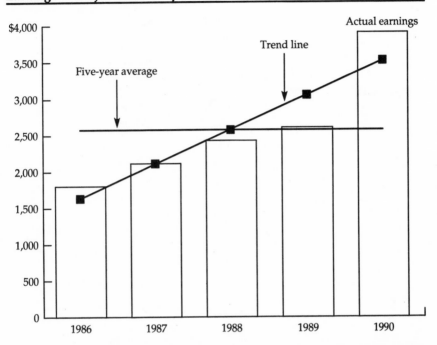

their actual bumpy path. In this way, the trend line both smoothes and normalizes the earnings stream. To the extent that the linear trend is deemed to be a reasonable model, the fitted values on the trend line can be interpreted as Stata's normalized earnings for each of the years. For instance, the normalized earnings for 1990 are $3,500.

In the context of the direct comparison approach, the key attribute of the trend line analysis is not that it produces an estimate of normalized earnings but that, like averaging, it smoothes the data and makes the V/x ratio less variable across firms. When using trend lines, as when using averages, the appraisal target and the comparable firms must be treated in the same fashion. If 1990 fitted earnings from the trend line ($3,500 in Stata's case) are to be used for the appraisal target, then fitted earnings from trend lines must be utilized when calculating the MV/E ratios for all the comparable companies.

TABLE 4–3
Earnings Data for Stata Corp

Year	Earnings (000s)	Fitted Values from Trend Line
1986	$1,800	$1,620
1987	2,100	2,090
1988	2,400	2,560
1989	2,600	3,030
1990	3,900	3,500
Five-year average	$2,560	

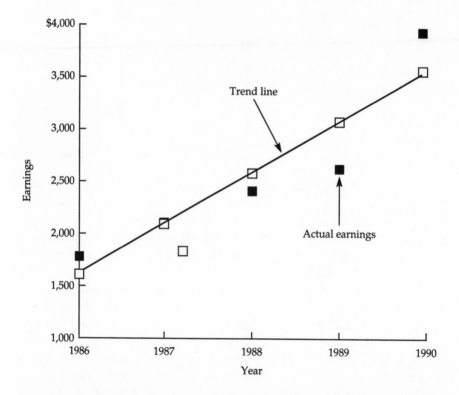

While there are statistical techniques that are much more power-
ful than averaging or fitting trend lines, with 5 years of data (or
even 10 years), attempting to use more sophisticated statistical
procedures to adjust the financial data is unlikely to be a worth-

while pursuit.[14] Unless a greater number of observations are available, application of high-powered techniques is as likely to uncover spurious correlations in the data as it to discern true patterns in the firm's earning power. Furthermore, such techniques have yet to gain widespread acceptance in appraisal practice.

Directly Adjusting the Financial Data

Whereas statistical adjustments are based largely on mechanical rules, direct adjustment of the data requires identifying the source, or sources, of aberrations and then deciding on the appropriate adjustments. For example, suppose that the appraiser decides to adjust the Bank Zero financial data to reflect normal operations instead of the aberrations that caused the $2 million loss. This requires both isolating the unique events that led to the loss and then recalculating what the financial results would have been if the unique events had not occurred. If the aberration is based on an accounting decision, such as Bank Zero's decision to write off bad loans, then the relevant financial variables must be recalculated using accounting conventions that more accurately mirror economic reality.

Because normalizing the financial statement requires identifying the unique factors that affect individual companies, the process is largely case specific. There are no general rules that can be laid down regarding how the data ought to be adjusted. This raises the specter of bias because the appraiser must determine what adjustments are required and how they are to be applied. Nonetheless, there are several standard situations that are worth reviewing and a couple rules of thumb that are helpful in dealing with complex cases.

If the sole source of aberration is the application of nonstandard accounting conventions, the adjustment process is conceptually straightforward, though frequently it is computationally tedious. The income statements and balance sheets for the appraisal target and the comparable companies must all be stated in

---

[14]For instance, time series analysis can be used. For an explanation of how time series analysis is applied, see C. R. Nelson, *Applied Time Series Analysis for Managerial Forecasting*, (San Francisco: Holden-Day, 1973).

terms of the same accounting conventions. For example, if most of the companies under consideration use LIFO inventory accounting, then the books of the few companies that use FIFO must be restated in terms of LIFO before computing V/x ratios.

One way to test whether specific adjustments are reasonable is to examine the behavior of the V/x ratio across comparable firms before and after adjustment. If an adjustment is successful, it should reduce variability in V/x by putting all the firms on the same basis. A study by Beaver and Dukes illustrates how this works.[15] Beaver and Dukes examined 123 firms, about half of which used accelerated depreciation for external reporting and the other half of which used straight-line depreciation. All the firms used accelerated depreciation for tax reporting. Beaver and Dukes found that the average price-earnings ratio for the firms using accelerated depreciation was 15.08, whereas the average price-earnings ratio for firms using straight-line depreciation was 16.61. Beaver and Dukes then recalculated the income statements for the firms using accelerated depreciation on a straight-line basis and found that the average P/E ratio rose to 16.20. They observe that this finding is consistent with the view that investors recognize which depreciation method a company uses and price the securities accordingly. To eliminate the spurious discrepancies between price-earnings ratios across firms, Beaver and Dukes argue, it is necessary to put all firms on a comparable basis because that is what investors do when valuing a company.

When the source of the aberration is a one-time change in accounting numbers, such as a loan write-off or realization of a capital gain, the adjustment process is more complex. Consider the case of Bank Zero discussed earlier. Because Bank Zero's loan write-off led to losses in the appraisal year, the direct comparison approach cannot be used unless the earnings data are adjusted. But which banks' earnings should be adjusted and for what years? Furthermore, how large should the adjustments be?

One possibility is to adjust the earnings of Bank Zero and Bank Three by eliminating the impact of the write-offs those banks

---

[15]W. H. Beaver and R. P. Dukes, "Interperiod Tax Allocation and Delta-Depreciation Methods: Some Empirical Results," *Accounting Review* 48 (July 1973), pp. 549–59.

took in 1990. However, eliminating the 1990 write-offs overstates the profitability of Bank Zero and Bank Three relative to the banks that took write-offs in earlier years. A solution more consistent with economic theory is to recalculate each bank's balance sheet and income statement in every year, replacing the book values of loans by estimates of the market value of the loans. This procedure eliminates the lumpiness of the write-off because the market value of the loans should change slowly over time. More importantly, marking loans to market should lead to a closer association between financial variables such as earnings and cash flow (calculated using market values) and the market value of the banks because in valuing the banks' securities, investors will look at the market value of the loans. Consequently, recalculating the balance sheet and income statement using market values for the loans should reduce variation in the V/x ratio across banks.

In this respect, the Bank Zero example illustrates a more general principle. A major goal of the adjustment process should be to restate accounting variables so that they more accurately reflect their economic counterparts. In the case of Bank Zero, restating loans to reflect their market value turns the accounting measure of earnings into true economic earnings. As another example, companies often report large profits associated with the sale of assets or the closing of divisions. However, the economic events that led to the sale or closing do not occur at the date of sale or closure, but are spread over prior years. Therefore, the adjustment process should distribute the reported gain or loss over the years in which it was actually realized in order to reflect true economic conditions.

Aside from accounting aberrations, the most common source of deviations in the financial variables is "abnormal" performance. The problem with defining abnormal performance is that a bad year in the eyes of management may be a good year in the eyes of the firm's critics. For instance, it is not uncommon for makers of computer software to attribute a bad year to the costs of introducing a new product, while critics are claiming that the problem is customer dissatisfaction with the new product. Nonetheless, it is indisputable that there are circumstances in which a firm's current performance fails to reflect its long-run earning power. In those situations, an adjustment is required.

Adjusting financial data to mitigate the impact of short-run variations has a long and glorious history in economics. The most famous example, which is directly applicable to valuation, is the consumption function. One of the key relations in macroeconomic models is that between national consumption and national income. Early macroeconomic models assumed that consumption was a linear function of income. Unfortunately, the data were inconsistent with this assumption. Consumers spent a larger fraction of their income during recessions and a smaller fraction of their incomes during expansions. In work for which he was cited when receiving the Nobel Prize, Milton Friedman offered an explanation for this observation. Consumers plan to spend a constant fraction of their "permanent" income. By permanent income, Friedman meant long-run normal income for the year in question. In years when actual income is above the long-run average, consumers add to savings. In years when income is below average, savings are reduced. Thus, the relation of current income to consumption varies from year to year even though the ratio of permanent income to consumption is virtually constant.

Friedman's work applies to valuation because the relation between earnings (or cash flow) and market value is similar to the relation between national consumption and national income. In valuing a company, the market looks to the firm's long-run earning power. Therefore, the ratio of current earnings to value will be high when current earnings are above normal and low when current earnings are below normal. This variation in the ratio, which invalidates the foundation on which the direct comparison approach is based, can be reduced by substituting normal or permanent earnings for current earnings. The difficulty is determining what normal earnings are in a given year. An approach suggested by Friedman is to use a weighted average or regression analysis, as discussed earlier. Another possibility is to rely on analyst and investment company reports. When dissecting a company's earnings record, analysts typically discuss whether or not earnings in a given year are abnormal. They also provide forecasts of the following year's earnings and state whether or not they expect it to be normal. If the future year is expected to be normal, an average of analyst forecasts for next year can be used as the financial variable, x, in constructing the V/x ratios. Recall that analyst forecasts were used by the investment bank to construct P/E ratios for the transportation companies reported in Table 4–1.

In many situations, however, the company and its comparables are not publicly traded or are not widely followed, so that analyst reports are unavailable. In that case, appraisers must turn to management or apply their own judgment to decide whether the financial variables used in the ratio analysis are normal, and if they are judged to be abnormal, to determine how they should be adjusted. These are not easy tasks and bias is a clear danger. Therefore, when adjustments are based on management input, a careful explanation is required.

CONTROL PREMIUMS AND THE DIRECT COMPARISON APPROACH

Whether or not a control premium is accounted for in the context of the direct comparison approach depends on how the ratios of value to the financial variable are developed. If the comparables are appraised using the stock and debt approach, a control premium is not included. If the values of the comparables are derived from sales of entire corporations, a control premium is included.

When investment banks are advising clients regarding corporate acquisitions, the direct comparison is often applied using both open market security prices and the price at which entire corporations were sold as value indicators for the comparable companies. Recall that Table 4–1 presents the ratio of equity value, calculated from stock market prices, to earnings for a variety of transportation companies as of December 1986. The investment bank also calculated similar ratios (not reported in the table) for a smaller sample of transportation companies that were purchased in corporate control transactions. The average price-earnings for the sample of corporate sales is 19.1 compared to the average ratio of 16.3 reported in Table 4–1. This is not uncommon; the appraised value is almost invariably greater when the corporate sales data are utilized because the value indicators derived from corporate sales are higher than those derived from the trading of minority positions.

It is tempting to interpret the difference between the value derived from the market prices of a comparable company's securities and the value derived from the sale of the complete comparable company as a control premium that should be added whenever the appraiser is trying to value a controlling interest in a company. However, such an interpretation is not correct. As discussed in Chapter 8, control premiums paid for other companies may not be applicable to the appraisal target because the factors that led investors to pay premiums in other situations may not characterize the appraisal target. Nonetheless, it is safe to say that the estimate of value derived from the market prices of securities establishes a floor beneath a company's value. Under certain circumstances, the appraiser may choose to elevate the appraised value above that floor to take into account a control premium.

A DIRECT COMPARISON APPRAISAL OF FORMS ENGINEERING COMPANY

To illustrate the preceding discussion, the direct comparison approach is applied to FEC. The appraisal of FEC is based on one value indicator (V), total firm value and three financial variables (x): (1) earnings before interest, depreciation, and taxes, EBIDT, (2) debt-free net cash flow (NCF), and (3) sales. Thus, there are three possible V/x ratios, one for each financial variable.

Total firm values is chosen as the measure of V because FEC is more highly leveraged than most printing companies. Consistent with choosing total firm value for V, all three measures of x, EBIDT, NCF, and sales, are selected because they reflect earnings and revenue available for all investors, not just stockholders. Therefore, these financial variables are independent of the firm's capital structure. Of the three variables, one would expect EBIDT and NCF to be more closely associated with value and, accordingly, to produce less variable V/x ratios, because sales are only a rough measure of a firm's earning power. Two companies can have identical sales and sharply divergent values if one company is an efficient, low-cost organization and the other squanders its revenue on high operating expenses. For this reason, the direct comparisons based on EBIDT and NCF are expected to generate more accurate appraisals.

Though there are dozens of printing companies that are comparable to FEC, virtually all of them are privately held. If privately held firms are selected as comparables, then each of them must be appraised by some method other than direct comparison before the direct comparison approach can be applied to FEC. Thus, choosing privately held companies as comparables simply exacerbates the appraisal problem. The problem with the publicly held printing firms is that they are a good deal larger than FEC and, therefore, tend to be growing more slowly. Nonetheless, from these larger firms, FEC management was able to select six that it judged to be comparable: American Business Products, Duplex Products, Ennis Business Forms, Moore Corporation, Standard Register, and Wallace Computer Services.

Although FEC's management believed that the business mix of the six firms was comparable to FEC, recent research in finance raises a question of whether they are of equal risk. As noted in Chapter 3, the average stock returns for small firms tend to be greater than the returns for large firms. Assuming that return is related to risk, this implies that small firms tend to be riskier than large firms. In a recent article, Fama and French have gone so far as to argue that firm size is a better measure of firm risk than the risk measures suggested by finance theory.[16] If this is the case, then multiples derived for large firms may not be applicable directly to small firms. In the appraisal of FEC, no account is taken of this size effect. Given the debate regarding the role of size in assessing firm risk, it is not possible to say at this point in time what adjustments should be made. Of course, controversy can be avoided by selecting comparables of approximately the same size as the appraisal target. Because publicly traded firms tend to be large, however, it is often not possible to find comparables for small companies that can be valued by the stock and debt

---

[16]The theoretical measures of risk are presented in Chapter 7.

approach. In that case, as with FEC, judgment must be employed in determining which comparables to use.

Because the comparable companies are publicly traded, they can be valued by applying the stock and debt approach. As described in Chapter 3, the value of the equity is computed by multiplying the published market price of a share on the appraisal date by the number of shares outstanding. Preferred stock is not included because none of the comparable companies had preferred outstanding. Turning to debt, there are not active markets for the debt of any of the comparable companies, so that published prices are not available. Therefore, bonds issued by the companies were valued by discounting the promised payments to present value at the yield to maturity on publicly traded bonds with an equal rating. (Two of the comparables had rated bonds outstanding; for the other four, an effective rating was calculated using Debt Rater.) The market value of bank debt was assumed to equal its book value. Adding the value of the outstanding bonds and the bank debt to the value of the equity gives the total market value for each of the comparable firms. These market values are used in the numerator of the direct comparison ratios.

Tables 4–4, 4–5, and 4–6 present the direct comparison appraisals of FEC using each of the three financial variables. In Table 4–4, the financial variable is EBIDT, in Table 4–5 the financial variable is NCF, and in Table 4–6 the financial variable is sales. At the top of each table, five years of historical data for the financial variable are shown for FEC and the comparables. Following the historical data are five-year averages and trend line fitted values for the financial variable. The market values of the comparable companies are listed in the next row, followed by rows showing the ratio of the market value of the comparable firm to its financial variable, to the five-year average of its financial variable, and to the fitted value of its financial variable. The last column of the table shows the average value of these ratios across the comparable firms. Finally, at the bottom of the table, the average ratio for the comparable companies is multiplied by the financial variable for FEC to arrive at an estimate of the market value of FEC. It is worth reiterating that the ratios must be applied consistently. If a ratio is developed utilizing five-year average data, then it must be applied to FEC's five-year average data.

Comparing the three tables, Table 4–5 is an obvious outlier. Because the cash flows for both FEC and the comparable companies are negative in some years and close to zero in others, the market value to NCF ratios are large in absolute value with fluctuating signs. For instance, the ratio of MV/NCF varies from 75.15 for Ennis Business Forms to − 245.15 for Wallace Computer Services. These peculiar cash flow figures and ratios arise because printing is a highly capital intensive business and because 1985 to 1989 was a time of aggressive expansion for FEC and its comparables. Due to this expansion, capital expenditures were large, but the full impact of those expenditures in terms of greater revenue was not yet fully realized. Therefore, cash flows are close to zero and negative on occasion. When cash flow is zero or negative, direct comparisons based on it do not produce reasonable value indicators for FEC.

Utilizing EBIDT instead of cash flow eliminates the problem because capital expenditures and changes in working capital, which are deducted when calculating NCF, are included in EBIDT. Whereas the MV/NCF ratio varies widely for the comparables, the MV/EBIDT ratio is bounded between 6.05 and 8.43 for the current EBIDT. The bounds for five-year average EBIDT and for the trend-line fitted values of EBIDT are similar. Furthermore, when the average ratio for the comparables is multiplied by FEC's EBIDT, the appraised values range from $9,388,000 for current EBIDT to $12,632,000 for the five-year average EBIDT. The trend line value at $9,393,000 is close to that for current EBIDT. The consistency of the results provides evidence in support of the view that the value of FEC is between $9.3 and $12.6 million.

The confidence produced by the EBIDT appraisal is undermined somewhat by the sales appraisal reported in Table 4–6. As shown in the table, the sales-based direct comparisons generate estimated values for FEC of between $14.5 million and $14.7 million. This tight range, in conjunction with the low variability of the MV/sales ratio for the comparables, gives credence to the sales-based comparisons and raised doubts about the EBIDT-based comparisons. Further investigation of the discrepancy is required.

A detailed investigation of FEC's operating strategy, in contrast to that of the comparables, provides an explanation for the

TABLE 4-4
A Direct Comparison of Appraisal of FEC Using Earnings before Interest, Depreciation, and Taxes (EBIDT)*

Year	Forms Engineering EBIDT (000s)	American Business Products EBIDT (000s)	Duplex Products EBIDT (000s)	Ennis Business Forms EBIDT (000s)	Moore Corporation EBIDT (000s)	Standard Register EBIDT (000s)	Wallace Computer Services EBIDT (000s)	Average
1985	$2,238	$ 25,285	$ 26,338	$ 17,399	$ 314,746	$ 69,990	$ 47,017	
1986	1,003	22,730	19,536	19,973	296,298	81,187	52,284	
1987	1,279	21,299	21,198	21,264	311,383	91,716	58,258	
1988	1,727	23,073	16,925	25,725	313,691	83,246	61,827	
1989	1,268	24,266	24,114	28,459	349,452	86,801	70,262	
Five-Year Average	$1,503	$ 23,331	$ 21,622	$ 22,564	$ 317,114	$ 82,588	$ 57,930	
Fitted 1989 values from trend line	$1,260	$ 22,992	$ 20,210	$ 28,138	$ 334,475	$ 89,724	$ 89,724	
Estimated market value (using stock and debt approach)		$161,473	$188,575	$206,438	$2,870,727	$525,498	$592,028	

MV/E (based on current EBIDT)	6.65	7.82	7.25	8.21	6.05	8.43	7.40
MV/E (based on five-year average)	6.92	8.72	9.15	9.05	6.36	10.22	8.40
MV/E (based on trend)	7.02	9.33	7.34	8.58	5.86	6.60	7.45

Implied value based on current year data = 7.40 × $1,268 = $9,388

Implied value based on five-year average data = 8.40 × $1,503 = $12,632

Implied value based on trend data = 7.45 × $1,260 = $9,393

*EBIDT is earnings before interest on debt, depreciation, and taxes.

TABLE 4-5
A Direct Comparison of Appraisal of FEC Using Debt-Free Net Cash Flow (NCF)*

Year	Forms Engineering NCF (000s)	American Business Products NCF (000s)	Duplex Products NCF (000s)	Ennis Business Forms NCF (000s)	Moore Corporation NCF (000s)	Standard Register NCF (000s)	Wallace Computer Services NCF (000s) Average
1985	$460	$3,128	$2,732	$2,747	$82,025	$9,459	$(2,415)
1986	(1,530)	(739)	(2,649)	(1,351)	65,656	(92,165)	(3,369)
1987	329	4,482	4,264	7,668	804	15,757	335
1988	(28)	1,958	1,909	21,939	70,870	17,994	885
1989	621	1,655	2,924	12,592	92,754	20,416	(2,818)
Five-Year Average	$(30)	$2,097	$1,836	$8,719	$62,422	$(5,708)	$(1,476)
Fitted 1989 values from trend line	$335	$2,047	$2,824	$17,315	$67,756	$20,707	$(787)
Estimated market value (using stock and debt approach)		$161,473	$188,575	$206,438	$2,870,727	$525,498	$592,028

MV/NCF (based on current NCF)	51.62	69.02	75.15	35.00	55.56	−245.15	6.87
MV/NCF (based on five-year average)	77.01	102.71	23.68	45.99	−92.07	−400.99	−40.61
MV/NCF (based on trend)	78.88	66.77	11.92	42.37	25.38	−752.45	−87.86

Implied value based on current year data = 6.87 × $621 = $4,265

Implied value based on five-year average data = − 40.61 × − $30 = $1,202

Implied value based on trend data = −87.86 × $335 = $(29,449)

*NCF is debt-free cash flow (see Table 6–3 for a detailed calculation of NCF).

TABLE 4–6
A Direct Comparison of Appraisal of FEC Using Sales

Year	Forms Engineering Sales (000s)	American Business Products Sales (000s)	Duplex Products Sales (000s)	Ennis Business Forms Sales (000s)	Moore Corporation Sales (000s)	Standard Register Sales (000s)	Wallace Computer Services Sales (000s)	Average
1985	$12,401	$300,400	$254,100	$110,500	$2,067,700	$441,000	$274,600	
1986	11,450	313,700	248,400	111,900	2,114,300	561,900	305,000	
1987	11,590	325,800	278,200	117,500	2,281,500	666,700	340,500	
1988	14,814	358,242	298,489	117,511	2,544,019	675,200	383,000	
1989	15,243	387,140	326,475	128,170	2,708,406	708,876	429,008	
Five-Year Average	$13,100	$337,056	$281,133	$117,116	$2,343,185	$610,735	$346,422	
Fitted 1989 values from trend line	$14,909	$380,661	$320,101	$125,306	$2,685,411	$740,546	$423,785	
Estimated market value (using stock and debt approach)	[ ]	$161,473	$188,575	$206,438	$2,870,727	$525,498	$592,028	

MV/S (based on current sales)	0.42	0.58	1.61	1.06	0.74	1.38	0.96
MV/S (based on five-year average)	0.48	0.67	1.76	1.23	0.86	1.71	1.12
MV/S (based on trend)	0.42	0.59	1.65	1.07	0.71	1.40	0.97

Implied value based on current year data = 0.96 × $15,243 = $14,701

Implied value based on five-year average data = 1.12 × $13,100 = $14,643

Implied value based on trend data = .97 × $14,909 = $14,503

discrepancy between the EBIDT appraisal and the sales appraisal. FEC's policy during the years from 1985 to 1989 was to aggressively compete for new business, even if it meant taking less profitable printing jobs. As a result of this policy, FEC's profit margins on sales were below industry averages. Consequently, the ratio of sales to EBIDT was high for FEC. This suggests that the EBIDT appraisal should be more reliable than the sales appraisal. As stressed throughout this book, value is ultimately derived from the spendable cash a business provides its investors. Two companies with comparable sales will be of equal value only if both companies are able to deliver the final product at the same cost. If one company is a more costly producer, it will be worth less. Such is the case with FEC. Its aggressive marketing strategy made it a relatively high-cost printer. For that reason, the ratio of sales to market value is less for FEC than for the comparables. Consequently, applying the comparable ratio to FEC's sales leads to an overstatement of value. This bias does not arise when EBIDT is utilized because EBIDT is calculated net of the cost of goods sold. Therefore, the relation between EBIDT and value should be similar for both FEC and the comparables.

It is possible to develop further direct comparison appraisals using other value indicators and additional financial variables. As noted earlier, however, the temptation to use a shotgun approach to appraisal should be avoided. It is better to select a limited group of variables that finance analysis suggests should produce accurate appraisals, rather than calculating value indicators for dozens of variables and choosing the one that "works best."

CONCLUDING OBSERVATIONS

In closing, it is worth reiterating that comparability is the key to the direct comparison approach. If the target company and the companies to which it is compared are comparable in *every respect*, then the choice of the value indicator, V, and the accounting variable, x, is largely irrelevant. The same appraised value will result because the V/x ratio will be identical for the target and the comparables. However, the real world is rarely so kind. Generally, the firms selected for comparison are only partially comparable to each other and to the appraisal target. In that case, it is possible to increase the accuracy of the appraisal by carefully selecting V and x, and by adjusting x so that comparability is maximized.

To review briefly, there are several specific steps an appraiser can take to increase effective comparability. First, the set of potential comparables can be reduced on the basis of a detailed study of each of them, including an analysis of financial ratios. Second, V and x can be chosen to highlight the similarities between the firms and to minimize differences. For instance, the impact of differing degrees of financial leverage can be minimized by using total firm value as a measure of V and using earnings before interest, depreciation, and taxes as the choice of x. Third, the x variable can be adjusted or normalized to mitigate the impact of aberrations that reduce comparability.

As a final word of warning, remember that extensive mining of the data can create the illusion of comparability when it does not in fact exist. By paring the sample of comparable companies, sifting through various candidates for V and x, and adjusting x in a variety of ways, the appraiser is certain to reduce variation in the V/x ratio. The drawback is that much of the reduction is likely to be spurious. Even highly dissimilar companies can be made to appear similar if the data are massaged enough. Thus, the fewer adjustments made to the data, the greater the confidence that generally can be placed in a direct comparison appraisal.

Chapter Five

The Discounted Cash Flow Approach

The discounted cash flow approach attempts to value directly the benefits that accrue to investors from their participation in the company. The strength of such an approach is that it can be applied in virtually any situation. If future cash flows to investors can be predicted, the discounted cash flow value can be applied. There are, however, three difficult practical problems that must be surmounted in order to apply the discounted cash flow approach. These problems are sufficiently detailed that three chapters are dedicated to the discounted cash flow model.

First, the benefits to investors must be precisely defined. As we shall see, this is the easiest problem to solve. The next section of this chapter demonstrates that the benefits to investors are the cash flows the company generates, net of all expenditures, including investment in plant, equipment, and working capital, that are available for distribution to investors.

Second, a method must be developed for forecasting the benefits to investors—now defined as net cash flow. Given the indefinite life of most corporations, this is no easy task. The standard approach, which is developed here, is to divide a company's life into two stages. During the first stage, when the company is changing rapidly, detailed cash flow forecasts are prepared on a year-to-year basis. Much of the remainder of this chapter is dedicated to analyzing methods for forecasting these annual cash flows.

At some point in the future, the company is assumed to reach an equilibrium state. In this equilibrium state, cash flows are assumed to be sufficiently stable and predictable that subsequent forecasts can be based on simplified rules of thumb. Chapter 6 examines how an appraiser decides when a firm reaches this equilibrium state and discusses what rules of thumb should be used to forecast cash flow at that point.

Third, a rate must be selected for discounting the predicted cash flows during the first stage of rapid evolution and during the second stage of equilibrium growth back to present value. Selection of the discount rate is complicated by a combination of two facts: (1) the cash flow forecasts are uncertain, so that the disbursements to investors are risky; and (2) investors demand a premium for bearing risk. Because of uncertainty and risk aversion, the discount rate used to calculate the present value of future cash flows must be greater than the risk-free rate by a "risk premium." Unfortunately, determining the proper magnitude of the risk premium is one of the most difficult problems in finance. This difficulty is compounded by the fact that risk premiums differ across classes of securities. For instance, bondholders typically bear less risk than stockholders because the cash flows they receive are more predictable. Consequently, risk premiums on bonds are typically smaller than those on stock. These and other issues related to the discount rate are the subject of Chapter 7.

The discounted cash flow approach to corporate valuation is conceptually identical to investment decision making based on net present value. When determining whether or not to purchase a new machine, the present value of the net cash flows the equipment is expected to produce is compared with the cost of the machine. If the present value exceeds the cost of the machine, the equipment is purchased; otherwise, it is not. From an appraisal standpoint, this investment rule amounts to comparing the value of the machine to the company, as measured by the present value of the expected future cash flows, with the cost of the machine in the marketplace. The company purchases the equipment if its value to the company exceeds its price. In the context of corporate acquisitions, the discounted cash flow approach to valuation can be seen as the net present value rule applied to an entire company. Potential buyers will choose to purchase a company only if the present value of the cash flows the target is expected to produce exceeds the cost of the acquisition.

VALUE IS BASED ON FUTURE CASH FLOW

Recall that the goal of an appraisal is to approximate the price at which a company would trade in a transaction between rational and informed buyers and sellers. The discounted cash flow approach to appraisal is based on the assumption that these hypothetical buyers and sellers will base their valuations of a company on cash flows the company is expected to produce. To understand the basis for this assumption, put yourself in the position of the hypothetical buyer and imagine that on the day you buy the company, you open a bank account to handle all company-related translations. (For the purposes of this illustration, it is assumed that there is only one buyer who purchases only one type of security, the company's equity. Later, the analysis will be complicated to include multiple investors and various types of securities.) Every receipt is deposited in the account, and all company payments, other than the original expenditure to purchase the firm, are deducted from the account. The account is used for no other purpose. On the day the company is purchased, the bank account is assumed to have a zero balance. In addition, an automatic overdraft provision is available in case withdrawals exceed deposits.

At the end of the first year of business, the balance in the account represents funds that the buyer can withdraw from the business and spend. (If the balance is negative, it represents the funds the buyer must put into the account to cover the overdrafts of the business.) To continue the example, assume that the buyer does in fact withdraw the funds, so that the bank balance is reset to zero by the start of the second year. In that case, the balance at the end of the second year represents the spendable cash generated in year 2. Proceeding in this fashion, it is clear that each year's ending balance represents funds that the buyers can withdraw and spend. Because it is assumed that value is ultimately derived from spendable cash, the value of the firm to the buyer will be determined by this sequence of year-end balances. But these year-end balances are precisely the company's annual net cash flows. Therefore, the value of a business can be estimated by forecasting future cash flows and discounting them to present value.

If value is determined by cash flow, does that mean that managers who focus on earnings per share (of which there are many) are foolish? The answer is yes and no, depending on what is meant by "focus on earnings." The fact is that earnings and cash flow are highly correlated, particularly over the long run. Companies that have consistently high earnings year after year also tend to produce large cash flows. Because earnings and cash flow are highly correlated, some executives fall into the habit of using the two measures interchangeably. To them, maximizing cash flow and maximizing long-run earnings are synonymous. The flaw in this thinking is that in some situations, cash flow and earnings diverge, at least in the short run. Under such circumstances, it is spendable cash, not accounting earnings, that determines value.

To draw an analogy, scoring and winning are highly correlated in football. For this reason, focusing on scoring is not an unreasonable coaching strategy. But scoring and winning are not perfectly correlated. A team with a terrible defense can score frequently and still lose a majority of its games. The ultimate measure of performance is games won, not points scored. Similarly, in corporate management, the ultimate measure of performance is spendable cash generated for investors, not accounting earnings reported. If accounting earnings are high but cash flow is low, the firm will be of little value to investors.

The correlation between cash flow and earnings also explains why the stock prices of companies are sensitive to earnings announcements even though value is determined by cash flow. In most cases, an announcement of higher earnings carries with it information about cash flow. The stock price responds to the implied information about cash flow, not the direct information about earnings.

At companies where maximizing cash flow and maximizing earnings are virtually equivalent, there is nothing wrong with management focusing on earnings. However, managers can get into trouble in situations where earnings and cash flow diverge in the short run. A classic example is the choice between LIFO (last-in, first-out) and FIFO (first-in, first-out) inventory accounting. In periods of rising prices, a company that switches from FIFO to LIFO will report lower earnings, because the cost of goods sold is now based on the more recently purchased, and more costly, items in inventory. Paradoxically, the decline in earnings leads to an increase in net cash flow, because firms with lower earnings pay less in taxes. Since the pre-tax cash flow is the same regardless of the choice of accounting method, the switch to LIFO accounting leads to a higher after-tax cash flow. In this situation, investors will prefer a switch to LIFO even though it causes earnings to drop.

The argument that "only cash matters" has more than theoretical backing; it is also supported by extensive research. This research focuses on listed companies for which it is possible to conduct direct tests of the relation between value and various measures of income, including cash flow and accounting earnings, because market values for listed companies can be estimated by the stock and debt approach. The results of these tests overwhelmingly support the view that corporate value is based on cash flow. When cash flow and earnings diverge, changes in value are associated with changes in cash flow, not changes in earnings. Though the literature is too extensive to review here, summaries of a few studies are presented to illustrate the general nature of the findings.

A 1975 study by Sunder examines the LIFO and FIFO inventory accounting decision discussed previously.[1] Sunder notes that if value is based on cash flow, the stock prices of companies switching from FIFO to LIFO should rise, while the stock prices of companies switching from LIFO to FIFO should drop. Conversely, Sunder observes, if value is based on earnings, the reverse should be true. Consistent with the cash flow theory, Sunder finds that on average, the stock prices of companies switching to LIFO rise, net of general market movements, and that the stock prices of those companies switching to FIFO fall.

A related 1978 study by Hong, Kaplan, and Mandelker focuses on corporate mergers.[2] In a merger, two types of accounting

---

[1] S. Sunder, "Stock Price and Risk Related Accounting Changes in Inventory Valuation," *Accounting Review* 50 (April 1973), pp. 302–15.

[2] H. Hong, R. S. Kaplan, and G. Mandelker, "Pooling versus Purchase: The Effects of Accounting for Mergers on Stock Prices," *Accounting Review* 53 (January 1978), pp. 31–74.

treatment are possible: pooling or purchase. In a pooling arrangement, the income statements and balance sheets of the merging firms are simply added together. Under purchase accounting, on the other hand, the assets of the acquired company are added to the acquiring company's balance sheet along with an addition to goodwill. The addition to goodwill equals the difference between the purchase price and the book value of the acquired company's assets. Regulations require that the added goodwill be written off as a charge against earnings after taxes over a period not to exceed 40 years. Because the write-off is after taxes, choosing purchase accounting does not affect cash flow, but it does cause earnings to decline. Thus, the cash flow theory predicts that the choice between purchase and pooling accounting is irrelevant, while the earnings theory predicts that purchase accounting will lead to lower earnings and, therefore, lower value. Hong, Kaplan, and Mandelker's findings support the cash flow theory. They find no evidence that choosing purchase accounting lowers the stock price of acquiring firms. Hong, Kaplan, and Mandelker conclude that investors see through the accounting shell game to the underlying value created by cash flow.

A 1985 study by the Office of the Chief Economist of the Securities and Exchange Commission (SEC) speaks not only to the question of earnings versus cash flow but also the question of "market myopia." Some critics argue that security markets are myopic in the sense that they focus on current earnings and cash flow and, as a result, discount future cash flow more sharply than the present value relation implies.[3] To test the myopia hypothesis, the SEC study examined the stock price reaction to announcements of new research and development projects by 62 companies.[4] Increased research and development reduces both current earnings and current cash flow because R&D expenditures are expensed. Nonetheless, if managers are rational, the present value of the expected long-run cash inflows produced by the research should exceed current R&D expenses. Thus, the

---

[3] This claim is made by M. E. Porter, "Capital Choices: Changing the Way America Invests in Industry," *Journal of Applied Corporate Finance* 5 (Summer 1992), pp. 4–17.

[4] "Institutional Ownership, Tender Offers and Long-Term Investment", Office of the Chief Economist, Securities and Exchange Commission, (1985 Washington, D.C.).

cash flow valuation model predicts that stock prices should rise, on average, when new R&D spending is announced, despite the associated decline in current earnings. (The stock price will not necessarily rise in response to every announcement of new R&D spending because the market may disagree with management and conclude that some projects are dogs.) This is exactly what the SEC study finds. The average stock price reaction to the announcement of new R&D projects by the 62 companies is significantly positive. Similar results are reported by McConnell and Muscarella and also Woolridge, who find that announcements of long-term strategic investments, which reduce current earnings, are associated with rising stock prices.[5]

The question of market myopia involves more than R&D spending. Recently, Michael Porter has argued that it is one reason for the decline of the competitiveness of American industry.[6] This is surprising because some simple calculations indicate that American investors and American capital markets are not myopic. For example, Rappaport calculates the fraction of the price of the Dow Jones 30 stocks that can be accounted for by the present value of dividends expected over the next five years.[7] He finds that only between 10 and 20 percent of the price is attributable to dividends expected in the next five years. Similarly, Bernstein points out that the yield on Treasury bonds typically exceeds that on stocks. If investors were myopic and unwilling to wait until dividends on stocks grew to the point where they exceed Treasury bond interest payment, they would shun stock in favor of bonds.[8] Bernstein calculates that in 1992, investors in the S&P 500 stocks would have to wait over 15 years until the dividends they

---

[5] J. J. McConnell and C. J. Muscarella, "Corporate Capital Expenditure Decisions and the Market Value of the Firm, *Journal of Financial Economics* 14 (March 1985), pp. 399–422; and R. Woolridge, "Competitive Decline and Corporate Restructuring: Is a Myopic Stock Market to Blame?" *Journal of Applied Corporate Finance* 1 (Spring 1988), pp. 26–36.

[6] Porter, "Capital Choices," pp. 4–16.

[7] A. Rappaport, "CFOs and Strategists: Forging a Common Framework," *Harvard Business Review*, May–June 1992, pp. 84–91.

[8] P. L. Bernstein, "Are Financial Markets the Problem or the Solution? A Reply to Michael Porter," *Journal of Applied Corporate Finance* 5 (Summer 1992), pp. 17–22.

received on a $1,000 investment surpassed the interest they would earn by holding a long-term Treasury bond. Finally, the fact that investors are willing to pay huge multiples to buy the stock of exciting growth companies such as Microsoft and Genentech indicates that they have a long-run horizon. (Microsoft and Genentech have grown so rapidly that they have become large companies and their growth rates have slowed.)

Perhaps the most dramatic evidence in favor of the cash flow theory of value comes from write-offs. When firms write off failed ventures, the short-term earnings impact is strongly negative. However, the cash flow impact is positive because write-offs reduce taxable income, thereby reducing a company's income tax bill. Accordingly, the cash flow model predicts that write-offs should be associated with stock price increases. This prediction is supported by the work of Mercer, who looked at 40 major write-downs between 1984 and 1986.[9] Mercer finds that 60 percent of the write-offs resulted in share price increases.

Though Mercer's results generally support the cash flow model, they also raise the question "Why did stock prices *decline* in reaction to write-offs 40 percent of the time?" The answer is that in some cases, write-offs provide information about *future* cash flow even though they do not alter *current* cash flow. The fact that a company is writing off an investment dashes any hopes the market might have entertained that the investment would eventually prove profitable. Write-offs associated with high-technology products that are never completed are a good example. If, prior to the write-off, the market knew with certainty that the product would never come to fruition, then the write-off would lead to an increase in the company's stock price because all it does is accelerate tax savings. However, if, prior to the write-off, the market believed there was a chance that the product might still prove successful, then the write-down may cause the company's stock price to drop because it dashes the hope of future success.

---

[9] G. Mercer, "A Review of Major Corporate Write-Offs: 1984–1986" (unpublished manuscript, 1987).

It is worth noting that these studies also provide support for the view that markets are efficient and rationally price securities. As the bank account analogy illustrates, economic theory predicts that investor value is derived from cash flow. If market prices reflected some other measure of income, such as accounting earnings rather than cash flow, that would be evidence that the market was inefficient. However, the evidence is just the reverse.

In addition to the fact that cash flow is what ultimately matters to investors, there is another reason why appraisers should feel more comfortable working with cash flow rather than with accounting earnings. Because cash flow is calculated by subtracting dollars received from dollars paid, it cannot be manipulated. Accounting earnings, on the other hand, are subject to adjustments associated with complicated amortization rules and arcane requirements for establishing reserves. In some situations, companies may take advantage of these accounting complexities to manipulate earnings.

To summarize, intuition, finance theory, and empirical research all support the view that corporate value is based on expectations of future cash flow. The next two sections deal with the problems of calculating and forecasting cash flow.

CALCULATING CASH FLOW

As the bank account analogy illustrates, calculating cash flow amounts to tracking the dollars that flow into and out of a company. Though the previous section made it clear that cash flows, not accounting earnings, are the ultimate source of value, the differences between cash flow and accounting earnings were not specified in detail. There are three major distinctions. First, accountants attempt to record revenue, or book sales, when the funds are "earned," such as when a product is shipped or a service is performed. Unfortunately, there can be a substantial difference between the time that a product is shipped and the time that the bill is paid. Cash flow does not occur until the bill is paid. Of course, the same is true of cash outflows, because the firm can also postpone payment of its own bills. On balance, therefore, the lag between the time receipts and costs are booked and the time cash is received or paid has little impact on net cash flow.

Second, accountants distinguish between *current* and *capital* expenditures. While current expenditures are expensed, capital expenditures are "depreciated" over time. The rationale for this procedure is that the original capital expenditure should be written off against earnings as the capital equipment is "used up" in the production of income. From a cash perspective, however, the outflows occur when the expenditure is made, not as the equipment is used up. Whereas accounting profits are stated net of depreciation, cash flow is calculated net of capital expenditure. Because capital expenditure rarely equals depreciation, a wedge is driven between accounting earnings and cash flow. (In a perfectly static world in which there is no growth, no inflation, and in which economic deterioration equals accounting depreciation, depreciation will equal its capital expenditures and accounting earnings will equal cash flow. Needless to say, this is not the world in which we live.)

Third, accountants keep track of special reserves, such as those for deferred taxes and bad loans. When reserves are altered—for example, when a bank increases its reserve for bad loans—accounting earnings are affected, but there is no impact on cash flow, because moving entries from one account to another does not involve payment or receipt of cash. When Citibank increased its reserve for bad loans by $3 billion, earnings tumbled a like amount, but cash flow was unaffected because the increase in reserves did not alter the rate at which Citibank was collecting or paying its bills. (This ignores taxes. If the write-off leads to lower tax payments, then cash flow will rise.)

Some Complications that Arise When Calculating Cash Flow

To undo accounting conventions and get back to the dollars that flow into and out of a company, a cash flow statement must be constructed from the income statement and the balance sheet. The procedure for constructing a cash flow statement is best illustrated by working through a detailed example. Before turning to the example calculations, however, there are several complications that need to be addressed.

Payments to investors and the interest tax deduction. There are two exceptions to the rule that cash flow equals the difference between the dollars that flow into a company and the dollars that flow out. First, payments to security holders are not deducted, because they are taken into account by the discounting process. The return to investors is reflected in the firm's weighted average cost of capital, WACC. Therefore, deducting payments to investors from the cash flow stream to be discounted is double counting. Put another way, the goal of a discounted cash flow analysis is to estimate the value of the stream of payments that the investors who "purchase" the firm can expect to receive and then to discount that stream to present value using the average rate of return required by investors. In this context, the "purchasers" of the firm include all investors, not just stockholders. Returning to the bank account example for an all-equity-financed firm, suppose that the owner of the company paid the entire balance of the bank account out to him- or herself as a dividend. If the cash flow stream were measured net of payments to investors, the net cash flow each year would be zero, implying that the firm had no value. However, the firm is clearly valuable to the owner because it provides him or her with spendable cash each year. In fact, the value of the firm to the owner is the present value of the spendable cash flow stream. This cash flow stream is precisely the same as the funds *available* for disbursement to investors.

With respect to interest payments, this introduces another complication—what happens to the interest tax deduction? Federal tax rules and the tax laws in most states allow companies to deduct interest payments when calculating taxes due. If interest payments are not considered to be a cash outflow, what happens to the interest tax deduction? The answer is that it also is included in the WACC by calculating the cost of debt on an after-tax basis. (The procedure for taking into account the interest tax deduction when calculating the WACC is discussed in detail in Chapter 7.) Because interest payments are deductible, the after-tax cost of debt is lower than the before-tax cost. This reduces the WACC. To avoid double counting, therefore, the interest tax deduction is not accounted for in the cash flow calculation. Instead, taxes due are computed as if the firm were all equity financed. For this reason, the cash flow that is calculated in this manner is often referred to as "debt free" cash flow. The calculation of debt-free cash flow is illustrated for the case of FEC later in the chapter.

Nonrecurring cash flows. Another complication involves extraordinary items. The value of the firm can be thought of as arising from two sources: the cash flow produced by normal operations and extraordinary cash flows from nonrecurring events, as shown in Equation (5–1).

Total value = Present value of operating + Present value
of the firm   cash flow   of extraordinary
                                                              cash flow   (5–1)

Extraordinary cash flows include income from sales of assets, revenues from discontinued operations, payments to settle outstanding lawsuits, and other nonrecurring sources and uses of cash. When calculating and forecasting cash flow, it is usually a good idea to treat extraordinary items separately. Including extraordinary items with operating cash flow makes trends in operating cash flow more difficult to spot and to project.

Separating the two sources of cash flow is also advisable because they may entail varying degrees of risk. The weighted average cost of capital measures the cost of financing the firm's normal operations. If the risk of the extraordinary cash flows is not equal to the risk of normal operations, then a different discount rate should be used to discount the extraordinary cash flows to present value. In practice, however, a separate discount rate is rarely used. Only if nonrecurring cash flow accounts for a significant fraction of the firm's value is it worthwhile to calculate a separate discount rate. For example, if a firm planned to downsize by selling off several divisions in future years, the receipts from those sales should be forecast and discounted separately. Whether a different discount rate is used depends on whether the appraiser believes that the receipts from the sales are more or less risky than normal cash flow from operations.

There is another reason why a separate discount rate generally does not have to be calculated for extraordinary income. Most extraordinary cash flows have a short horizon; many occur only in the current year. Therefore, they are not sensitive to small changes in the discount rate.

Income from excess marketable securities. Cash flows produced by excess marketable securities should also be separated from normal operating cash flow. Because every firm must hold some cash and marketable securities as part of its normal operations, the income from these normal holdings is included as part of the cash inflow from operations. However, some companies use cash and marketable securities as a repository for excess funds. For example, at one point, IBM built up over $5 billion in cash and marketable securities before deciding to use the excess funds to buy back its own stock. These unusually large holdings of securities constitute an investment that is distinct from the cash held to facilitate normal operations.

Excess marketable securities can be valued as part of the overall firm by simply including the income from the securities as a component of the total cash flow. The problem with this approach is that the income from marketable securities is less risky than the revenue produced by normal operations. For this reason, it is appropriate to discount the income from excess marketable securities at a lower rate than the company's cost of capital. As a result, excess cash and marketable securities should be valued separately, as shown in Equation (5–2).

Total value	= Present value of	+ Market value of cash and
of the firm	cash flow excess	marketable
	operating	securities (5–2)

Fortunately, the discounting process can usually be avoided because the market and book values of cash and marketable securities are generally equal.[10] Therefore, excess marketable secu-

---

[10] This is true as long as the marketable securities are short-term money market instruments. If the company holds long-term securities or equity securities, the book and market values may diverge. However, the securities can still be valued easily if market prices are available.

rities can be valued by deducting an estimate of the company's required normal holdings from the cash and marketable securities reported on the balance sheet. The only difficult issue is determining the level of cash and marketable securities "required" for normal operations, so that the "excess" is defined properly. The FEC example discussed subsequently illustrates this problem.

Deferred taxes. As noted in Chapter 2, the provision for income taxes reported on the income statement will not equal taxes paid in cash if different depreciation methods are used for reporting purposes and tax purposes. To calculate cash flow, the appraiser must "undo" deferred tax accounting and get back to taxes paid in cash. This is accomplished by deducting the change in deferred tax, which is included in the provision for income taxes, but is not paid in cash, from the income tax provision. Remember that the change in deferred taxes is deducted from the taxes calculated on a debt-free basis. Fortunately for most companies, the change in deferred tax on a debt-free basis equals the change in deferred tax computed from the balance sheet. This is so because the increase in deferred tax depends solely on depreciation. If the company is profitable after interest expense, and if tax rates are relatively constant (which corporate taxes are), the change in deferred tax is not affected by the interest deduction. Put another way, the change in deferred tax equals the added depreciation available in a given year due to accelerated depreciation times the effective tax rate.

Leases. The fact that there are two types of leases leads to confusion as to how they should be treated. Capital leases are those that transfer ownership of the asset to the lessee. All other leases are considered operating leases. The treatment of operating leases is straightforward. The lease payment is an operating expense that is included in the cost of goods sold or selling and administrative expenses. Therefore, the lease payment is automatically deducted when computing cash flow.

When a lease is capitalized, the present value of the lease payments (at the interest rate implicit in the lease) is added to both the company's fixed assets and to its liabilities. Therefore, capital leases should be treated like other forms of debt. Rather than deducting the lease payments from cash flow, the payments are treated as disbursements to investors and included as an element of debt in the firm's weighted average cost of capital.

It is also possible to capitalize operating leases. In that case, the market value of the lease, which equals the present value of the lease payments, is added to both the assets and liabilities of the company. The lease payments are then treated as disbursements to investors. In most cases, however, capitalizing operating leases unnecessarily complicates the appraisal process without adding accuracy. Unless operating leases account for a large fraction of the company's assets, it is more practical to treat them as operating expenses.

Pensions. Because pension costs are included in the cost of goods sold or selling and administrative expenses, an adjustment to the cash flow calculation typically is not required. An exception arises when a pension fund is significantly under- or overfunded. In that case, future cash flows associated with the pension fund will differ from those reflected in the current cost of goods sold. These added costs or benefits must be taken into account when forecasting future cash flow.

It is worth noting that in some cases, under- or overfunded pension funds can have a significant impact on the value of the firm. For instance, when Kaiser Industries was involved in a battle for corporate control, one of the assets suitors sought most aggressively was the firm's overfunded pension plan.

AN EXAMPLE: CALCULATING AND FORECASTING CASH FLOW FOR FEC

To see how all the pieces fit together, a detailed cash flow analysis of FEC is presented. This analysis encompasses both the calculation of FEC's historical cash flow and predictions of future cash flow. The historical calculations and the future predictions are linked in two ways. First, the mechanics of the calculations are identical. In both cases, computing cash flow amounts to tracking the dollars that flow into and out of a company on an annual basis. Second, history provides a guide to the future. The patterns, if any, discernible in the historical calculations are a valuable tool in making future predictions. Furthermore, the past can be used to "check" the future. If future predictions are markedly different than past performance, a reconsideration of the cash flow forecasts is in order.

To emphasize the relation between the past and the future, the dependence of future predictions on historical calculations is highlighted throughout the FEC example. Of course, there are also situations in which the future is expected to diverge from the past. For example, growth must eventually slow as a firm matures. Therefore, the example also highlights situations in which elements of the future cash flow predictions diverge from their historical precedents.

The Historical Calculations for FEC

The information necessary to calculate historical cash flow is contained in the income statement, the balance sheet, and the related notes. The income statement provides data on income and expenses for the year in question. Balance sheet information is required at both the beginning and the end of the year in order to compute changes in quantities such as plant and equipment, working capital, and deferred taxes.

The income statement and balance sheets necessary to calculate FEC's cash flow for fiscal 1989 are reproduced in Tables 5–1 and 5–2. The cash flow calculation based on this financial information is presented in Table 5–3. Table 5–3 also presents historical data on FEC's cash flow for the years from 1980 to 1988. The calculations for 1989 are discussed in depth below. The calculations are similar for all the prior years.

As shown in Table 5–3, the cash flow calculation begins with sales revenue as reported on the income statement. By starting with sales revenue, the appraiser is implicitly assuming the difference between sales booked and sales collected is negligible. For all but the most aberrant companies, this is a reasonable assumption. Next, the cost of goods sold, depreciation, and selling and administrative expense are deducted to arrive at income from operations. For FEC, the figure is $449,131 in 1989. Though

TABLE 5–1
Forms Engineering Income Statement for Fiscal Years Ending
June 30, 1988 and 1989

	1988	1989
Sales	$14,813,981	$15,243,196
Cost of goods sold	10,795,327	11,796,820
Depreciation	711,054	756,526
Selling and administrative expense	2,373,248	2,240,719
Income from operations	$ 934,352	$ 449,131
Other Income (expense):		
Interest expense	$ (250,374)	$ (295,953)
Interest income	45,329	26,822
Total other income	$ (205,045)	$ (269,131)
Income before taxes	$ 729,307	$ 180,000
Provisons for income taxes:		
Current payable	$ 371,813	$ 80,386
Deferred	12,456	51,378
Total provisions for income tax	384,269	131,764
Net income	$ 345,038	$ 48,236

depreciation is not a cash outflow, it must be deducted at the initial stage of the calculation in order to properly account for tax payments. Once taxes have been calculated, the depreciation is added back.

Because FEC has no reported extraordinary income or expenses, the only difference between operating income and taxable income is the interest earned on cash and marketable securities. What makes FEC difficult to handle is the wide swings in the holdings of cash and marketable securities. For example, the 1989 holdings are almost $500,000 less than the holdings in 1988. After discussion with management, it was concluded that the 1989 holdings represent "normal" requirements. Based on management's assertion that the build-up in 1988 was unique, FEC's holdings of cash and marketable securities in all other years is assumed to be normal. Thus, no special adjustment is necessary to account for excess cash when computing cash flow in 1989.

TABLE 5–2
Forms Engineering Balance Sheets for the Fiscal Year Ending June 30, 1988 and 1989

	1988	1989		1988	1989
Cash	$ 865,182	$ 383,168	Accounts payable	$ 536,604	$ 510,258
Accounts and notes receivable	2,307,075	2,885,742	Accrued commissions	74,409	78,934
Inventories	1,258,641	933,087	Accrued payroll	46,171	101,475
Tax claim receivable	0	117,318	Accrued vacation pay	140,554	157,838
Prepaid income taxes	0	80,386	Employee benefit plan	22,822	20,330
Prepaid expenses	16,749	6,961	Notes payable	581,942	581,146
Deposits	17,811	43,244	Income taxes payable	325,978	0
Deferred income taxes	39,718	47,136	Other liabilities	15,460	35,496
Current assets	$4,505,176	$4,497,042	Current liabilities	$1,743,940	$1,485,477
			Notes due after one year	$2,360,671	$1,768,929
Leasehold improvements	$ 169,015	$ 169,015	Deferred income taxes	176,304	227,682
Machinery and equipment	5,626,309	6,166,997			
Office equipment	138,887	141,868	Total	$2,536,975	$1,996,611
Automotive	171,268	162,683			
Computer equipment	197,863	201,807	Total liabilities	$4,280,915	$3,482,088
Deposit on new press	382,500				
Total	$6,685,842	$6,842,370	Preferred stock	$1,055,580	$1,055,580
			Common stock/paid in capital	58,000	58,000
Accumulated depreciation	3,281,868	4,029,501	Retained earnings	2,512,869	2,714,243
			Total shareholders' equity	$3,626,449	$3,827,823
Net property and equipment	$3,403,974	$2,812,869			
Total assets	$7,909,150	$7,309,911	Total liabilities and shareholders' equity	$7,907,364	$7,309,911

TABLE 5-3
Historical Cash Flow Calculations for FEC (1980–1989)

	1980	1981	1982	1983	1984	1985	1986	1987	1988	1989
Sales revenue	$4,008,223	$4,555,080	$6,268,866	$6,591,688	$10,458,272	$12,400,665	$11,049,654	$11,590,100	$14,813,981	$15,243,196
Less: Cost of goods sold	2,676,960	3,149,557	4,397,599	4,706,418	7,294,676	8,399,322	8,069,953	8,429,514	10,795,327	11,796,820
Less: Depreciation	209,000	295,000	320,000	369,000	410,000	530,000	698,000	689,000	711,054	756,526
Less: Selling and administrative expense	789,988	773,349	1,117,100	1,267,088	2,092,584	1,997,892	2,114,671	1,996,117	2,373,248	2,240,719
Income from operations	$ 332,275	$ 337,174	$ 434,167	$ 249,182	$ 661,012	$ 1,473,451	$ 167,030	$ 475,469	$ 934,352	$ 449,131
Add: Interest on marketable securities	7,053	8,015	11,031	11,599	18,402	21,820	19,443	20,394	45,329	26,822
Debt-free taxable income (EBIT)	$ 339,328	$ 345,189	$ 445,198	$ 260,781	$ 679,414	$ 1,495,271	186,473	495,863	$ 979,681	$ 475,953
Less: Provision for income taxes (assuming 40% tax rate)	129,731	138,576	175,079	106,812	271,766	580,108	97,589	159,345	393,972	202,381
Add: Increase in deferred taxes	2,398	8,134	2,980	3,210	6,892	14,568	23,986	9,876	12,456	51,378
Net operating profit after adjusted tax	$ 209,597	$ 206,613	$ 270,119	$ 153,968	$ 407,649	$ 915,163	$ 88,884	$ 336,518	$ 585,709	$ 273,572
Add: Depreciation add-back	209,000	295,000	320,000	369,000	410,000	530,000	698,000	689,000	711,054	756,526
Less: Increase in working capital	(23,000)	(56,000)	(140,000)	(184,000)	(268,000)	(298,000)	(229,450)	(302,000)	(287,000)	(266,597)
Less: Capital expenditures	(85,000)	(298,000)	(49,000)	(56,000)	(78,000)	(669,196)	(2,113,077)	(357,679)	(1,028,383)	(153,519)
Net cash flow	$ 310,597	$ 147,613	$ 401,119	$ 282,968	$ 471,649	$ 477,977	$(1,555,643)	$ 365,839	$ (18,620)	$ 609,982

The distinction between normal and excess holdings of cash is important because, as noted earlier, interest earned on excess holdings is treated separately. Furthermore, some assumption must be made about FEC's cash holdings in the future. The assumption made here is that FEC will not hold excess cash in the future. Given this assumption, and based on management's statement that 1989 holdings are normal, future holdings of cash are estimated by multiplying the ratio of marketable securities to sales in 1989 by the predicted sales in future years. This procedure relies on the assumption that cash holdings are dependent on the level of business activity as measured by sales.

Whereas the historical interest earned on marketable securities is known, it must be estimated in future years. In the case of FEC, which holds very short-term liquid securities, the cash and marketable securities are assumed to earn interest at the average expected future Treasury bill rate. Based on the forecasting methodology developed in Chapter 7, that rate is assumed to be 7 percent. Because the income from marketable securities is relatively small, reasonable changes in this assumption would have only a minute effect on the cash flow forecasts.

FEC is somewhat unique in that it has no extraordinary income or expenses. It is common for firms to report extraordinary sources of items such as proceeds from discontinued operations, profits from asset sales, and loss write-offs. These extraordinary items drive a wedge between income from operations and taxable income. As noted previously, it is wise to exclude these nonrecurring items from the cash flow calculation. If nonrecurring income or expense is expected to have an impact on future cash flow, the value of the extraordinary income stream can be calculated separately. Management is usually the best source of information on future cash flows from nonrecurring sources.

At this point, it is worth reiterating that the taxable income reported in Table 5–3 is calculated on a debt-free basis. The impact of interest expense and the interest deduction is included in the discount rate.

Given the taxable income, the next step is to calculate taxes paid in cash. The calculations in Table 5–3 assume that the tax rate was 40 percent throughout the period from 1980 to 1989. Though this is not exactly correct, it makes the historical calculations consistent with the future forecasts, which are based on a 40 percent tax rate. This makes it easier to see the relation between past cash flow and future forecasts. Using this assumption, the provision for income taxes on a debt-free basis equals debt-free taxable income times the tax rate.

Because FEC takes advantage of accelerated depreciation, the income tax provision does not all have to be paid in cash. As discussed previously, the cash tax payment equals the provision for income taxes minus the change in deferred taxes. The historical change in deferred taxes is reported in Table 5–3 on an as is basis taken directly from FEC's balance sheets. Because FEC is profitable and tax rates are relatively constant, no adjustment to the change in deferred taxes is required. Notice that because FEC was growing through the 1980s, deferred taxes rose consistently. For example, deferred taxes increased from $176,304 in 1988 to $227,682 in 1989, reducing FEC's cash outlay for taxes in 1989 by $51,378.

Estimation of future tax payments requires two assumptions. First, a tax rate must be assumed for each future year. For FEC, the total tax rate, state and federal, is assumed to be a constant 40 percent. That rate closely approximates what the firm expects to pay under the current tax regulations. Of course, both the federal government and the state of California may change the rules, but attempting to forecast future tax policy is beyond the scope of this book.

Second, future changes in deferred taxes must be forecast. This is complicated because it depends on current and past investments, the assumed tax rate, and the depreciation method and schedules used by the firm on all of its investments. When forecasting future deferred taxes, all of these elements, in principle, must be taken into account, though appraisers often use simplifying assumptions. One common simplifying assumption is to project past increases in deferred taxes using a simple trend line analysis, as described for earnings in Chapter 4. In the case of FEC, it was not necessary to employ a simplifying assumption because Mr. Bergstrom, the CFO, maintains a detailed computer model of the firm's capital spending plans. Two of the outputs of this model are future depreciation and the amount of deferred income taxes. Because the company is projected to be profitable and because tax rates are assumed to be constant, the output from the model is used without adjustment to calculate the change in deferred taxes.

Deducting taxes paid in cash and from debt-free taxable income and adding back the increase in deferred taxes gives net operating profit after adjusted tax, or NOPAT. NOPAT differs from cash flow in three respects. First, depreciation, which was deducted in order to compute taxes payable but which is not a cash charge, must be added. Second, net increases in working capital, which constitute a cash drain, must be deducted. (Working capital is defined as the difference between current assets and current liabilities.) Table 5–3 shows that FEC's working capital rose in every year throughout the 1980s. The increases, furthermore, exceed 50 percent of after-tax operating income in several years. (Printers are required to maintain large inventories of paper, ink, and supplies. In addition, they usually have large accounts receivable. The increase in FEC's working capital is attributable primarily to the rise in inventories and accounts receivable.) Such sharp increases in working capital are not uncommon for rapidly growing companies. Third, capital expenditures are subtracted. FEC's capital expenditures, like those for many small companies, are "lumpy." In some years, capital expenditures are minimal, while in other years, such as 1986, when a large new press was purchased, they exceed operating income.

Interpreting the Cash Flow Calculations

Insight into FEC's historical cash flow statement for the 1980s can be gained by relating it to developments at the company. Understanding the relation between cash flow and corporate developments is critical for forecasting future cash flow. Without knowledge of the company's fundamentals, trends are difficult to separate from random fluctuations.

In 1978, FEC moved into a new plant in La Palma, California, that was five times the size of its old facility. The move was part of a corporate plan to increase market share dramatically. The corporate plan also called for the firm to launch a new marketing

TABLE 5–4
Historical Data on Key Ratios

Data for FEC

Date	FEC Sales	COGS/Sales	Selling and Administrative Expenses/Sales	Working Capital/Sales
1980	4,008,223	66.8%	19.7%	11.2%
1981	4,555,080	69.1%	17.0%	7.9%
1982	6,268,866	70.1%	17.8%	13.4%
1983	6,591,688	71.4%	19.2%	18.5%
1984	10,458,272	69.8%	20.0%	14.6%
1985	12,400,665	67.7%	16.1%	17.4%
1986	11,049,654	73.0%	19.1%	19.8%
1987	11,590,100	72.7%	17.2%	19.7%
1988	14,813,981	72.9%	16.0%	18.6%
1989	15,243,196	77.4%	14.7%	19.8%
Ten-year average		71.1%	17.7%	16.1%
Five-year average		72.8%	16.6%	19.1%

Data for Comparable Companies (five-year averages ending in 1989)

	COGS/Sales	Selling and Administrative Expenses/Sales	Working Capital/Sales
American Business Products	68.7%	16.2%	16.2%
Duplex Products	69.5%	16.8%	19.5%
Ennis Business Forms	67.9%	16.8%	19.0%
Moore Corporation	69.2%	15.9%	19.9%
Standard Register	71.0%	16.0%	20.5%
Wallace Computer Services	70.5%	16.5%	19.0%
Industry average	69.5%	16.4%	19.0%

effort that included bidding aggressively for jobs and offering successful salespeople generous commissions.

FEC's marketing strategy was a resounding success. Between 1980 and 1985, FEC's sales tripled and EBIT and cash flow both rose markedly. The dark side of the drive to increase sales was that it led to a high ratio of selling and administrative expenses to sales. As shown in Table 5–4, FEC's ratio was above the industry average, particularly in the early part of the decade.

By 1984, management came to realize that the company was taxing its equipment to the limit and that sustained rapid growth would require significant new investment. Therefore, in 1985, FEC initiated an unprecedented capital spending program. Between 1985 and 1989, the company purchased two large new presses and associated support equipment. Plans were also made to import a massive German press in 1991. To keep the new presses busy, the company continued its aggressive sales effort. As a result, cost of goods sold and selling and administrative expenses remained above industry averages. In 1985, the company also loosened its credit policy to promote sales further. The easier credit resulted in a buildup of accounts receivable, and, therefore, working capital. The rising working capital ratios are evident in Table 5–4.

Unfortunately, FEC's new capital spending program coincided with a downturn in the company's business. Two of the firms largest customers went bankrupt in 1986, and in 1987, a third important customer turned to a competing firm. Due to this series of disasters, cash flow declined markedly. Not until 1989, when sales picked up and capital expenditures declined, did the firm's cash flow achieve levels obtained in 1985.

In summary, the historical record indicates that FEC is a rapidly growing company whose cash flow depends to a large degree on the pattern of capital expenditures. Going forward, a key question for the company is whether it can generate sufficient sales, without incurring undue selling expense, to justify the large recent capital expenditures and the capital expenditures planned for the immediate future. Another important question is how long the rapid growth can be expected to continue.

Forecasting Cash Flow

Corporate value is based on future cash flow, not historical cash flow. The appraiser's task, therefore, is to produce an analog to Table 5–3 that begins with the present year and extends into the future. That task involves understanding the company, its products, and its customers well enough to forecast the income statement and the balance sheet up to 10 years into the future.

Unfortunately, financial economics provides no set rules on how such forecasts are to be constructed. Cash flow forecasting is more in the domain of industrial economics, accounting, statistics, and management science than finance. It also involves a good deal of judgment and practical experience. Perhaps it is for these reasons that financial valuation models based on discounted cash flow begin with the assumption that cash flow forecasts are given. Whatever the explanation, only general issues related to forecasting future cash flow are discussed here. To help keep track of the issues, a checklist is developed.

A Cash Flow Forecasting Checklist

At the core of any cash flow forecast lies a sales forecast. Sales to a company are like gross national product to a country. They are a measure of overall economic activity. All other sources and uses of cash, including production costs, capital expenditures, and interest income, are related, either directly or indirectly, to sales. The first problem an appraiser faces, therefore, is developing a sales forecast. Unfortunately, this is also likely to be the most difficult task.

Consider, for instance, the task of forecasting sales for the PS/2 line of personal computers when IBM introduced them in 1987. A reasonable sales forecast would have to take into account *at least* the following factors:

- The technical capabilities of the IBM machines in relation to current and future competitors. These capabilities include the power of processor, the storage capacity of the disk drives, the speed of the data bus, and the like.
- The software available for the IBM machines compared to competing machines.
- The ease with which third-party products could be used on the IBM machines.
- The opportunity to expand or improve the IBM machines compared with competing computers.
- The extent to which customers would be willing to pay a premium for the IBM name.
- The relative pricing of the IBM machines compared to their competing machines, and the general sensitivity of the market to price.

IBM no doubt considered these and many other factors in its decision to release the PS/2 line. Nonetheless, the company was disappointed. Buyers decided that the features provided by the PS/2 machines were not sufficiently innovative. They felt they could get more computing power for their money by buying clones of IBM's old line of computers rather than the new PS/2s. Furthermore, IBM's name carried less weight than the firm had hoped, and the market proved to be more price sensitive than IBM had estimated. To make matters worse, third-party producers chose to support IBM's old line and the clones of the old line more actively than the PS/2s. Due to all these factors, IBM's market share fell sharply and profitability declined. As a result, the value of the division turned out to be less than an appraisal based on 1987 forecasts would have indicated. As the stock market became aware of this fact, IBM's stock price dropped significantly in inflation-adjusted terms.

Though the PS/2 line was new, IBM did have a history of making personal computers. In some situations, such as when valuing start-up companies, appraisers must develop sales forecasts without the benefit of prior history. Consider, for example, the litigation that arose over the valuation of a proposed instant sign franchising company. The franchise company went bankrupt following the collapse of negotiations with a venture capital firm. The franchise company then sued the venture capital firm on the grounds that its business had been destroyed by the failure of the venture capitalist to provide necessary financing. Putting aside the legal merits of the claims, the economic question that arose in the litigation was "What would have been the value of the franchise company if the financing had been provided?" To estimate the value of the firm, business valuation experts for both sides used the discounted cash flow approach and agreed on the discount rate. Nonetheless, the resulting appraisals differed by 2,500 percent. One expert predicted a dynamic "McDonald's-like" future for the instant sign business, with sales and outlets doubling every few years. The other foresaw stagnant sales for a struggling company sandwiched between instant printers and home computer users. This difference in sales forecasts alone accounted for virtually all of the 25-fold discrepancy.

Both the IBM and instant printing examples illustrate the first point on the checklist:

1. The sales forecast is generally the most critical element of a cash flow forecast. As the examples show, changes in a sales forecast often lead to dramatic changes in value. The examples also demonstrate that sales forecasting generally requires a detailed knowledge of the company being appraised, including the following, among other things: the industry in which the company operates; the products the company produces; the relationship of the company with its customers, suppliers, and servicers; and the nature of the company's competition.

Because sales forecasting is difficult, the process is subject to potential abuse depending on the goal of the appraiser. In the instant sign printing example, the two appraisers were able to reach dramatically different conclusions by making different assumptions regarding future sales growth. Wherever possible, historical data, either for the firm or its industry, should be examined to assess the reasonableness of the sales forecasts— which leads to the second point on the checklist.

2. The sales forecast should be consistent with the firm's historical performance and the historical performance of the industry. While it is always possible that a company will develop in unexpected ways, so that the future does not resemble the past, this is not the best way to bet. Appraisals based on forecasts that depart markedly from historical patterns are suspicious. In particular, predictions of dramatic turnarounds should be viewed with skepticism. One useful warning is "Beware of hockey sticks." Hockey sticks arise when historical sales are flat or declining, but future sales are predicted to take off. Therefore, plotting historical sales and forecast sales against time results in a chart that looks like a hockey stick. Hockey stick forecasts are a simple way for an appraiser to create value out of thin air. Consequently, if a turnaround is predicted, all of the actions necessary to produce the expected success should be specified.

Another way for an appraiser to create value is to assume that a company will grow faster than other firms in its industry for a sustained period. Such sustained growth implies that the appraisal target will eventually become the dominant firm in the industry. This is usually not a reasonable assumption.

3. The sales forecast and the forecasts for the items that depend on sales must be internally consistent. Once a sales forecast has been developed, it is often relatively easy to forecast other cash flows because those other flows are related to and dependent on the level of sales. For instance, most of the predicted cash flows into and out of FEC, which are estimated in the next section, are dependent on the sales forecast. Other cash flow items for which predictions are not derived directly from the sales forecast must still be consistent with the sales forecast. For instance, rapid growth in sales can rarely be achieved without significant capital expenditures and a buildup of working capital. Therefore, appraisals that forecast a rapid rise in sales without an associated increase in capital spending should be viewed with suspicion. In addition, costs must bear a reasonable relation to sales. The tendency to assume that increased volume will naturally lead to lower per unit costs should be resisted unless the appraiser can find convincing evidence that such is the case. Assuming that costs per unit will inevitably fall as sales rise is one way to produce a hockey stick forecast for net cash flow.

It is worth noting that the advent of the electronic spreadsheet makes it *less* likely that checking for consistency will detect faulty appraisals. With a computer, any appraisal can easily be made internally consistent. If the appraiser's goal is to produce a high or low value, that can be done, without introducing any inconsistencies, by building a cash flow model on an electronic spreadsheet and then adjusting the key assumptions such as the sales growth rate until the desired value is achieved. In this way, an internally consistent but still biased appraisal can be produced.

One consistency check is so important that it is worth adding to the checklist as a separate point. As stressed in Chapter 2, interest rates, and therefore the cost of capital, reflect expectations regarding future inflation. For an appraisal to be consistent, the same inflation forecast must be incorporated in the cash flow forecasts—which yields the fourth point on the checklist.

4. The cash flow forecast must reflect the same expected inflation rate impounded in the discount rate. Saying that the cash flow forecast must reflect expected inflation does not mean that every revenue and expense item should be adjusted upward each year by exactly the same percentage. In a dynamic economy, the prices of some goods and services will rise more quickly than inflation, while the prices of others lag behind. Furthermore, some items such as depreciation are contractually fixed in terms of nominal dollars and do not vary with inflation at all. The point is that the expected rate of inflation should be taken as the baseline assumption around which price variation occurs. For example, if the expected rate of inflation impounded in interest rates is 5 percent, then all prices that are not fixed in nominal terms should be assumed to grow at 5 percent unless specific information to the contrary is available.

Treating inflation consistently means that the appraiser must attempt to estimate the expected rate of inflation incorporated in interest rates. Though the procedure for doing this is discussed in detail in Chapter 7, a thumbnail sketch is required at this point in order to proceed with the cash flow forecasting examples. To illustrate the procedure, suppose that it is necessary to estimate the expected rate of inflation (on average) over the next 10 years. Because the interest rate on a 10-year Treasury security is a nominal rate, it is comprised of two items: (1) an expected real rate of interest; plus (2) the expected average rate of inflation over the next 10 years. Therefore, the expected average rate of inflation equals the nominal rate minus the expected real interest rate. Consequently, estimating expected inflation amounts to estimating the expected real interest rate. One straightforward and widely employed method for estimating the real interest rate is to assume that it equals its long-run historical average. Table 7–2 (from Chapter 7) shows that the average real return on long-term Treasury securities over the period 1926 to 1990 was 1.7 percent. (This equals the difference between an average nominal return of 4.9 percent and an average inflation rate of 3.2 percent. Subtracting this historical real interest rate of 1.7 percent from the current 10-year bond rate provides an estimate of expected inflation over the next 10 years. For instance, a current 10-year rate of 6 percent would be consistent with an expected inflation rate of 4.3 percent.

The drawback of this simple approach is that it assumes that the real rate of interest is constant despite evidence indicating that real rates vary in response to changing economic conditions and shifting government policy. In the long run, however, the real rate does tend to revert toward its historical average.[11] Therefore, it is reasonable to deduct the average historical real rate from the current long-term rate on government securities when forecasting inflation over the long run. If there is convincing evidence that the current real rate is not equal to its historical average, the appraiser may decide to make an adjustment.

5. Employ sensitivity analysis to isolate those assumptions that have the largest impact on the cash flow forecasts. The rationale for those key assumptions should then be double-checked. Although a discounted cash flow model involves many assumptions, all assumptions are not created equal. Some, such as the assumed choice of depreciation method, may have a minor impact on value, while others, such as the assumed growth rate in sales, almost invariably have a major impact on the final appraised value. Because it highlights the assumptions on which the cash forecasts are most critically dependent, sensitivity analysis is a valuable tool for assessing a cash flow forecast. Once the key assumptions have been isolated, their rationale can be reviewed.

The best way to perform sensitivity analysis is to reduce the cash flow forecast to an electronic spreadsheet model. This procedure not only facilitates sensitivity analysis, it also forces the appraiser to specify the quantitative relations between the various elements of the cash flow forecast. Once the spreadsheet has been developed, the assumptions can be altered, and the impact on future cash flow is recalculated automatically.

Although sensitivity analysis is useful for isolating key assumptions, it is not of much help in determining whether a given set of assumptions is reasonable. In the case of FEC, for instance, the sensitivity analysis discussed in the next section points to one key assumption—the growth rate in sales—but it offers no insight into whether or not management's sales forecast is reasonable—which is the subject of our last checklist guideline.

---

[11] For a detailed analysis of the behavior of real interest rates, see E. F. Fama and K. French, "Business Conditions and Expected Returns on Stocks and Bonds," *Journal of Financial Economics* 25 (November 1989), pp. 23–49.

6. Compare the DCF value indicator with the value indicators produced by other approaches. A discounted cash flow model and the cash flow forecasts on which it depends can be assessed directly by comparing the DCF value indicator with value indicators produced by alternative appraisal approaches. If the DCF indicator is significantly different from the alternative value indicators, the critical assumptions isolated by the sensitivity analysis should be reviewed carefully. In conducting the review, a good question to ask is what alterations of key assumptions are necessary to bring the DCF value indicator into line with the other indicators. The answer to this question will help the appraiser understand whether a discrepancy exists between the DCF model and competing approaches. Without such knowledge, it is difficult for an appraiser to decide whether the DCF approach or the alternative approaches are on stronger footing and should be given greater weight in making a final judgment as to the value of the firm.

Though comparison with other approaches is an excellent method for evaluating DCF models, it is least applicable when it is needed most. If the company being appraised is a publicly traded firm with a long history, such as IBM, then a DCF appraisal can be checked against both stock and debt and direct comparison valuations. However, the cash flow forecasts for publicly traded firms with long histories are also likely to be relatively uncontroversial. Conversely, if the appraisal target is small, privately held, and has virtually no history, such as the instant printing franchise, then it is impossible to do a stock and debt appraisal and difficult to find comparables for a direct comparison appraisal. But it is in this situation, when the most weight must be placed on the DCF approach, that the cash flow forecasts are likely to be the most controversial. Without an historical record, appraisers are more free to peer into their crystal balls and come up with radically different views regarding the future of the company and its industry.

The instant printing example is not unique. Courts are littered with lawsuits involving disputes over the value of start-up business in rapidly evolving industries such as computers, biotechnology, and environmental control. In these lawsuits, it is not uncommon for the appraisals produced by the opposing sides to differ by a factor of 10 or more. Lacking an historical record, and without the ability to apply alternative appraisal methods, the competing parties are free to make radically different, but still internally consistent, forecasts of future sales and future cash flows. In such situations, the only way to evaluate an appraisal is to conduct a comprehensive, point-by-point analysis of the assumptions on which the forecasts are based.

The FEC Cash Flow Forecast

The first step in forecasting cash flow is to determine the horizon over which forecasts are to be developed. Though the general question of selecting a forecast horizon is not addressed until the next chapter, in the case of FEC, a seven-year horizon, 1990 to 1996, is selected (see Table 5–5). (Recall that the lien date is July 1, 1989, the beginning of fiscal year 1990.) The reason for this choice is straightforward. By 1996, the company expects to be operating its plant at full capacity, and there are no plans to expand the current production facilities. Once the capacity constraint becomes binding, management expects that nominal growth in sales will drop sharply from approximately 14 percent per year to a long-run equilibrium level of 6 to 7 percent per year, or 1 to 2 percent in real terms. It is reasonable, therefore, to assume that by the end of 1996, FEC will have reached its equilibrium state, thereby allowing simple rules of thumb to be used to estimate cash flows in the subsequent years. Detailed item-by-item forecasts are required only for the seven years following the lien date.

Forecasting future sales. Following the checklist, the DCF appraisal of FEC begins with a sales forecast. This starting point is consistent with the nature of FEC's business. In repeated conversations, FEC management stated that in the printing business, sales are the key to success. Because the technology is relatively well developed, production costs, working capital, and capital expenditures are all closely tied to sales. If the sales can be accurately forecast, then a successful DCF model can be developed.

Because sales are reported in nominal dollars, a preliminary step in predicting future sales is to forecast the future rate of

TABLE 5–5
Predicted Cash Flows for FEC (1990–1996)

	1989 (actual)	1990	1991	1992	1993	1994	1995	1996
Sales revenue (from management schedule)	$15,243,196	$17,857,709	$20,694,227	$23,504,090	$26,374,409	$29,075,149	$31,780,591	$33,446,530
Less: Cost of goods sold (70% of sales)	11,796,820	12,500,396	14,485,959	16,452,863	18,462,086	20,352,604	22,246,414	23,412,571
Less: Depreciation (from management schedule)	756,526	720,000	1,020,000	975,000	895,000	880,000	950,000	910,000
Less: Selling and administrative expense (16.5% of sales)	2,240,719	2,946,522	3,414,548	3,878,175	4,351,778	4,797,400	5,243,798	5,518,677
Income from Operations	$ 449,131	$ 1,690,791	$ 1,773,721	$ 2,198,052	$ 2,665,545	$ 3,045,145	$ 3,340,380	$ 3,605,282
Add: Normal interest on securities*	26,822	31,422	36,413	41,358	46,408	51,160	55,921	58,852
Debt-free taxable income (EBIT)	$ 475,953	$ 1,722,213	$ 1,810,134	$ 2,239,410	$ 2,711,953	$ 3,096,305	$ 3,396,301	$ 3,664,134

Less: Taxes (40% total tax rate)	190,381	688,885	724,054	895,764	1,084,781	1,238,522	1,358,520	1,465,653
Add: Increase in deferred taxes (based on capital expenditures)	51,378	14,750	79,854	29,865	21,654	14,987	31,000	28,750
Net operating profit after adjusted tax (NOPAT)	$ 285,572	$ 1,033,328	$ 1,086,080	$ 1,343,646	$ 1,627,172	$ 1,857,783	$ 2,037,780	$ 2,198,480
Add: Depreciation add-back	756,526	720,000	1,020,000	975,000	895,000	880,000	950,000	910,000
Less: Increase in working capital (19% of change in sales)	(266,597)	(496,757)	(538,939)	(533,874)	(545,361)	(513,141)	(514,034)	(316,528)
Less: Capital expenditures (from management schedule)	(153,519)	(50,000)	(3,450,000)	(150,000)	(175,000)	(225,000)	(650,000)	(375,000)
Net cash flow	$ 621,982	$ 1,206,570	$(1,882,858)	$ 1,634,772	$ 1,801,811	$ 1,999,643	$ 1,823,746	$ 2,416,952

*The normal holdings of cash and marketable securities is assumed to maintain the same ratio to sales as obtained in 1989. The yield on those securities is forecast to average 7 percent.

inflation. If unit sales remain unchanged, and if the relative price of the goods sold remains constant, then sales will grow at precisely the rate of inflation. Of course, unit sales and relative prices typically vary, and this must also be taken into account. Nonetheless, the inflation forecast provides a baseline to which the impacts of changing unit sales and changing relative prices are added.

FEC's management believed that 5 percent was a reasonable forecast for future inflation. Before accepting this forecast, it is necessary to see if it is consistent with the level of interest rates prevailing at the time. On the lien date of July 1, 1989, the true annual yield on 10-year Treasury bonds was 8.27 percent. Subtracting the 1.7 percent historical real return on long-term bonds produces an inflation forecast of 6.57 percent, about 150 basis points higher than the inflation forecast chosen by FEC's management. There is reason to believe that the FEC forecast may nonetheless be a reasonable choice. In 1989, economists were arguing that real interest rates were above their long-run historical average. If the real rate were assumed to be about 3 percent, then the implied inflation forecast falls to 5 percent. Interestingly, both the President's Council of Economic Advisers and Data Resources, Inc., were predicting inflation rates of approximately 5 percent and real interest rates on long-term Treasury bonds of 3 to 5 percent over the next decade. In light of these predictions, FEC's inflation forecast of 5 percent seems reasonable and is adopted here.

Taking account of an inflation rate of 5 percent, Mr. Bergstrom, in conjunction with Jill Gwaltney, the head salesperson at FEC, produced a detailed sales forecast. The schedule of future sales predicted by Mr. Bergstrom is presented in Figure 5–1. For comparison, sales forecasts based on extrapolation of FEC's 10-year compound growth rate of 14.29 percent and on extrapolation of the 5 percent inflation rate are also shown. The figure makes it clear that management is assuming that sales will continue to grow at approximately historical rates until 1993. At that point, limitations on plant and equipment begin to bind, and the sales growth rate starts declining toward its long-run level of 6 to 7 percent in nominal terms, or 1 to 2 percent in real terms. This is the real growth rate that management feels is sustainable by replac-

FIGURE 5–1
FEC Sales Forecast Analysis

Year	Sales (000s)	CPI	Growth Rate	Growth Rate Extrapolation	Inflation at 5 Percent
1980	$ 4,008	78.5			
1981	4,555	87.7	13.64%		
1982	6,269	94.8	37.62%		
1983	6,592	98.2	5.15%		
1984	10,458	101.8	58.66%		
1985	12,401	105.1	18.57%		
1986	11,050	109.0	−10.89%		
1987	11,590	110.2	4.89%		
1988	14,814	114.7	27.82%		
1989	15,243	120.0	2.90%		
1990	17,858	Geometric	Geometric	17,422	16,005
1991	20,694	average	average	19,911	16,806
1992	23,504	growth	growth	22,757	17,646
1993	26,374	4.34%	14.29%	26,009	18,528
1994	29,075			29,726	19,455
1995	31,781			33,974	20,427
1996	33,447			38,830	21,449

FEC Sales Forecast

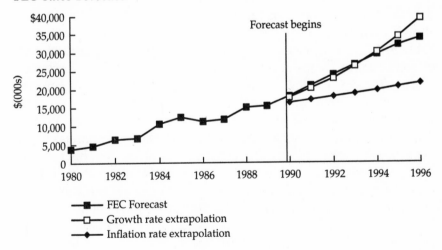

—■— FEC Forecast
—□— Growth rate extrapolation
—♦— Inflation rate extrapolation

ing old equipment with more productive machines and by improving operating efficiency without moving to a larger plant.

Overall, Mr. Bergstrom's sales forecast appears to be reasonable. It is consistent with FEC's historical sales record and takes into account future constraints on capacity. There are no hockey sticks in which a dramatic change in performance is predicted. Nonetheless, it should be noted that other than checking for consistency, it is extremely difficult for an outside appraiser to offer a critique of a sales forecast such as that prepared by Mr. Bergstrom. Mr. Bergstrom, like key managers at most firms, has a thorough knowledge of the company, its customers, and the industry. Based on this knowledge, he is in a position to produce sales forecasts that an outside appraiser, with only a cursory knowledge of the business, will find difficult to replicate. This makes it easy for a clever manager to mislead an appraiser. Consequently, it is wise to proceed with care and cross-check a management sales forecast wherever possible. With this warning in mind, Mr. Bergstrom's forecasts are utilized in the remainder of the example. They are shown in the top line of Table 5–5.

Forecasting operating costs. Once a sales forecast has been developed, operating costs must be estimated and deducted. Operating costs include the cost of goods sold, administrative and selling expenses, and depreciation. The estimates for the cost of goods sold and the selling and administrative expense shown in Table 5–5 are based on the ratio analysis presented in Table 5–4. Turning to Table 5–4, notice that the ratios both of cost of goods sold to sales and of selling and administrative expenses to sales for FEC exceed the average ratios for comparable companies. These higher ratios for FEC can be attributed to the company's ambitious efforts to increase market share. As the company matures, and as capacity is approached, management expects both ratios to drop to industry averages. For this reason, cost of goods sold is forecast to average 70 percent of future sales, and selling and administrative expenses are forecast to average 16.5 percent of future sales. Both the ratios chosen for application to FEC are slightly above the industry average but below historical levels for FEC. Multiplying these ratios by Mr. Bergstrom's sales forecast gives the cost of goods sold and selling and administrative expenses for each of the next seven years.

Forecasting future depreciation. The depreciation forecast includes future depreciation on equipment purchased prior to July 1, 1989, and still in service on the lien date, as well as depreciation on anticipated new investments. New investments are assumed to be made in accord with the company's capital spending plan. In conjunction with his sales forecast, Mr. Bergstrom, in consultation with the President Gwaltney, estimated what new equipment would be required to ensure that future production could keep pace with future sales. Notice in Table 5–5 that the impact on future depreciation of the company's anticipated purchase of a large German press in 1991 is clearly evident. Except for the German press, no other significant expansion of the stock of capital equipment is projected through 1996, though the company does expect to replace old machines as they wear out with new, electronically controlled printing equipment.

From operating income to debt-free taxable income. Subtracting cost of goods sold, selling and administrative expense, and depreciation from sales gives the forecast future income from operations. Table 5–5 shows that FEC expects continuing growth in operating income at a healthy and relatively consistent rate through 1996.

Two entries, extraordinary items and earnings on security investments, distinguish operating income from debt-free taxable income. Extraordinary items do not appear in Table 5–5 because FEC has not had, and does not expect to have, extraordinary income or expenses. However, even if such items existed, they should probably be excluded from the cash flow forecast and valued separately. As discussed previously, mixing nonrecurring items with normal operating income and expenses makes cash flow more difficult to forecast.

Turning to income from marketable securities, recall that FEC expects to hold only those marketable securities that it needs to ensure that the firm has sufficient liquidity to meet short-run contingencies. As stated earlier, management believes that the normal ratio of marketable securities to sales in the future will approximate the 1989 ratio. Furthermore, those security holdings are predicted to earn interest at an average rate of 7 percent. Therefore, the interest income from investments for any future year is calculated by multiplying the ratio of cash holdings to sales in 1989 by the sales forecast for the year in question and then applying an interest rate of 7 percent.

Because there are no extraordinary items, adding predicted interest income to operating income gives debt-free taxable income. Debt-free taxable income also equals earnings before interest and taxes, EBIT, net of extraordinary items. EBIT measures the earning power of the firm prior to making payments to the government, to investors, to purchase new equipment (net of depreciation), and to add to working capital.

Estimating future tax payments. For simplicity, FEC is assumed to face a total tax rate, both state and federal, of 40 percent. Applying that rate to the debt-free taxable income gives FEC's predicted provision for income taxes shown in Table 5–5. The income tax provision exceeds taxes paid in cash because FEC is a growing company that expects to take advantage of accelerated depreciation. This leads to rising deferred taxes. The annual increase in deferred taxes represents that fraction of the provision for income taxes that is not paid in cash. To arrive at cash tax payments, an estimate of future increases in deferred taxes must be deducted from the provision for income taxes. This is complicated because future changes in deferred taxes depend on a company's past capital expenditures, its future capital expenditures, the depreciation methods employed, and the tax rate. In FEC's case, Mr. Bergstrom's model, which assumed a tax rate of 40 percent, takes all of those factors into account. Given the past record of capital spending and the projected future capital expenditures, the model calculates FEC's expected depreciation and deferred taxes for each of the next seven years. These projections are shown in Table 5–5.

Forecasting capital expenditures and estimating cash flow. Subtracting cash taxes paid yields net operating profit after adjusted taxes, or NOPAT. As noted earlier, there are three items that distinguish NOPAT from cash flow: depreciation, changes in working capital, and capital expenditures. First, depreciation is added to NOPAT because it was deducted when calculating taxable income, but it is not a cash expense.

Second, the expected increase in working capital is deducted. Generally, working capital is closely related to sales. This is the situation in the printing industry. The ratio analysis in Table 5-4 indicates that working capital averaged about 19 percent of sales for both FEC and the comparable companies. On this basis, future increases in working capital are assumed to equal 19 percent of future increases in sales.

Finally, capital expenditures are deducted to arrive at net cash flow. As described earlier, the capital expenditure forecasts are based on the company's strategic financial model developed by Mr. Bergstrom. The capital expenditures are lumpy at the start of the seven-year forecasting interval because FEC is still making periodic large investments in new equipment to expand production.

FEC's expected net cash flow reported in Table 5-5 represents the dollars that will be available to pay investors in each of the next seven years. The cash flow forecasts have two notable characteristics. First, cash flow is predicted to grow sharply. This reflects primarily the continued rapid real growth in sales in the years from 1990 to 1994. Second, the cash flow stream is irregular because of the erratic nature of the planned capital expenditures. In particular, the huge expenditure planned for 1991 leads to a predicted net cash flow of negative $1.88 million. However, by the end of the forecast horizon, capital spending is swamped by the continued growth in sales.

Checking the consistency of the cash flow forecast. Because the individual items that go into the cash flow forecast are not typically estimated simultaneously, or even produced by the same person or procedure, it is possible that they are inconsistent. To check this possibility for FEC, a number of tests were conducted. First, it was noted that by construction, the forecast ratios of cost of goods sold to sales, selling and administrative expense to sales, and working capital to sales are all close to industry averages. On this score, there is no evidence that FEC's management is predicting that the company can generate future sales without paying the requisite costs. Second, the planned capital expenditures were reviewed and compared to the sales forecasts. Though the planned expenditures occur at irregular times, management has recognized clearly that sales growth cannot be sustained without purchasing necessary equipment. Finally, the sales forecast was checked to see that it was consistent with FEC's historical performance. Though sales growth is predicted to be rapid in the years 1990 to 1994, it is not out of line with FEC's track record. In addition, the forecast growth in sales is not so rapid that FEC's position in the industry is transformed. Furthermore, the sales forecast takes into account the constraint on growth imposed by the size of FEC's production facility.

Overall, the FEC forecasts are reasonable. They are internally consistent and in line with FEC's historical performance.

Applying sensitivity analysis to the FEC cash flow forecast. For an assumption to play a critical role in a cash flow forecast, two conditions must be satisfied. First, the assumption must be important in the sense that alterations in the assumption will have a significant impact on the cash flow forecasts. Second, there must be a relatively wide range of values that reasonably can be chosen.

In the case of FEC, the sales forecast clearly satisfies both criteria. First, sales revenue is the main source of cash flow. Furthermore, most of FEC's cash outflows are tied directly or indirectly to sales, so that changes in the sales forecast are passed through to net cash flow more or less proportionally. Second, because forecasting sales for a small company in a competitive industry is inherently speculative, a wide range of sales forecasts can reasonably be selected. A pessimistic analyst might argue that FEC's period of rapid growth was over by 1989 and that the firm could not expect to grow at more than 1 to 2 percent in real terms in the future. Conversely, an optimist might project two decades of high growth based on the view that the company could open plants similar to its La Palma facility throughout the country. Ex ante, neither view can be dismissed as unwarranted.

The cost assumptions, on the other hand, satisfy only the first condition. Like changes in sales revenue, variation in the cost of goods sold or in selling and administrative expense has a large impact on net cash flow. However, relative to the sales forecast, the cost forecasts are tightly constrained. Though there is some leeway, the relation between costs and sales in the printing business is quite predictable. Ratios of costs to sales that deviate significantly from industry averages can quickly be rejected as unreasonable. This need not, however, be true of every industry.

The same is true of the capital expenditure and working capital assumptions. Though the timing of expenditures is subject to some discretion, the investment schedule is largely determined by the sales forecast. If sales fail to rise, capital spending plans will be altered. Working capital is even more closely tied to sales and production. If new sales do not materialize, neither inventories, accounts receivable, nor accounts payable are likely to be altered significantly.

In short, a brief qualitative analysis points directly to the sales forecast as the key determinant of the value of FEC. To the extent that independent appraisers forecast significantly different cash flows for FEC, it is almost certainly because they disagree about the prospects for future sales. In this way, FEC is not unique. For companies with uncertain prospects, most of the variation in DCF appraisals will be due to disagreements regarding projections of future sales. Such debates persist because even with a detailed knowledge of the business and the industry, it is extraordinarily difficult to accurately predict the success of one firm. In the case of the computer software industry, for instance, a few firms have flourished while many others have disappeared. At the outset, how is an appraiser to tell which is which?

CONCLUDING OBSERVATIONS

Whereas the key to the direct comparison approach is comparability, the key to the discounted cash flow approach is the cash flow forecasts on which it is based. Though the DCF value depends on the cost of capital as well as the cash flow forecasts, most of the variation in competing DCF valuations can generally be traced to different forecasts of future cash flow. The problem is that relatively small alterations in critical assumptions, such as the growth rate in sales and the ratio of operating costs to sales, can have an immense impact on estimated value. Furthermore, it is difficult for an appraiser or a financial economist to verify cash flow forecasts. Whereas estimates of the cost of capital generally are based on standard financial calculations using historical data on stock and bond returns, cash flow forecasts are based on inherently nebulous predictions regarding the future success of a business. Developing such forecasts requires a detailed understanding of the business, rather than an understanding of finance theory. Though the appraiser can test to see whether the cash flow forecasts are internally consistent and conform with the historical record, it is much more difficult to determine whether a consistent forecast is reasonable. With the aid of a microcomputer, producing a consistent but misleading forecast is as simple as 1-2-3.

While the message of this chapter is simple from an economic standpoint—corporate value depends on expected cash flow—from a practical standpoint, forecasting future cash flow is a daunting task. Cash flow forecasting is difficult for corporate planners in staid industries with long histories. It is an extraordinarily difficult task for outside appraisers dealing with companies in rapidly evolving competitive industries. As a result, the DCF approach to valuation may be abused in practice. Because they are so difficult to contradict, cash flow forecasts can be tailored to satisfy the needs of the client, rather than to produce the most accurate appraisal.

The litigation that erupted following the Interco restructuring illustrates the problems that can arise. To fight off a takeover bid, Interco formulated a restructuring plan that involved the company issuing a great deal of high-yield debt. On the basis of the cash flow forecasts it was presented, the Interco board decided that the company could safely issue the debt. Unfortunately, soon after the restructuring, the company's business slowed and the huge interest burden forced the firm into bankruptcy. As a result, Interco filed a lawsuit against Wasserstein-Pirella, the company's investment banker, claiming that Wasserstein-Pirella was professionally negligent because it presented the board with unrealistically high cash flow forecasts to promote the restructuring. Wasserstein-Pirella responded by arguing that the cash flow forecasts utilized in their valuation analysis were based on assumptions provided by management. If the forecasts were biased, it was because management had provided faulty information.

As of this writing, the lawsuit remains unresolved, but for our purposes, the resolution is beside the point. The issue is not whether Wasserstein-Pirella or the Interco board is to blame for mistakes that might have been made with regard to the restructuring, but to illustrate the hazards of forecasting cash flow in a highly uncertain world where there are clear rewards for pushing the forecasts in one direction or another. Quite possibly, both the board and Wasserstein-Pirella were willing to accept optimistic projections because both had an incentive to see the restructuring proceed.

Although the DCF approach depends on potentially speculative cash flow forecasts, it does have the advantage that it is applicable in virtually any situation. It is not required that the appraisal target be publicly traded or that easily identifiable comparables exist. All that is necessary is that estimates of future cash flows are available and that a reasonable estimate of the discount rate can be derived. That is both the virtue of the discounted cash flow approach and its vice.

Chapter Six

Estimating the Continuing Value at the Terminal Date

There is an apparent paradox in the discounted cash flow approach to valuation. First, a great deal of effort is expended to forecast future cash flows on an annual basis up to a terminal date. Second, the continuing value of the firm at the terminal date is estimated. Third, the present values of both the annual cash flow forecasts and the continuing value are calculated and summed to obtain an estimate of the total value of the firm. This procedure suggests an obvious simplification: Why not define the current time to be the terminal date and value the firm today using whatever procedure is employed to estimate the continuing value? Such a simplification would eliminate both the need to forecast cash flows and the need to calculate present values.

The answer, as suggested in the previous chapter, is twofold. First, because the life of a firm is indefinite, simplified procedures must be used to compute the continuing value at the terminal date. However, these simplified procedures are applicable only when the firm has reached an "equilibrium state" and is no longer evolving rapidly. In many situations, it is inappropriate to assume that the firm is in an equilibrium state on the appraisal date. Second, the simplified procedures used to estimate continuing value are less accurate than valuations based on explicit cash flow forecasts. By postponing the date at which the simplified models are applied, the impact of errors produced by these models is mitigated by the discounting process.

The preceding suggests two criteria for selecting the terminal date. First, the terminal date should not precede the point at which the firm can be said to have reached an equilibrium state. Second, the terminal date should be sufficiently far in the future that valuation errors caused by using simplified procedures to estimate the continuing value are mitigated by the discounting process.

Despite the impact of discounting, in many discounted cash flow appraisals the continuing value accounts for a large percentage of the total value. Copeland, Koller, and Murrin report that for a series of appraisals produced by McKinsey and Company, the continuing value accounted for 56 percent of the total value of tobacco companies, 81 percent of the total value of sporting goods companies, 100 percent of the total value of skin care companies, and 125 percent of the total value of high-tech companies.[1] Continuing value can account for more than 100 percent of firm value if predicted cash flows are negative during the early years in which annual cash flow forecasts are developed. The greater the fraction of total value attributable to the continuing value, the more important it is that the continuing value be estimated carefully.

The fact that the continuing value accounts for a large share of the total value for many firms does not mean that value is not being created during the cash flow forecasting period. During this period, some firms, particularly high-tech firms, are making large investments in capital equipment and research and development. Due to these expenditures, the net cash flow is negative. Assuming that they are successful, capital expenditures undertaken during the forecasting period will also produce higher revenues in the years following the terminal date. Once the firm matures and capital spending and research and development slows, net cash flow rises sharply. These high cash flows in years following the terminal date produce the large continuing value.

---

[1] T. Copeland, T. Koller, and J. Murrin, *Valuation: Measuring and Managing the Value of Companies* (New York: John Wiley & Sons, 1990), p. 208.

To estimate the continuing value of the firm, the appraiser must make two interrelated decisions: selecting the terminal date and deciding what valuation model to apply at the terminal date. The decisions are interrelated because the procedure used to estimate the continuing value defines what is meant by the firm's equilibrium state, which in turn defines the terminal date. For ease of presentation, the models for estimating continuing values are presented first, and then the selection of the terminal date is discussed.

MODELS FOR ESTIMATING CONTINUING VALUE AT THE TERMINAL DATE

Because firms have indefinite lives, at some point, cash flow forecasts must stop and a simplified rule must be employed to estimate the continuing value of the firm. Three basic approaches are employed for estimating continuing value: the constant growth approach, the value-driver approach, and the direct comparison approach. Each approach is based on the assumption that by the terminal date, the firm has reached an equilibrium state. However, the approaches differ in defining what is meant by equilibrium.

THE CONSTANT CASH FLOW GROWTH MODEL

The first approach utilizes the constant growth model. The constant growth model is based on the assumption that in equilibrium at the terminal date, the growth in the firm's real (inflation-adjusted) cash flow has converged to a constant level that is maintained indefinitely. Several observations are in order about this definition of equilibrium and the associated long-run growth rate in cash flow.

- The equilibrium condition is more appropriately defined in terms of real cash flow than nominal cash flow because nominal cash flow depends on the general rate of inflation, a factor unrelated to the fate of the appraisal target. Once the equilibrium growth rate in real cash flow has been estimated, the nominal growth rate can be calculated by compounding the forecast rate of inflation and the expected real growth rate using the formula (1+ nominal rate) = (1+ real rate) · (1+ inflation rate). (The formula nominal rate = real rate + inflation rate is an approximation that works when rates are low.) This approach has the added benefit that the same expected inflation rate can be used in appraisals for different companies.

- Because the real growth rate is assumed to continue forever, special care should be taken to ensure that the estimated growth rate is reasonable. The long-run real rate of growth for the U.S. economy is only on the order of 2 to 3 percent per year. If a company is assumed to grow at a higher rate indefinitely, its cash flow would eventually exceed America's GNP. Too often, appraisers assume that short-run high rates of growth can be maintained forever.
- It is important that the forecast cash flow for the year ending at the terminal date be properly normalized. As will become evident, errors in the normalized cash flow forecast at the terminal date translate into equal percentage errors in the continuing value. The cash flow forecast for the year ending on the terminal date may not be normal if extraordinary expenditure or receipts are anticipated in that year.

Given the assumption of constant real growth in cash flow, the continuing value at the terminal date is calculated from the formula:

$$\text{Continuing value at time } t = \frac{E(\text{NCF}_{t+1})}{\text{WACC} - [(1+g) \cdot (1+\pi) - 1]}$$

$$(6\text{--}1)$$

In Equation (6–1):

Time t = End of the forecasting horizon

$E(\text{NCF}_{t+1})$ = Normalized cash flow expected during period $t + 1$. This equals the normalized cash flow for the year ending on the terminal date multiplied by $[(1 + g) \cdot (1 + \pi)]$

WACC = Weighted average cost of capital (see Chapter 7)

g = Long-run real growth in cash flow

π = Expected inflation rate impounded in the WACC

The formula is derived by projecting a constantly growing stream indefinitely and discounting it to present value at the WACC.[2]

Using the cash flow forecasts from Chapter 5 and the WACC, which will be estimated in Chapter 7 (see Table 7–8), Equation (6–1) can be applied to Forms Engineering. In FEC's case, the terminal date is the end of fiscal 1996. By the end of 1996, FEC's management expects the plant to be operating at capacity, so that future growth in sales and cash flow must come from technological improvements in the equipment and increased operating efficiency. Management felt that these continuing enhancements would produce a real growth rate of between 1 and 2 percent. To be conservative, g is assumed to equal 1 percent. This 1 percent real growth compounded with an expected inflation rate of 5 percent produces a 6.05 percent growth rate for nominal cash flow. Finally, FEC's weighted average cost of capital, using the company's target capital structure weights, as shown in Table 7–8, is 13.98 percent. The cash flow forecast through fiscal 1996, reproduced in Table 6–1, reveals that for fiscal 1996, the estimated net cash flow is $2.42 million. However, this is more than $400,000 greater than the highest previous year and involves a relatively low level of capital expenditures. After conversations with Mr. Bergstrom, it was determined that this figure may be somewhat in excess of normalized net cash flow in the terminal year. This is important because the terminal year cash flow is the starting point for all future growth. In light of this, Mr. Bergstrom felt it would be reasonable to reduce the terminal year cash flow to a round value of $2.25 million. He admitted, however, that the reduction was only a rough estimate. This is to be expected, be-

---

[2]For a derivation of this formula, see S. A. Ross, R. W. Westerfield, and J. F. Jaffee, *Corporate Finance*, 2nd ed. (Homewood, Ill.: Richard D. Irwin, 1990), p. 93.

cause no one can make fine adjustments to cash flow seven years into the future. It should be noted in his defense that Mr. Bergstrom's adjustment is conservative in the sense that it reduces the appraised value of FEC. Applying the expected growth rate of 6.05 percent, the normalized cash flow for 1997 comes to $2.39 million.

Substituting the numbers for FEC into Equation (6–1) gives:

$$\text{Continuing value at time } t = \frac{\$2.39}{(.1398 - .0605)} = \$30.14 \text{ million}$$

Notice that the continuing value is sensitive to the parameters that determine long-run nominal growth. If the real growth rate is increased to 3 percent and the expected inflation rate to 7 percent, the continuing value more than doubles, to over $63 million. In addition, errors in the normalized cash flow are magnified because they are divided by .0793. An error of $200,000 in the normalized cash flow produces an error of about $2.5 million in the estimate of the continuing value.

The impact of these potential errors is ameliorated by the fact that the continuing value is discounted back seven years at 13.98 percent. Consequently, an error in the continuing value of $1 million translates into an error in the current value of only about $400,000.

An Extended Version of the Cash Flow Growth Model

For the constant growth model to be applicable, explicit cash flow forecasts are required up to the point where the real growth in cash flow converges to a constant rate. Unfortunately for many firms, particularly recent start-ups and high-technology enterprises, it may take 20 years or more for growth rates to fall to a constant level. Rather than abandoning the growth model under such circumstances, it is often possible to extend it along the lines described in the discussion of the dividend growth model in Chapter 7. Specifically, individual cash flows are forecast up to an equilibrium point where the cash flow growth becomes

TABLE 6-1
Predicted Cash Flows for FEC (1990–1996)

	1989 (actual)	1990	1991	1992	1993	1994	1995	1996
Sales revenue (from management schedule)	$15,243,196	$17,857,709	$20,694,227	$23,504,090	$26,374,409	$29,075,149	$31,780,591	$33,446,530
Less: Cost of goods sold (70% of sales)	11,796,820	12,500,396	14,485,959	16,452,863	18,462,086	20,352,604	22,246,414	23,412,571
Less: Depreciation (from management schedule)	756,526	720,000	1,020,000	975,000	895,000	880,000	950,000	910,000
Less: Selling and administrative expense (16.5% of sales)	2,240,719	2,946,522	3,414,548	3,878,175	4,351,778	4,797,400	5,243,798	5,518,677
Income from operations	$ 449,131	$ 1,690,791	$ 1,773,721	$ 2,198,052	2,665,545	$ 3,045,145	$ 3,340,380	$ 3,605,282
Add: Normal interest on securities*	26,822	31,422	36,413	41,358	46,408	51,160	55,921	58,852
Debt-free taxable income (EBIT)	$ 475,953	$ 1,722,213	$ 1,810,134	$ 2,239,410	$ 2,711,953	$ 3,096,305	$ 3,396,301	$ 3,664,134

Less: Taxes (40% total tax rate)	190,381	688,885	724,054	895,764	1,084,781	1,238,522	1,358,520	1,465,653
Add: Increase in deferred taxes (based on capital expenditures)	51,378	14,750	79,854	29,865	21,654	14,987	31,000	28,750
Net operating profit after adjusted tax (NOPAT)	$ 285,572	$ 1,033,328	$ 1,086,080	$ 1,343,646	$ 1,627,172	$ 1,857,783	$ 2,037,780	$ 2,198,480
Add: Depreciation add-back	756,526	720,000	1,020,000	975,000	895,000	880,000	950,000	910,000
Less: Increase in working capital (19% of change in sales)	(266,597)	(496,757)	(538,939)	(533,874)	(545,361)	(513,141)	(514,034)	(316,528)
Less: Capital expenditures (from management schedule))	(153,519)	(50,000)	(3,450,000)	(150,000)	(175,000)	(225,000)	(650,000)	(375,000)
Net cash flow	$ 621,982	$ 1,206,570	($1,882,858)	$ 1,634,772	$ 1,801,811	$ 1,999,643	$ 1,823,746	$ 2,416,952

*The normal holdings of cash and marketable securities is assumed to maintain the same ratio to sales as obtained in 1989. The yield on those securities is forecast to average 7 percent.

predictable though not necessarily constant. That predictability is then used to forecast the trend in cash flow without developing an item-by-item cash flow forecast.

Consider, for instance, the case of Symantec, a rapidly growing manufacturer of utility software for personal computers. Even using a long forecasting period such as 10 years, it still may be unrealistic to conclude that Symantec will grow at a constant real rate from the terminal date onward. One way to solve this problem is to extend the terminal date, but producing a detailed item-by-item cash flow forecast such as that shown in Table 6–1 more than 10 years into the future is a difficult and often futile task. Beyond a certain point, the future is too hazy for forecasts to be reliable. In fact, when applying the DCF approach, many investment banks define the terminal date as the date beyond which item-by-item forecasting is no longer reasonable.

Although Symantec's cash flow growth may not fall to a constant rate for 20 years, it may be possible to use simple approximation to forecast beyond a given horizon. For example, if the terminal date at which item-by-item forecasting ceases is 10 years, the real growth rate in Symantec's cash flow might be assumed to be 5 percent in years 11 through 15 and 3 percent in years 16 to 20 before settling down to a constant level of 2 percent in the 21st year. Given these growth rates, the cash flows for years 11 through 20 can be projected and discounted to present value. Finally, the constant growth model is applied to estimate the continuing value as of year 21, and that continuing value is also discounted to present value.

Such an extended growth model can be thought of as a compromise between constructing a detailed item-by-item cash flow forecast and assuming that the rate of growth in cash flow is constant. This takes into account the investment bankers' observation that beyond a certain point, it may no longer be reasonable or feasible to attempt to forecast all the elements that determine cash flow. However, it may still be premature to assume that the real growth rate is constant. A middle ground is to estimate the real growth rate in cash flow directly between the end of the explicit forecasting period and the date at which constant growth begins.

TABLE 6–2
Calculating the Continuing Value of FEC Using an Extended Growth Model

Year			Discounted Values
1990	$1,206,570		
1991	($1,882,858)		
1992	$1,634,772		
1993	$1,801,811	Net cash flow forecasts from Table 6–1.	
1994	$1,999,643		
1995	$1,823,746		
1996	$2,416,952		
1997	$2,480,625	= $2,250,000 · Assumed nominal growth rate, 10.25%	$2,176,369
1998	$2,708,843	= $2,480,625 · Assumed nominal growth rate, 9.2%	$2,085,098
1999	$2,929,613	= $2,708,843 · Assumed nominal growth rate, 8.15%	$1,978,447
2000	$3,137,616	= $2,929,613 · Assumed nominal growth rate, 7.1%	$1,859,025
			$8,098,938
2001	$3,327,441	= $3,137,616 · Assumed nominal growth rate, 6.05%	
2002	$3,528,752	= $3,327,441 · Assumed nominal growth rate, 6.05%	

The terminal date is 1996. The continuing value at the terminal date is computed in four steps, using a cost of capital of 13.98 percent. First, the cash flows during the period from 1997 to 2000 are discounted back to 1996. Second, the value at the beginning of the constant growth period is computed using the constant growth model. Third, the value at the beginning of the constant growth period is discounted back to the terminal date. Finally, the continuing value equals the sum of the present values as of 1996.

Year 1996 present value of cash flows from 1997 and 2000 $8,098,938
Year 1996 present value of cash flows for years 2001 and beyond $24,861,231

Total continuing value as of 1996 $32,960,168

The procedure can be illustrated by applying it to Forms Engineering. In the previous section, it was assumed that FEC's real growth rate dropped immediately to its long-run rate of 1 percent at the terminal date in 1996. It might be more reasonable to assume that the capacity constraints bind slowly over time, so that the real growth rate declines from 5 percent in 1996, to 4 percent in 1997, to 3 percent in 1998, and to 2 percent in 1999, before leveling off at 1 percent in the year 2000. The cash flow forecasts under those assumptions are presented in Table 6–2. The table shows the cash flow forecasts for three periods—the period during which item-by-item cash flow forecasts are developed, the period during which the growth rate in cash flow is declining, and the period of constant growth. Once again, the normalized cash flow for fiscal 1996 is assumed to be $2.25 million. Therefore, the cash flow forecast for 1997 is $2.48 million, which equals $2.25 million increased by 10.25 percent. (The 10.25 percent increase reflects real cash flow growth of 5 percent compounded with inflation of 5 percent.)

The continuing value is the sum of the present values, *as of the terminal date in 1996*, of the cash flows forecast during the period of declining growth and the period of constant growth. First, the cash flows during the period of declining growth are discounted on a year-by-year basis. Second, the constant growth formula is applied to the cash flow stream once constant growth begins. Third, the number that results from applying the constant growth formula is discounted back to the terminal date. Finally, the present values are summed to arrive at the continuing value. It is worth reiterating that this continuing value is discounted a second time to calculate the present value at the lien date. This procedure produces a continuing value at the terminal date that can be compared with the continuing value produced by competing approaches. However, it is also possible to discount the cash flow forecasts following the terminal date directly to present value on the lien date.

This procedure is applied to FEC in Table 6–2. As shown in the table, the continuing value for FEC comes to $32.96 million. This exceeds the continuing value of $30.14 million estimated using the constant growth model for two reasons. First, cash flows are greater during the years from 1997 to 2000 because of the higher rates of real growth during that period. Second, once constant growth begins in 2001, it starts at a higher base level because of the faster growth in the years from 1997 to 2000.

THE VALUE–DRIVER MODEL

The value-driver model attempts to account explicitly for the profitability of investments made after the terminal date. The value-driver approach begins with net operating profits after adjusted tax, NOPAT, instead of net cash flow. NOPAT differs from net cash flow in that depreciation is not added back and capital expenditures (including expenditures for working capital) are not deducted. To calculate NOPAT from net cash flow, therefore, it is necessary to subtract depreciation and add capital expenditures and changes in working capital. Interpreting the depreciation charge as the cost of maintaining current facilities, the difference between NOPAT and net cash flow is the new investment in fixed assets and working capital. (This interpretation must be made with care because in an inflationary environment, depreciation will understate the cost of replacing existing assets.)

Future growth in NOPAT is a function of the amount of new investment the firm undertakes and the return on that investment. A firm that invests little in addition to that required to replace assets, or that does not earn in excess of the cost of capital on new investments, will experience little growth in NOPAT. Consequently, the continuing value depends on the fraction of NOPAT reinvested and the rate of return on investment in relation to the cost of capital. For this reason, these two variables are referred to as value drivers.

In the early stages of a firm's life, when the company is evolving rapidly, both new investment and the return on new investment are likely to be changing rapidly. As a result, the relation between the value of the firm, the growth in NOPAT, and the value drivers is extraordinarily complicated. However, as the firm matures, the variation in the value drivers typically declines. In the limit, when the value drivers are constant, a simple formula can be used to calculate the value of the firm. Thus, the value-driver approach consists of two steps: (1) forecasting cash flow until the terminal date at which the value drivers can be assumed to be approximately constant; and (2) applying the value-driver formula for continuing value at the terminal date.

The value-driver formula for continuing value is similar to that produced by the constant growth model. The formula states that the continuing value of the firm is given by the equation:[3]

$$\text{Continuing value at time } t = \frac{E(NOPAT_{t+1})(1 - gnom/r)}{WACC - gnom} \quad (6\text{--}2)$$

where:

WACC $\quad = $ Weighted average cost of capital

$E(NOPAT_{t+1}) = $ Expected normal net operating profit after adjusted tax during the year following the terminal date, $t + 1$

$r \qquad\qquad = $ Expected rate of return on new investment in equilibrium

$gnom \qquad = $ Expected *nominal* rate of growth in NOPAT in equilibrium.

The similarity between the value-driver formula and the constant growth formula is a result of the fact that both are based on the same economic concept of equilibrium at the terminal date. If the firm reinvests a constant fraction of its after-tax operating profit, and if the return on investment is constant, then after-tax operating profit and cash flow, as well as NOPAT, will grow at a constant rate. (Note that for the return on investment to be constant, other key drivers such as operating margins must also be constant.)

In practice, the constant growth model and the value-driver approach may not produce the same continuing value because of discrepancies in the normalized starting point. In the case of FEC, the normalized cash flow at the terminal date was assumed to be $2.25 million, and the resulting continuing value was $30.14

---

[3]See Copeland, Koller, and Murrin, *Valuation*, p. 210, for a derivation of the equation.

million. For the value-driver approach to yield the same continuing value, the starting normalized NOPAT must be consistent with a cash flow of $2.25 million. That is, margins and new investment must be at their long-run equilibrium values, and the difference between replacement investment and depreciation must be such that when cash flow is calculated from NOPAT, the answer is $2.25 million. In addition, the expected rate of return on new investment must be consistent with the forecast growth rate of cash flow. Because these conditions rarely hold exactly for real companies, some discrepancy between the continuing value produced by the two approaches is to be expected.

To calculate the NOPAT level consistent with FEC's terminal cash flow of $2.25 million, it is necessary to subtract depreciation and to add investment expenditures and changes in working capital. Because FEC is operating at capacity, it may appear that investment expenditures will equal depreciation and working capital will be constant, but this is not true because of inflation. Utilizing the 5 percent inflation forecast and assuming that the average life of FEC's new equipment is 10 years, investment expenditure will exceed depreciation by 30 percent in equilibrium. In addition, working capital will grow at the inflation rate of 5 percent.

To see why capital expenditure will exceed depreciation by 30 percent, assume that FEC's assets last 10 years from the purchase date to retirement and cost I (in current dollars). Assume, furthermore, that the ages of the assets currently owned by FEC are equally distributed, so that $1/10$ are new, $1/10$ are one year old, and so on. Therefore, $1/10$ must be replaced this year at a cost proportional to I. With an inflation rate of π, and assets that last n years, depreciation in the current year equals $(1/n)[\$I/\pi + \$I/\pi^2 \ldots + \$I/\pi^n]$. Applying the formula for summing a geometric series, the total depreciation, per dollar of replacement costs, can be shown to be $\frac{\pi n}{1 - 1/(1+\pi)^n}$ when the inflation rate is π and the life of new equipment is n years. Substituting $\pi = 5$ percent and $n = 10$ years, the ratio of replacement cost to new investment is found to be approximately 1.3. Thus, capital expenditure will exceed depreciation by 30 percent even though the firm is not growing.

The calculation of NOPAT for FEC is illustrated in Table 6–3. Assuming that FEC's normalized depreciation for 1996 is approximately $1 million, the normalized investment expenditure would be $1.3 million. Therefore, when computing equilibrium NOPAT, $1 million is subtracted from net cash flow and $1.3 million is added back for a net increase of $300,000. In addition, an adjustment must be made to account for the inflationary growth in working capital. A straightforward way to estimate the inflationary growth in working capital is to multiply predicted sales by the product of the expected inflation rate and the ratio of working capital to sales. Using this procedure, Table 6–3 shows that in 1996, the inflationary growth in FEC's working capital equals $317,742. The total adjustments for inflation thus come to $617,742. Adding this to FEC's normalized cash flow in 1996 of $2.25 million gives an estimated NOPAT of approximately $2.87 million.

The nominal growth rate in NOPAT is assumed to be 6.05 percent, 1 percent real growth compounded with 5 percent inflation, which equals the assumed nominal growth rate in cash flow. To achieve real growth of 1 percent without expanding capacity, the rate of return on new investment must exceed the cost of capital. Therefore, it is assumed that the return on investment, r, equals 20 percent, whereas the cost of capital is only 13.98 percent. Finally, the value-driver formula applies to NOPAT in 1997, which equals $3.04 million ($2.87 · 1.0605). Substituting these numbers into equation (6–2) gives:

$$\text{Continuing value at time } t = \frac{(\$3.04)(1 - .0605/.20)}{.1398 - .0605} = \$26.70 \text{ million}$$

The constant growth model and the value-driver model do not produce identical continuing values despite the adjustments. There is a wide variety of possible reasons for the discrepancy. For example, the inflation adjustment for capital expenditures may be incorrect. It was assumed that all the equipment FEC purchases has a 10-year life when new. In fact, large presses last a good deal longer, while the expected life of electronic equipment is less. Additionally, the return on investment of 20 percent may not be exactly consistent with real growth of 1 percent. Further-

TABLE 6-3
Calculating the Continuing Value of FEC Using a Value-Driver Model

Continuing value at time $t + 1$ for FEC = (using Equation 6-2 and NOPAT derived in step 2)	**$26,737,264**

Step 1: Determining NOPAT for FEC as of 1996

Normalized cash flows	$2,250,000	*Estimate*
Subtract normalized estimate of depreciation	$1,000,000	*Estimate*
Add estimated investment expenditures	$1,300,000	*See A below*
Add inflation adjustment to working capital	$317,742	*See B below*
NOPAT for FEC as of 1996	$2,867,742	

Step 2: NOPAT for FEC as of 1997 (assuming a 1% real growth rate and 5% inflation rate)

$3,039,807

Calculations

A. Wedge between depreciation and investment expenditures:
   Estimate ratio of depreciation to investment expenditures:

$$\frac{\pi \cdot n}{1 - 1/(1+\pi)^n}$$

where:
   π = inflation rate
   n = Life span of investment

For FEC, applying this formula using π = 5% and n = 10 years:

$$\frac{5\% \cdot 10}{1 - 1/(1+5\%)^{10}} = 1.3$$

Depreciation	$1,000,000
Ratio	× 1.3
Investment expenditure	$1,300,000

B. Inflation adjustment to working capital:

Working capital to sales ratio	19%
Inflation	× 5%
	0.95%
1996 sales projection	$33,446,530
.95% of 1996 sales projection	$317,742

more, the inflationary adjustment in working capital may not mirror the rate of increase in FEC's current assets and liabilities. The bottom line is that although the constant growth model and value-driver model rely on similar definitions of equilibrium, they are not based on identical assumptions about the behavior of capital expenditures, working capital, and the return on investment. It is not surprising, therefore, that the two approaches do not produce precisely the same estimate of continuing value.

Unfortunately, there is no formula for deciding whether the constant growth model or the value-driver model is superior in any particular situation. In fact, under some circumstances, neither one may be a reasonable choice. Once again, the appraiser must bring judgment to bear. The key questions that should temper that judgment are "Is the firm in equilibrium, as defined by the chosen model, at the terminal date? Are reasonable estimates available of the variables on which the continuing value is based?"

THE DIRECT COMPARISON MODEL

Both the constant growth and value-driver models rely on a strict definition of equilibrium. The firm must have reached a mature state such that sales growth, margins, and return on investment are all constant. A less restrictive definition is to say that a firm is in equilibrium when it becomes a mature member of its industry. Based on this definition of equilibrium, the continuing value of the firm is estimated by applying the direct comparison approach using currently mature firms as comparables. That is, the appraisal target at the terminal date is assumed to be comparable to mature firms today.

For example, suppose that an appraiser is asked to value AST Computer as of July 1, 1991. AST is a maker of clones of IBM personal computers and peripheral equipment for PCs. By July 1991, the company had been in business for eight years. Though the first six years had been up and down, AST had grown dramatically in the two years prior to July 1991 to emerge as a significant computer company with a full line of PCs, from laptops to high-powered file servers.

Despite its dramatic growth, AST could not be called a mature company on the appraisal date. Its track record as a major computer manufacturer was limited, and it had few proven customers. Most of its increase in sales could be attributed to AST undercutting the prices charged by high-priced manufacturers such as IBM and Compaq. If IBM or Compaq were to respond to AST's challenge by introducing new products or sharply lowering prices, AST's position could be undermined. On the other hand, AST had shown itself to be an innovative and energetic company that was able to get new products out the door quickly at competitive prices. It is quite possible that the company could withstand a counterattack by IBM and Compaq while building a loyal customer following. In short, as of July 1991, the fate of AST was still in doubt; both rapid growth and sharp decline were distinct possibilities. Under such circumstances, it clearly would be misleading to value AST by applying multiples derived from mature companies such as IBM or Compaq. (As described in Chapter 4, multiples could be developed by selecting companies that are currently comparable to AST, such as Dell, Gateway, and Northgate.)

The solution to this problem is to forecast future cash flow up to the point where AST can be interpreted as having become a mature company. What the mature company will look like, of course, depends on the cash flow forecast. AST may be seen as becoming a bit player in the industry or a major producer of personal computers. Whatever the forecast, the continuing value is estimated by selecting companies that are currently comparable to the company AST is expected to become. Financial ratios are calculated for those comparable companies and multiplied by the forecast value of AST's corresponding financial variables at the terminal date. For instance, if AST were anticipated to become a major producer of PCs by the terminal date, ratios currently calculated for IBM and Compaq would be multiplied by AST's forecast financial variables at the terminal date.

It may seem as if it would be extraordinarily difficult to find companies *today* that are comparable to what the appraisal target is *expected to become in the future.* However, the reverse can be true for small and rapidly growing companies. It is often easier to find comparables to what the firm is likely to become than comparables to the firm in its current condition. For example, Genentech and Biogen are both biotechnology firms, but their products are evolving so rapidly that it is unclear how comparable the firms are today. This is a common problem that arises when the value of a company depends heavily on its growth opportunities. Because growth opportunities are intangible and because they involve products that are yet to be produced, it is difficult to determine whether one set of growth opportunities possessed by one firm is comparable to a related set possessed by another firm. As firms mature, their cash flow comes to depend more on proven products and assets in place and less on intangible opportunities. As a result, comparability is easier to assess. For example, it is not difficult to determine that Ford and General Motors are comparable.

The direct comparison approach to estimating continuing value can be illustrated by applying it to FEC. As noted in Chapter 4, one difficulty that arose when applying the direct comparison approach to FEC was that the comparable firms were larger and more mature than FEC. By the terminal date in 1996, this is not a difficulty because FEC is anticipated to be a mature firm with few growth opportunities due to binding capacity constraints. For this reason, it may be more appropriate to apply the financial ratios derived from the comparable companies to FEC as it is expected to look in 1996 than to the FEC as it looked in July 1989.

With respect to the choice of a financial variable, recall from Chapter 4 that the ratio that gave the most meaningful valuation results was total market value divided by EBIDT. FEC's EBIT in 1996 is predicted to be about $3.66 million. Adding back depreciation of approximately $910,000 gives EBIDT of $4.57 million. This does not, however, represent normalized EBIDT. To be consistent with the cash flow forecast, it must be adjusted downward by at least $170,000, the amount Mr. Bergstrom subtracted from net cash flow. Consequently, a figure of $4.4 million is used for FEC's EBIDT in 1996.

Table 4–4 in Chapter 4 shows three ratios of market value to EBIDT: 7.40 for current values, 7.45 for trend line values, and 8.40

for five-year average values. Because the 8.40 ratio seems to be an outlier, a multiple of 7.45 is selected for FEC at the terminal date. Multiplying this average ratio by the EBIDT of $4.5 million gives a continuing value of approximately $32.8 million.

Aside from questions of comparability, changing economic conditions may make it misleading to apply ratios calculated for the comparables at one point in time to an appraisal target at another point in time. While changes in a wide variety of economic variables could render a direct comparison misleading, two possibilities are of paramount importance.

- First, the macroeconomic environment at the current date (July 1989 for FEC) may differ from the long-run economic conditions that are expected to prevail at the terminal date (July 1996 for FEC). Indicators such as real GNP, industrial production, and unemployment can be used to assess the general economic activity. If economic conditions are different at two points in time, ratios calculated on the first date may not be applicable on the second date. For instance, financial ratios are usually different at the height of economic expansions than they are at the bottom of a recession.

- Second, the current inflation rate may differ from the inflation rate expected to prevail at the terminal date and beyond. Because the rate of inflation affects the rate of growth in both revenues and expenses, as well as the cost of capital, it has an impact on many financial ratios. Therefore, the appraiser either must be sure that the inflationary environment on the lien date and the terminal date are expected to be similar or develop ratios that are not affected by inflation.

Fortunately in the case of FEC, economic conditions on the lien date were relatively "average." This is important because given the difficulty of long-term economic forecasting, it is usually reasonable to assume that economic conditions on the terminal date will be average. In July 1989, the economy was growing at a rate about equal to its long-run average rate of 2 percent to 3 percent. In addition, the rate of inflation that prevailed in the prior year was close to the expected inflation of 5 percent. On this score, there is no reason why ratios calculated in 1989 cannot be applied at the terminal date.

CHOOSING A TERMINAL VALUE FOR FEC

To review the results, the constant growth model produced a continuing value of $30.14 million; the value-driver model produced a continuing value of $26.70 million; and the direct comparison approach produced a continuing value of $32.80 million. In light of these three estimates and recognizing the inherent difficulty in estimating value seven years into the future, a round figure of $30 million is chosen for FEC's continuing value.

SELECTING THE TERMINAL DATE

As noted at the outset, the choice of terminal date depends on the model used to estimate continuing value and on the associated definition of equilibrium. For instance, if the constant growth model is picked to value the company at the terminal date, then the terminal date must be far enough in the future so that it is reasonable to assume that the company will be growing at a constant real rate.

The selection of a terminal date is complicated by the fact that most companies engage in numerous business activities, not all of which reach equilibrium at the same time. For example, by 1986, IBM's mainframe computer business was mature, but its personal computer was only two years old and personal computer sales were exploding. While one part of the company could be valued using a constant growth model, the other clearly could not. Overall, the constant growth model would not be applicable to IBM. In situations such as this, the appraiser has two alternatives. First, the forecast period can be extended until a point in time at which each part of the business is expected to be growing at a constant rate. Second, the two divisions can be appraised separately. In that case, a constant growth model could be used to value the mainframe business at the terminal date, while a direct comparison model could be employed to appraise the personal computer division.

Business cycle effects must also be considered when selecting the terminal date. A forecast period that begins during a recession and ends during an expected boom will produce a misleading estimate of the continuing value. The continuing value should reflect average business conditions that are expected to prevail over the long run. The simplest way to achieve this is to lengthen the forecast period so that it extends beyond the end of the current business cycle.

Selecting the Terminal Date for the Constant Growth and Value-Driver Models

The constant growth model is based on the assumption that by the terminal date, the firm will have reached an equilibrium state in which it is growing at a constant rate in real terms. For the growth rate to be constant, a number of conditions must hold. Specifically, as the company approaches the terminal date, the cash flow forecasts should have the following characteristics:

- Real sales growth should be approaching a constant. Rapid growth in sales indicates that the company is still exploiting new opportunities, which is inconsistent with the constant growth model.
- Investment should be declining to the point where the company is simply replacing current capacity and making ordinary improvements and upgrades. If a dramatic change in capacity or technology is anticipated, the cash flow forecasting period should be extended to include it. In addition, by the terminal date, the firm's real rate of return on capital should be approximately constant.
- The company's cost structure should have settled down so that margins are constant.

Because the value-driver model is economically similar to the constant growth model, the same criteria apply for selecting the terminal date. The value-driver model requires that the fraction of NOPAT reinvested, the return on investment, and profit margins should all be constant. If these conditions obtain, then sales growth and cash flow growth also will be constant.

Selecting the Terminal Date for the Direct Comparison Model

In the context of the direct comparison approach, the terminal date is the date by which the appraisal target has become comparable to mature firms in the industry. Once this date is reached, industry average multiples can be applied.

What makes the criterion difficult to apply is that the word *mature* is ambiguous. Nonetheless, there are several useful characteristics that indicate that a firm has matured to the point where the direct comparison approach can be applied confidently. First, the forecast cash flows should be converging to a somewhat stable growth path, even though growth need not have fallen to a constant level. Second, growth opportunities should have declined in importance relative to income produced by existing assets and products. Third, the company's position in the industry should be clearly defined. If a question remains whether the company is going to become a major player or decline into insignificance, as was noted earlier in the case of AST, the firm can hardly be considered mature.

The definition of maturity will also differ across industries. Mature computer companies such as Compaq may still have numerous growth opportunities, while mature auto manufacturers have few. The key question, therefore, is not whether the appraisal target is mature in some abstract sense, but whether by the terminal date it will be comparable to established publicly traded firms that can be valued using the stock and debt approach. That comparability can be assessed by applying the techniques described in Chapter 4.

One important benefit of the direct comparison approach is that it allows the appraiser to employ a shorter forecast period. To apply the constant growth model or the value-driver model, cash flows must be forecast to the point at which the firm has reached a steady state, with constant margins and constant return on investment. To apply the direct comparison model, it is only necessary to forecast cash flow to the point where the company has become an established member of its industry, so that ratios derived from other mature firms can be applied in the valuation process. For rapidly evolving firms, this distinction is important. Returning to the AST example, AST will clearly become an established firm long before it settles down to a constant growth rate. This is because even relatively mature firms in the personal computer industry, such as Compaq, still have significant growth opportunities.

It is for this reason that the direct comparison approach is widely employed by investment banks. As observed earlier, many bankers feel that forecasting cash flow on an item-by-item basis into the distant future is a futile task. The direct comparison approach to estimating terminal value offers the benefit of limiting the cash flow forecasting period.

CONCLUDING OBSERVATIONS

Because the life of a company is indefinite, at some point a simplified model is required to estimate its continuing value. The difficult issue is deciding when it is appropriate to apply a simplified model and determining what model to apply. If a growth model is utilized, then the firm must have progressed to the point where future growth in cash flow is constant, or soon to become constant. If the value-driver model is used, then the firm must have matured to the point where the factors that determine the drivers, such as profit margins and the percentage of NOPAT reinvested, are constant. Finally, if the direct comparison model is employed, the appraisal target must have developed to the point where it is comparable to established, publicly traded firms in the industry.

Comparing the alternatives, the advantage of the direct comparison model is that it allows the appraiser to shorten the cash flow forecasting period, because a company will become comparable to established firms in the industry before either the growth rate in cash flow or the value drivers become constant. The drawback of the direct comparison model is that comparability must be assessed both across companies and over time. The appraiser must determine what firms *today* are comparable to what the appraiser anticipates the target firm will become by the *terminal* date.

Given the strengths and weaknesses of each procedure, it is wise to use more than one model to calculate the continuing value. If the different models produce similar continuing values, confidence in the estimate rises. If the different models produce different values, further research is suggested to reconcile the discrepancies.

Chapter Seven

The Cost of Capital

With the estimates of the annual future cash flows to the terminal date and the continuing value in hand, the final step in a DCF appraisal is to discount those estimates to present value at the firm's cost of capital. Unfortunately, estimating the cost of capital is not a simple task for three reasons. First, companies issue a variety of securities to finance their operations, including common stock, preferred stock, public debt, and bank debt. To estimate the company's cost of capital, the costs of the various types of financing it employs have to be averaged.

Second, the payments companies make to investors occur in the future. Therefore, the cost of capital, which is determined by the price that investors will pay for a company's securities, must take into account the time value of money to investors. In addition, the future payments investors receive are in deflated dollars. As a result, the price that investors will pay for a company's securities, and thus, the firm's cost of capital, depends on the rate of inflation expected by investors.

Third, it is possible that investors will not receive the payments they expected when they purchased the company's securities. For example, the dividend on common stock may be unexpectedly cut or even eliminated. Because they are aware of such possibilities, risk averse investors will demand a premium to compensate for the risk of buying corporate securities. That premium increases the cost of capital. Therefore, to estimate the cost of capital, it is necessary to estimate the size of the risk premium.

What makes calculating the cost of capital difficult is that each of the preceding three issues involves complexities that, despite the publication of hundreds of professional articles, remain the subject of active dispute. The goal of this chapter is to provide an intuitive understanding of the issues and offer practical solutions to the problem of estimating the cost of capital. Nonetheless, given the nature of the issues, it is impossible to avoid theoretical analysis and mathematical presentation altogether.

One response to the complexity involved with estimating the cost of capital is to rely on rules of thumb. Some analysts, dismayed at plowing through the theory underlying asset pricing models, have jokingly said, "Why bother with all the complexity, the cost of equity capital is always between 10 percent and 15 percent anyway." The problem with rules of thumb is that once disagreement arises, there is no way to resolve the dispute except by appeals to authority. If your rule of thumb says that the cost of capital is 10 percent and my rule of thumb says that it is 15 percent, how is a third party to decide who is correct? Though the asset pricing models may be dauntingly complex, they are based on fundamental economic reasoning that can be tested empirically. For this reason, courts and regulatory authorities, as well as financial managers, have come to rely on the models with increasing regularity. An analogy illustrates the point. Until recently, drug treatment was based on rules of thumb derived from experience. Thousands of drugs would be tested until one that worked was discovered. With the development of modern biochemistry, it has become possible, for the first time, to design drugs from the ground up. Though manufacturers still commonly use the rule of thumb approach, the tide is turning in favor of more sophisticated theoretical procedures. The same is true in financial economics. Though many financial managers still rely on rules of thumb to estimate the cost of capital, the tide is running in favor of asset pricing theory.

To present the material in the most intuitive fashion possible, the chapter is organized as follows. The first section introduces the weighted average cost of capital, or WACC. The next section focuses on estimating the cost of fixed income securities such as debt and preferred stock. By necessity, it includes a detailed discussion of the determination of interest rates and the relation between interest rates and inflation. The third section deals with the pricing of risk and the cost of equity capital. The fourth section analyzes how the costs of various financing sources are averaged to calculate the WACC for a company. The fifth section presents a step-by-step example of the calculation of the WACC for FEC. Forms Engineering's WACC is then used to discount the cash flows estimated in Chapters 5 and 6 to their present values. The final section offers some concluding comments on estimating the cost of capital.

THE WEIGHTED AVERAGE COST OF CAPITAL: AN INTRODUCTION

The three fundamental sources of funds that American firms use to finance operations are debt (including bank borrowing), equity (including retained earnings), and preferred stock. Only these three types of securities are considered in this chapter. For a discussion of the cost of capital associated with more sophisticated securities such as options, warrants, and convertible bonds, see Hull.[1]

In terms of the three basic securities, the formula for calculating the weighted average cost of capital, WACC, is given by:

$$\text{WACC} = k_d(1 - t_c)w_d + k_p w_p + k_s w_s \qquad (7\text{--}1)$$

where:

k_d = Cost of debt capital
t_c = Corporate tax rate for the appraisal target
k_p = Cost of preferred stock
k_s = Cost of common stock
w_d = Fraction of debt in the firm's long-run capital structure
w_p = Fraction of preferred stock in the firm's long-run capital structure
w_s = Fraction of common stock in the firm's long-run capital structure

Equation (7–1) states that the cost of capital for a corporation is the weighted average of the after-tax costs of all its financing sources. As will be discussed later in this chapter, the weights represent the long-run financing mix that the firm employs. For

---

[1] J. Hull, *Options, Futures and Other Derivative Securities* (Englewood Cliffs, N.J.: Prentice Hall, 1993).

example, if the firm is typically financed 60 percent with debt and 40 percent with equity, w_d is 0.60 and w_s is 0.40. Viewed in this light, the WACC can be interpreted as a company's after-tax cost of raising funds, assuming that funds are raised by issuing a mix of securities with proportions equal to the long-run financing weights. This is not meant to imply that every time a company raises money it will issue securities in amounts proportional to the long-run financing weights. In fact, most companies commonly issue only one type of security at a time. However, over time and across a number of issues, the financing weights will be maintained so that the firm's average cost of funds is given by the WACC.

Whose Cost of Capital?

When calculating a company's WACC, the business being appraised must be considered in isolation. To see why this is important, consider the following situation. AT&T requests a DCF appraisal of a small, high-risk computer company that we will call Altos. AT&T is considering acquiring Altos. As part of the job, the appraiser must estimate the cost of capital. But whose cost of capital should be estimated? Should it be AT&T's cost of capital because AT&T is purchasing Altos, or should it be Altos's cost of capital?

The answer to the question will have a significant impact on the appraisal, because AT&T is in a low-risk business and, therefore, has a low WACC, while Altos is in a high-risk business and has a high WACC. Though it may appear that it is appropriate to use AT&T's cost of capital because it measures "what it will cost AT&T to finance the purchase of Altos," such reasoning is incorrect. The erroneous logic is revealed by the paradox it produces. Suppose that it was appropriate to use AT&T's cost of capital. Because AT&T has a lower cost of capital than Altos, the appraised value of Altos using AT&T's WACC will be larger than the appraised value of Altos using Altos's WACC. This means that AT&T should be willing to pay more for Altos than it is worth to the current owners. Furthermore, the same argument holds for every small computer company because they all have higher WACCs than AT&T. It follows, therefore, that AT&T should buy every small computer company. But AT&T has acquired only a select few computer companies. Is antitrust regulation the reason for AT&T's reticence? Is AT&T foolish? Or is there a financial economic explanation for AT&T's behavior?

The paradox arises because the wrong cost of capital was employed. The cost of capital that AT&T should use in valuing Altos is Altos's WACC, the same number that Altos's current management would use. If both companies use Altos's WACC, there is no reason, at least from an appraisal standpoint, for AT&T to acquire Altos. Of course, AT&T may still choose to acquire Altos for other reasons. For instance, AT&T may conclude that there is synergy between the computer business and the telephone business. However, these considerations do not affect the estimate of the cost of capital. Instead, the synergies will be reflected in forecasts of higher cash flows for Altos once it becomes part of AT&T.

To see further why Altos's cost of capital is the appropriate choice, think of the postacquisition AT&T as consisting of two parts: its huge telephone business and Altos. Assume that the WACC for the telephone business is 10 percent and the WACC for Altos, considered in isolation, is 20 percent. Assume, furthermore, that Altos represents 1 percent of AT&T's total business. Before the merger, AT&T's cost of capital is 10 percent. After the merger, AT&T's cost of capital, including the computer company, is 10.1 percent. The WACC rises because AT&T is now a blend of 99 percent telephone operations and 1 percent computer operations. (The new WACC = (0.99)(10%) + (0.01)(20%) = 10.1%). Because the increase in the WACC is so small, it can easily be overlooked, and the appraiser can falsely conclude that acquiring Altos has no impact on AT&T's cost of funds. This is analogous to concluding that throwing a gallon of yellow dye in the Pacific Ocean has no effect because there is no observable yellow tint to the ocean afterwards. There is a small effect, and if you tossed enough dye in the ocean, it would be noticeable.

The upshot of the AT&T example is that the cost of capital depends only on the cash flows of the firm being appraised. If the cash flows produced by a computer company are sufficiently risky that the financing cost is 20 percent, the financing cost is 20 percent whether the firm is owned by AT&T or Brad Cornell. However, if Brad Cornell owns the firm, it will be clear that the cost of capital is 20 percent. If AT&T owns the firm, its individual cost of capital will no longer be observable, because it is blended with the cost of capital for AT&T's other operations. That is why the firm must be considered in isolation when estimating its weighted average cost of capital, even if the firm is a subsidiary of a larger corporation.

THE COST OF DEBT

The starting point for estimating the cost of debt is the one factor that affects the cost of all three types of financing—the interest rate. Interest rates are direct determinants of the cost of debt and indirectly affect the cost of preferred and common stock because equity securities compete with fixed income securities for investors' dollars. An analysis of interest rates, in turn, must begin with a brief review of the market for U.S. Treasury securities. Because Treasury securities are highly liquid and free of default risk, the interest rates on these securities are used to measure the risk-free rate that serves as the benchmark from which the cost of capital is calculated on more complicated and riskier securities.

U.S. Treasury Securities: A Brief Review

As Table 7–1 shows, there are two types of Treasury securities, Treasury bills and Treasury notes and bonds. Treasury bills have a maturity of one year or less, while Treasury notes range in maturity from 2 to 10 years, and Treasury bonds have maturities from 10 to 30 years. Because the U.S. Treasury can pay principal and interest on its securities by printing new money as well as collecting taxes, Treasury securities are considered to be free from default risk.

The data reported in Table 7–1 are based on prices quoted in the secondary market. After their initial auction, Treasury securities are actively traded through a network of government securities dealers. Each of these dealers quotes prices at which the firm is willing to buy or sell outstanding Treasury issues. The dollar volume of trading in Treasury securities far outstrips the volume of trading on the New York Stock Exchange despite the fact that there are a relatively limited number of issues. This makes the market one of the most liquid in the world.

TABLE 7–1

Treasury Bonds, Notes, and Bills

Monday, June 1, 1992

Representative Over-the-Counter quotations based on transactions of $1 millon or more.

Treasury bond, note and bill quotes are as of mid-afternoon. Colons in bid-and-ask quotes represent 32nds; 101:01 means that 101 1/32. Net changes in 32nds, n-Treasury note. Treasury bill quotes in hundredths, quoted on terms of a rate of discount. Days to maturity calculated from the settlement date. All yields are to maturity and based on the asked quote. Latest 13-week and 26-week bills are boldfaced. For bonds callable prior to maturity, yields are computed to the earliest call date for issues quoted above par and to the maturity date for issues below par. *-When issued.

Source: Federal Reserve Bank of New York.

U.S. Treasury strips as of 3 p.m. Eastern time, also based on transactions of $1 million or more. Colons in bid-and-ask quotes represent 32nds; 101:01 means 101 1/32. Net changes in 32nds. Yields calculated on the asked quotation. ci-stripped coupon interest. bp-Treasury bond. stripped principal. np-Treasury note, stripped principal. For bonds callable prior to maturity, yields are computed to the earliest call date for issues quoted above par and to the maturity date for issues below par.

Source: Bear, Stearns & Co. via Street Software Technology Inc.

GOVT. BONDS & NOTES

Rate	Maturity Mo/Yr	Bid	Asked	Chg.	Ask Yld.
8 1/4	Jun92n	100:12	100:14	....	2.26
8 3/8	Jun92n	100:12	100:14	– 1	2.38
10 3/8	Jul92n	100:25	100:27	....	2.26
8	Jul92n	100:21	100:23	– 1	3.37
4 1/4	Aug87-92	98:11	98:27	+ 1	10.00
7 1/4	Aug92	100:21	100:23	– 1	3.56
7 7/8	Aug92n	100:25	100:27	....	3.55
8 1/4	Aug92n	100:27	100:29	– 1	3.61
8 1/8	Aug92n	101:00	101:02	– 1	3.62
8 1/8	Sep92n	101:11	101:13	– 1	3.55
8 3/4	Sep92n	101:17	101:19	– 2	3.73
9 3/4	Oct92n	102:03	102:05	– 1	3.73
7 3/4	Oct92n	101:15	101:17	– 1	3.91
7 3/4	Nov92n	101:21	101:23	– 1	3.84
8 3/8	Nov92n	101:29	101:31	– 1	3.89
10 1/2	Nov92n	102:28	102:30	– 1	3.82
7 3/8	Nov92n	101:20	101:22	– 1	3.88
7 1/4	Dec92n	101:26	101:28	– 1	3.92
9 1/8	Dec92n	102:27	102:29	– 1	3.96
8 3/4	Jan93n	102:25	102:27	– 2	4.03
7	Jan93n	101:26	101:28	– 2	4.09
4	Feb88-93	95:19	96:03	+ 5	9.88
6 3/4	Feb93	101:24	101:28	– 3	4.01
7 7/8	Feb93	102:15	102:19	– 2	4.09
8 1/4	Feb93n	102:24	102:26	– 2	4.14
8 3/8	Feb93n	102:27	102:29	– 1	4.13
10 7/8	Feb93n	104:18	104:20	– 2	4.12
6 3/4	Feb93n	101:26	101:28	– 2	4.16
7 1/8	Mar93n	102:10	102:12	– 1	4.17
9 5/8	Mar93n	104:10	104:12	– 2	4.18
7 3/8	Apr93n	102:19	102:12	– 2	4.22
7	Apr93n	102:12	102:14	– 2	4.24
7 5/8	May93n	102:31	103:01	– 3	4.33
8 5/8	May93n	103:29	103:31	– 3	4.31
10 1/8	May93n	105:11	105:13	– 2	4:25
6 3/4	May93n	102:09	102:11	– 2	4.31
7	Jun93n	102:20	102:22	– 4	4.41
8 1/8	Jun93n	103:26	103:28	– 3	4.39
7 1/4	Jul93n	102:30	103:00	– 4	4.47
6 7/8	Jul93n	102:18	102:20	– 4	4.53
8	Aug93n	103:29	103:31	– 4	4.57
8 5/8	Aug93	104:20	104:22	– 4	4.57
8 3/4	Aug93n	104:25	104:27	– 4	4.56
11 7/8	Aug93n	108:14	108:16	– 5	4.53
6 3/8	Aug93n	102:02	102:04	– 4	4.60
6 1/8	Sep93n	101:25	101:27	– 5	4.68
8 1/4	Sept93n	104:16	104:18	– 5	4.66
7 1/8	Oct93n	103:03	103:05	– 5	4.71
6	Oct93n	101:19	101:21	– 6	4.77
7 3/4	Nov93n	104:01	104:03	– 5	4.79
8 5/8	Nov93	105:09	105:11	– 6	4.76
9	Nov93n	105:23	105:25	– 6	4.82
11 3/4	Nov93n	109:19	109:21	– 5	4.77
5 1/2	Nov93n	100:28	100:30	– 6	4.84
5	Dec93n	100:03	100:05	– 5	4.90
7 5/8	Dec93n	104:01	104:03	– 5	4.89
7	Jan94n	103:02	103:04	– 6	4.96
4 7/8	Jan94n	99:25	99:27	– 6	4.97
6 7/8	Feb94n	102:28	102:30	– 6	5.05
8 7/8	Feb94n	106:06	106:08	– 5	5.00
9	Feb94	106:09	106:13	– 9	5.03
5 3/8	Feb94n	100:15	100:17	– 5	5.05
5 3/8	Mar94n	101:01	101:03	– 6	5.12
8 1/2	Mar94n	105:24	105:26	– 7	5.13
7	Apr94n	103:07	103:09	– 6	5.13
5 3/8	Apr94n	100:08	100:10	– 6	5.20
4 1/8	May89-94	96:23	97:07	+ 9	5.65
7	May94n	103:05	103:07	– 6	5.24
9 1/2	May94n	107:23	107:25	– 6	5.25
13 1/8	May94n	114:18	114:20	– 6	5.14
5 1/8	May94n	99:22	99:24	– 6	5.26
8 1/2	Jun94n	106:03	106:05	– 7	5.33
8	Jul94n	105:07	105:09	– 6	5.33
6 7/8	Aug94n	102:31	103:01	– 6	5.40
8 5/8	Aug94n	106:18	106:20	– 6	5.39
8 3/4	Aug94	106:27	106:31	– 6	5.35
12 5/8	Aug94n	114:29	114:31	– 6	5.33
8 1/2	Sep94n	106:16	106:18	– 6	5.46
9 1/2	Oct94n	108:20	108:22	– 8	5.53
6	Nov94n	101:01	101:03	– 1	5.52
8 1/4	Nov94n	106:02	106:04	– 7	5.54
10 1/8	Nov94	110:09	110:11	– 7	5.55
11 5/8	Nov94n	113:22	113:24	– 7	5.54
7 5/8	Dec94n	104:25	104:27	– 7	5.58
8 5/8	Jan95n	107:01	107:03	– 7	5.67
3	Feb95	94:10	95:10	– 3	4.87
5 1/2	Feb95n	99:16	99:18	– 7	5.68
7 3/4	Feb95n	105:02	105:04	– 7	5.68
10 1/2	Feb95	111:28	111:28	– 7	5.70
11 1/4	Feb95n	113:20	113:22	– 8	5.71
8 3/4	Apr95n	106:20	106:22	– 9	5.81
5 7/8	May95n	100:05	100:07	– 7	5.79
8 1/2	May95n	107:02	107:04	– 8	5.84
10 3/8	May95	112:01	112:03	– 6	5.85
11 1/4	May95n	114:11	114:13	– 9	5.86
12 5/8	May95	118:10	118:14	– 8	5.47
8 7/8	Jul95n	108:04	108:06	– 9	5.96
8 1/2	Aug95n	107:04	107:06	– 9	6.00
10 1/2	Aug95n	112:26	112:28	–10	6.02
8 5/8	Oct95n	107:16	107:18	– 9	6.11
8 1/2	Nov95n	107:06	107:08	– 9	6.14
9 1/2	Nov95n	110:10	110:12	– 9	6.12
11 1/2	Nov95	116:16	116:20	– 7	6.08
9 1/4	Jan96n	109:20	109:22	– 8	6.22
7 1/2	Jan96n	104:02	104:04	– 7	6.22
7 7/8	Feb96n	105:07	105:09	– 9	6.25
8 7/8	Feb96n	108:15	108:17	– 9	6.26
7 1/2	Feb96n	104:00	104:02	– 9	6.27
7 3/4	Mar96	104:25	104:27	– 9	6.31
9 3/8	Apr96n	110:08	110:10	– 8	6.33
7 5/8	Apr96n	104:12	104:14	– 9	6.33
7 3/8	May96n	103:15	103:17	– 9	6.35
7 5/8	May96n	104:12	104:14	– 8	6.35
7 7/8	Jun96n	105:06	105:08	– 8	6.39
7 7/8	Jul96n	105:05	105:07	– 9	6.41
7 7/8	Jul96n	105:05	105:07	– 8	6.43
7 1/4	Aug96n	102:26	102:28	–10	6.46
7	Sep96n	101:28	101:30	–10	6.48
8	Oct96n	105:18	105:20	–10	6.50
6 7/8	Oct96n	101:13	101:15	– 9	6.49
7 1/4	Nov96n	102:25	102:27	– 9	6.50
6 1/2	Nov96n	100:02	100:04	– 8	6.47
6 1/8	Dec96n	98:17	98:19	– 9	6.49
8	Jan97n	105:17	105:19	–10	6.58
6 1/4	Jan97n	98:21	98:23	– 9	6.57
6 3/4	Feb97n	100:17	100:19	– 9	6.60
6 7/8	Mar97n	100:28	100:30	– 9	6.64
8 1/2	Apr97n	107:15	107:17	–10	6.66
6 7/8	Apr97n	100:27	100:29	– 9	6.66
8 1/2	May97n	107:15	107:17	–10	6.69
6 3/4	May97n	100:08	100:10	–10	6.68
8 1/2	Jul97n	107:18	107:20	–10	6.71
8 5/8	Aug97n	108:05	108:07	–10	6.73
8 3/4	Oct97n	108:24	108:26	–10	6.76
8 7/8	Nov97n	109:10	109:12	–11	6.79
7 7/8	Jan98n	104:26	104:28	–12	6.82
8 1/8	Feb98n	105:29	105:31	–10	6.84
7 7/8	Apr98n	104:23	104:25	–11	6.87
7	May 93-98	100.16	100.24	– 8	6.17
9	May98n	110:02	110:04	–12	6.90
8 1/4	Jul98n	106:13	106:15	–10	6.93
9 1/4	Aug98n	111:11	111:13	–11	6.95
7 1/8	Oct98n	100:25	100:27	–10	6.96
3 1/2	Nov98	92:24	93:24	–27	4.63
8 7/8	Nov98n	109:17	109:19	– 9	7.00
6 3/8	Jan99n	96:20	96:22	–10	7.01
8 7/8	Feb99n	109:17	109:19	– 9	7.05
7	Apr99n	99:25	99:27	–10	7.03
8 1/2	May94-99	105:04	105:12	– 9	5.55
9 1/8	May99n	110:27	110:29	–11	7.11
8	Aug99n	104:25	104:27	–11	7.13
7 7/8	Nov99n	104:00	104:02	–11	7.16
7 7/8	Feb95-00	102:31	103:03	– 9	6.61
8 1/2	Feb00n	107:09	107:11	–12	7.24
8 7/8	May00n	109:16	109:18	– 9	7.27
8 3/8	Aug95-00	105:06	105:10	– 7	6.51
8 3/4	Aug00n	108:24	108:26	– 9	7.30
8 1/2	Nov00n	107:05	107:07	–10	7.34
7 3/4	Feb01n	102:12	102:14	– 9	7.37
11 3/4	Feb01	127:25	127:29	–12	7.35
8	May01n	103:27	103:29	–10	7.40
13 1/8	May01	137:06	137:10	–12	7.36
7 7/8	Aug01n	102:30	103:00	–11	7.42
8	Aug96-01	103:14	103:18	– 7	7.01
13 3/8	Aug01	139:16	139:20	–12	7.37
7 1/2	Nov01n	100:15	100:17	–11	7.42
15 3/4	Nov01	156:19	156:23	–13	7.33
14 1/4	Feb02	147:03	147:07	–11	7.36
7 1/2	May02n	100:25	100:27	–13	7.38
11 5/8	Nov02	129:20	129:24	–16	7.47
10 3/4	Feb03	123:11	123:15	–15	7.52
10 3/4	May03	123:20	123:24	–15	7.53
11 1/8	Aug03	126:18	126:22	–15	7.55
11 7/8	Nov03	132:18	132:22	–15	7.56
12 3/8	May04	137:05	137:09	–17	7.58
13 3/4	Aug04	148:11	148:15	–19	7.59
11 5/8	Nov04	131:08	131:12	–18	7.67
8 1/4	May00-05	104:06	104:10	–17	7.52
12	May05	134:28	135:00	–19	7.96
10 3/4	Aug05	124:29	125:01	–16	7.70
9 3/8	Feb06	114:06	114:10	–16	7.67
7 5/8	Feb02-07	100:05	100:09	–15	7.58
7 7/8	Nov02-07	101:11	101:15	–15	7.67
8 3/8	Aug03-08	104:23	104:27	–16	7.72
8 3/4	Nov03-08	107:12	107:16	–16	7.76
10 3/8	May04-09	110:12	110:16	– 9	5.55
9 1/8	Nov04-09	120:12	120:16	–17	7.78
11 3/4	Feb05-10	131:18	131:22	–21	7.78
10	May05-10	117:26	117:30	–17	7.78
12 3/4	Nov05-10	140:29	141:01	–18	7.78
13 7/8	May06-11	151:08	151:12	–23	7.78
14	Nov06-11	153:08	153:12	–22	7.78
10 3/8	Nov07-12	122:04	122:08	–20	7.78
12	Aug08-13	137:05	137:09	–24	7.89
13 1/4	May09-14	149:17	149:21	–26	7.89
12 1/2	Aug09-14	142:27	142:31	–25	7.89
11 3/4	Nov09-14	136:07	136:11	–22	7.88
11 1/4	Feb15	134.17	134:19	–25	7.94
10 5/8	Aug15	128:06	128:08	–26	7.94
9 7/8	Nov15	120:10	120:12	–25	7.95
9 1/4	Feb16	113:23	113:25	–24	7.95
7 1/4	May16	92:18	92:20	–20	7.94
7 1/2	Nov16	95:04	95:06	–20	7.95
8 3/4	May17	108:19	108:21	–24	7.95
8 7/8	Aug17	109:30	110:00	–23	7.95
9 1/8	May18	112:27	112:29	–24	7.94
9	Nov18	111:17	111:19	–24	7.94
8 7/8	Feb19	110:04	110:06	–24	7.95
8 1/8	Aug19	101:28	101:30	–22	7.95
8 1/2	Feb20	106:03	106:05	–24	7.95
8 3/4	May20	109:00	109:02	–24	7.94
8 3/4	Aug20	109:01	109:03	–24	7.94
7 7/8	Feb21	99:09	99:11	–22	7.93

TREASURY BILLS

Maturity	Days to Mat.	Bid	Asked	Chg.	Ask Yld.
Jun 04 '92	1	3.68	3.58		3.64
Jun 11 '92	8	3.67	3.57	+0.04	3.63
Jun 18 '92	15	3.72	3.62	+0.04	3.69
Jun 18 '92	15	3.75	3.65		3.71
Jun 25 '92	22	3.30	3.20	+0.03	3.26
Jul 02 '92	29	3.61	3.57	+0.01	3.64
Jul 09 '92	36	3.62	3.58	+0.01	3.65
Jul 16 '92	43	3.62	3.58	+0.02	3.66
Jul 23 '92	50	3.64	3.60	+0.03	3.68
Jul 30 '92	57	3.65	3.63	+0.02	3.71
Aug 06 '92	64	3.68	3.66	+0.01	3.75
Aug 13 '92	71	3.69	3.67	+0.03	3.76
Aug 20 '92	78	3.71	3.69	+0.04	3.78
Aug 27 '92	**85**	**3.75**	**3.73**	**+0.05**	**3.83**
Sep 03 '92	92	3.74	3.72	+0.05	3.81
Sep 10 '92	99	3.37	3.71	+0.04	3.80
Sep 17 '92	96	3.73	3.71	+0.04	3.80
Sep 24 '92	113	3.74	3.72	+0.05	3.83
Oct 01 '92	120	3.75	3.73	+0.05	3.83
Oct 08 '92	127	3.77	3.75	+0.04	3.85
Oct 15 '92	134	3.79	3.77	+0.05	3.88
Oct 22 '92	141	3.80	3.78	+0.04	3.90
Oct 29 '92	148	3.80	3.78	+0.04	3.89
Nov 05 '92	155	3.82	3.80	+0.04	3.92
Nov 12 '92	162	3.85	3.83	+0.07	3.95
Nov 19 '92	169	3.86	3.84	+0.06	3.98
Nov 27 '92	**177**	**3.89**	**3.87**	**+0.06**	**4.00**
Dec 17 '92	197	3.87	3.85	+0.06	3.99
Jan 14 '93	225	3.91	3.89	+0.08	4.04
Feb 11 '93	253	3.98	3.96	+0.08	4.12
Mar 11 '93	281	4.02	4.00	+0.07	4.16
Apr 08 '93	309	4.07	4.05	+0.08	4.22
May 06 '93	337	4.09	4.07	+0.08	4.25
Jun 03 '93	365	4.13	4.11	+0.07	4.30

Treasury bills. Treasury bills are discount securities, which means they are issued at a price less than par and appreciate to par at maturity. For example, a 91-day Treasury bill with a par value of $10,000 discounted at 11.87 percent will be issued at a price of $9,700. Between the issuance date and maturity, no other payments are made to the holders of the bills. The Treasury issues bills with three different maturities: three months, six months, and one year. New three- and six-month bills are offered each week; one-year bills are offered once a month. Because the secondary market is highly liquid, bills with any maturity up to one year can easily be purchased with minimal transaction costs.

The bid and ask quotes for Treasury bills such as those shown in the far right-hand column of Table 7–1 are stated in terms of the bank discount, which is quoted on a 360-day basis. The bid price is the price at which a government security dealer is willing to purchase the security, and the ask price is the price at which a government security dealer will sell the security. The bid and ask quotes reported in *The Wall Street Journal* are indicative. Actual bid-ask spreads on round lot trades of $5 million or more, which are obtained by contacting government securities dealers, typically are narrower.

The bank discount and the price of the bill per hundred dollars of par value are related by the following formula:

$$p = 100 - d \cdot (n/360) \tag{7-2}$$

where:

p = Price of the Treasury bill per $100 par value
d = Bank discount
n = Number of days until the bill matures

For example, consider the bill maturing August 27, 1992, that is underlined in Table 7–1. As of June 1, 1992, that bill had a maturity of 85 days and was selling at an ask bank discount of 3.73. Substituting these numbers into Equation (7–2) gives:

$$p = 100 - 3.73 \cdot (85/360) = 99.119$$

Though it looks like an interest rate when reported in the newspaper, the bank discount is not a yield, it is simply a convention used by government securities dealers to quote prices.

For this reason, bond equivalent yields on Treasury bills are also reported. These bond equivalent yields, which are shown in the last column of Table 7–1, are comparable to the yield to maturity on bonds. The bond equivalent yield for a bill with a maturity of 182 days or less is calculated using the following formula:

$$\text{Bond equivalent yield} = [(100 - p)/p] \cdot 365/n \qquad (7\text{–}2a)$$

where the variables are as defined above.[2] Bond equivalent yields are calculated from the perspective of a buyer of securities and, therefore, are based on ask prices. Utilizing the data above for the 85-day bill, the bond equivalent yield comes to 3.83 percent as shown in Table 7–1.

Neither the bank discount nor the bond equivalent yield measures the true economic return on a Treasury bill. The true economic return is that rate that investors would earn over the course of a year if they invested in Treasury bills of a given type and reinvested the proceeds in identical bills until the end of the year. Because of the assumed reinvestment, the true annualized yield takes account of compound interest. Therefore, the true annualized yield is the rate of interest that should be used when calculating the cost of capital.

The true annualized yield on a Treasury bill can be computed by a two-step procedure. First, Equation (7–2) is solved for the price of the bill. Second, the true annualized yield is calculated from the price (per hundred), p, the par value, 100, and the maturity in days, n, using the following formula:

$$\text{True annualized yield} = [(100/p)^{(365/n)}] - 1. \qquad (7\text{–}3)$$

Applying Equation (7–3) to the 85-day bill with a price of 99.119 discussed above, the true annualized yield is 3.87 percent. Notice that the true annualized yield is 14 basis points greater than the bank discount and 4 basis points greater than the bond equivalent yield. Though these differences are small, they grow rapidly as rates rise. For example, at a bank discount on the order of 12.00

---

[2]For a more detailed discussion of the mathematics of Treasury yields, see Chapter 3 of F. J. Fabozzi and T. D. Fabozzi, *Bonds Markets, Analysis and Strategies* (Englewood Cliffs, N.J.: Prentice Hall, 1989).

for 90-day bills, the discrepancy between the discount and the true annualized yield is over 50 basis points. When the Treasury bill rate is used as the risk-free rate in an economic model, the appropriate measure of return is the true annualized yield because it takes proper account of the compounding of interest.

Treasury notes and bonds. Unlike Treasury bills, Treasury notes and bonds pay interest in the form of semiannual coupons. The bonds come in units with a par value of $1,000, but the prices are quoted per hundred. For example, consider the last Treasury bond listed in Table 7–1, the 8 percent coupon maturing in November 2021. As of June 1, 1992, the date the data were collected by *The Wall Street Journal*, this was the most recently issued 30-year Treasury bond. The most recently issued 30-year bond is often called the *long* bond or the *bellwether* bond and is closely followed as a benchmark of the market for long-term funds. As shown in the table, the long bond is quoted at prices of 101 5/32 (per hundred) and 101 7/32 ask.

The semiannual interest payments on a Treasury bond are determined by the coupon rate. Each interest payment equals the coupon rate times the par value of the bond divided by two. In the case of the long bond, the coupon is 8 percent, which means that the bond pays $40 in interest per $1,000 in par value every six months for the next 30 years.

The final number shown in the right-hand column is the yield to maturity. The yield to maturity is defined as twice the internal rate of return, calculated at the ask price. The factor of two is included to adjust for the fact the payments are received semiannually. As will become apparent, however, this adjustment does not take into account compound interest.

The internal rate of return on an investment is that rate that discounts the cash flows from the investment back to the purchase price.[3] It can be quickly computed using spreadsheet software such as Excel and 1-2-3. For instance, the internal rate of

---

[3]Each of the four finance texts cited in Chapter 1 of this book contains a detailed discussion of the internal rate of return. It is worth noting that some of the difficulties associated with the internal rate of return do not apply to bonds. Most importantly, a bond cannot have multiple internal rates of return because there is only one cash outflow—the initial purchase price of the bond.

return (IRR) on a $100 investment that provides three annual payments of $40, $50, and $60 is the discount rate, r, which solves the equation;

$$100 = \frac{40}{(1 + r)} + \frac{50}{(1 + r)^2} + \frac{60}{(1 + r)^3}$$

Application of the IRR function in Excel reveals that r equals 21.6 percent.

In the case of Treasury bonds, the IRR is that rate that discounts the promised stream of interest and principal payments back to the price of the bond. Returning, for instance, to the long bond, and assuming that its maturity is exactly 30 years, the bond provides 60 interest payments of $40 and a final principal payment of $1,000.[4] The current ask price of the bond is 101 7/32 per hundred, or $1,012.18 per bond. Thus, the IRR is that rate that discounts a stream involving 59 payments of $40.00 and then one payment of $1,040.00 back to a present value of $1,012.18. Using Excel, that rate is found to be 3.947 percent. Because the cash flows are semiannual, the resulting internal rate of return is a semiannual rate. This semiannual rate is multiplied by 2 and rounded to two decimal places to calculate the yield to maturity, which is 7.89 percent in the example. As noted above, this last step is incorrect in that it ignores compound interest. To calculate the true annualized yield, account must be taken of compounding.

The internal rate of return of 3.947 percent is a true yield, but it is stated per six months. The problem, therefore, is to annualize the rate. There is a general formula for annualizing interest rates that are stated in terms of fraction, $1/n$, of a year. The formula is:

Annual rate $= (1 + \text{Rate for fraction } 1/n \text{ of a year})^n - 1$ (7—4)

In the case of a semiannual yield, this formula becomes:

Annual rate $= (1 + \text{Semiannual IRR})^2 - 1$

---

[4]The actual maturity is slightly less than 30 years because the bond has been outstanding for a while. This means that the first coupon payment will be made in less than six months and complicates the calculation of the IRR. These complications are not considered here. Fabozzi and Fabozzi, *Bond Markets*, presents the more complicated calculations.

Applying the formula to a semiannual rate of 3.947 percent gives a true annualized rate of 8.05 percent, which is 16 basis points greater than the yield to maturity. It is this higher rate that should be used as an input in cost of capital calculations.

The Determination of Interest Rates

The purpose of this section is to develop some basic principles regarding the behavior of interest rates that prove useful in appraisal practice. The presentation is intuitive rather than formal, and the principles developed are only approximations.[5] Nonetheless, they can prove invaluable when attempting to estimate the cost of capital.

Following Fama, the interest rate on a short-term, risk-free security such as a Treasury bill can be broken into two components—its expected real return and a premium to compensate the lender for expected inflation—as shown in equation (7–5).[6]

Short-term risk-free rate = Expected short-term real rate
                               + Short-term inflation
                                 premium   (7–5)

For simplicity, the compounding term has been omitted from Equation (7–5) and is omitted from all the following equations. More correctly the equation should be $(1 + i) = (1 + r)(1 + \pi)$, where i is the nominal rate of interest, r is the real rate of interest, and π is the expected rate of inflation. Solving the equation for i gives, $i = r + \pi + r\pi$. For low rates of interest and inflation, the cross product term, $r\pi$, which results because of compounding, is small and can safely be ignored.

Equation (7–5) holds not only for current short-term securities, it also holds for short-term securities that will be issued in the future. It follows, therefore, that the expected average short-term

---

[5]There is a huge formal literature on the determination of interest rates and the term structure of interest rates. A good introduction to that literature is provided by R. W. McEnally, "The Term Structure of Interest Rates," in *The Handbook of Fixed Income Securities*, 2nd ed., ed. F. J. Fabozzi and I. M. Pollack (Homewood, Ill.: Dow Jones-Irwin, 1987).

[6]E. F. Fama, "Short-Term Interest Rates as Predictors of Inflation," *American Economic Review* 65 (June 1975); pp. 269–82.

rate over any future period—say, for example, the next 10 years—equals the sum of the expected average short-term real rate plus the expected average inflation premium, as shown in equation (7–5a).

Expected average short-term = Expected average
risk-free rate over the   short-term real rate
long run   + Expected average
                                          inflation premium   (7–5a)

The role of inflation in Equations (7–5) and (7–5a) is easy to understand. In an inflationary environment, lenders recognize that they are being repaid in dollars with reduced purchasing power. To compensate for this anticipated drop in purchasing power, lenders require a premium that they expect will make them whole before committing their funds. For example, if expected inflation is 5 percent, lenders require a premium of 5 percent.

Compensation for inflation, while necessary, is not sufficient to induce lenders to part with their cash. Borrowers must also offer a real return in excess of the inflation premium. The question of what determines the real rate of interest is complicated. Though it is widely agreed that consumer preferences, economic activity, investment demand, and fiscal and monetary policy all affect the short-term real rate, the relative importance of these and other factors and the manner in which they are related has not been resolved. Fortunately, this is not a major issue in appraisal practice because corporate valuation depends on the average short-term risk-free rate over the long run. Transitory variations in the short-term rate, which tend to cancel out over time, do not have a significant impact on the value of long-term cash flow streams such as those produced by corporations. All that the appraiser needs to forecast is the long-run average of the short-term interest rate. A market-based source of the information necessary to forecast that average is contained in the long-term rate.

The rate on a long-term default-free security such as a 30-year Treasury bond consists of three components:

Long-term risk-free rate = Expected long-term real rate
                                    + Long-term inflation premium
                                    + Term (or maturity) premium   (7–6)

The term premium arises because investors require added compensation for the risk of investing in long-term securities. Unlike short-term default-free securities whose prices are pinned down by their imminent maturity, the prices of long-term securities can swing dramatically over time. The term premium is the compensation investors require for bearing the risk associated with such price fluctuations.

In an efficient bond market, the expected long-term real rate will approximately equal the expected average of short-term real rates over the life of the long-term bond, and the long-term inflation premium will approximately equal the average expected inflation over the life of the bond. Therefore, the expression for the long-term, risk-free rate can also be written as:

Long-term risk-free rate = Expected average short-term
real rate over the life of the bond
+ Expected average inflation rate
over the life of the bond
+ Term (or maturity)
premium[7]   (7–6a)

Combining Equations (7–5a) and (7–6a) suggests a procedure for estimating the term premium. Over the long run, the returns on both short-term and long-term securities will be similar because they will both reflect average expectations regarding real rates and inflation. Thus, the only difference between the average return on long-term Treasury bonds and the average return on short-term Treasury bills is the term premium, as shown in Equation (7–7).

Term premium = Average return on long-term Treasury
bonds
− Average return on Treasury bills   (7–7)

Equation (7–7) holds for any pair of securities. For example, suppose the appraiser wants to estimate the term premium on

---

[7]The term premium is assumed to be constant, so it is not affected by the averaging process. To the extent that the term premium varies, a much more complicated model of the behavior of interest rates is required. See, for instance, J. C. Cox, J. Ingersoll, and S. A. Ross, "The Term Structure of Interest Rates," *Econometrica* 53 (May 1985); pp. 385–407.

long-term Treasury bonds (average maturity 20 years) with respect to 1-month Treasury bills. The average return for the period 1926 to 1989 on long-term Treasury bonds, shown subsequently in Table 7–6, is 4.88 percent, while the average return on 1-month Treasury bills over the same period is 3.66 percent.[8] Accordingly, the term premium associated with long-term Treasury bonds, in comparison with one-month Treasury bills, is approximately 1.2 percent.

Thus far, the discussion has focused on default-free securities. Default risk adds two new elements to the basic equations. In the short-term case, the analog to Equation (7–5) is given by Equation (7–8).

$$\text{Short-term risky rate} = \text{Expected short-term real rate}$$
$$+ \text{ Short-term inflation premium}$$
$$+ \text{ Default premium}$$
$$+ \text{ Risk premium} \qquad (7\text{–}8)$$

It may seem surprising that Equation (7–8) includes both a default premium and a risk premium. A simple example illustrates how the default premium and the risk premium differ and why both are necessary. Assume that there are two possible future states of the world, a good state and a bad state. The good state occurs with a probability of 0.90, and the bad state occurs with a probability of 0.10. In the good state, a risky security, call it commercial paper, pays principal and interest in full; but in the bad state, the investor receives only 50 percent of the principal and no interest. The risk-free security, a Treasury bill, pays full principal and interest at a rate assumed to be 7 percent in both states. As shown in Table 7–2, the promised payout on the commercial paper—that is, the return the investor receives if there is no default—must equal 13.3 percent for the expected return on the paper to be 7 percent. Thus, a premium of 6.33 percent is required to compensate investors for the possibility of a default.

If the risky security offers only a default premium, then investors have no incentive to hold it instead of Treasury bills. Bills

---

[8]Data on Treasury security returns taken from a data base maintained by Dimensional Fund Advisers, a Santa Monica-based investment management firm. The data is the same as that provided by Ibbotson and Associates.

will pay 7 percent with certainty. Investors who purchase the commercial paper, in the example, face the risk of loss and still expect to earn only 7 percent. Under such circumstances, risk averse investors will always prefer to hold the bills. Consequently, an added premium is required to induce investors to buy the risky security. For illustrative purposes, this added risk premium is assumed to be 1.7 percent. Adding the 1.7 percent risk premium to the 6.33 percent default premium brings the total premium to approximately 8.0 percent. Given a total premium of 8.0 percent and a risk-free rate of 7 percent, the promised yield on the risky security must be 15 percent.

It is also possible to write an averaged version of Equation (7–8). Because of the possibility of default, averages should be computed using actual returns, not promised returns. When expected average returns are calculated, the default premium disappears. Remember that the role of the default premium is to compensate investors for the defaults that they suffer in bad states of the world. Over the long run, the good states and the bad states should occur with their expected frequencies so that the average default premium is zero, as shown in Equation (7–8a).

$$
\begin{aligned}
\text{Expected average return on a} &= \text{Expected average short-} \\
\text{short-term risky security} &\quad\text{term real rate} \\
&+ \text{Expected average inflation} \\
&\quad\text{premium} \\
&+ \text{Risk premium.} \qquad (7.8a)
\end{aligned}
$$

Comparison of Equations (7–5a) and (7–8a) suggests a procedure for estimating the risk premium. Notice that the equations are identical except for the risk premium. Thus, the long-run average difference between the return on a risky security and the return on a Treasury security with the same maturity, as given by Equation (7–9), provides an estimate of the risk premium for that security.

$$
\begin{aligned}
\text{Risk premium} &= \text{Long-run average return on the risky} \\
&\quad\text{security} \\
&- \text{Long-run average return on a risk-free} \\
&\quad\text{security} \qquad\qquad\qquad\qquad\qquad (7\text{–}9)
\end{aligned}
$$

TABLE 7–2
An Illustration of the Default Premium versus the Risk Premium

The matrix shows the payoff per $1 invested in two alternative investments in each of two possible future states. The Treasury bill pays principal and full interest in both the good and bad state, whereas the commercial paper pays only 50 percent of the principal in the bad state.

	Good State (90% chance)	Bad State (10% chance)
Treasury Bill	$1.07	$1.07
Commercial Paper	ϕ	$0.50

The default premium equals the excess promised yield required to make the expected return on the risky security equal to the expected return on the risk-free security. In the above example, the default premium is calculated using the equation:*

$$0.90 \cdot (\phi) + 0.10 \cdot (\$0.50) = \$1.07$$

Solving for ϕ gives:

$$\phi = [\$1.07 - 0.10 \cdot (\$0.50)] / .90 = \$1.133$$

	Good State (90% chance)	Bad State (10% chance)
Treasury Bill	$1.07	$1.07
Commercial Paper	$1.133	$0.50

The calculation shows that the promised payoff per dollar invested must be $1.133 for the expected return to equal that of the Treasury bill's 7 percent rate. The promised return—that is, the return the investor earns in the absence of default—must be 13.3 percent. Thus, the default premium is 6.33 percent.

In order to induce investors to choose this security over the T-bill, a risk premium must also be offered above. Therefore, for the expected return to exceed that of the Treasury bill, the promised return must be greater than 13.3 percent. For example, a risk premium of approximately 1.7 percent increases the promised return to 15 percent.

---

*Probability of the "good"   + Probability of the "bad"   = Default-free rate of return
state occurring times the   state occurring times the   on $1 invested
return on $1 invested in   return on $1 invested in
a risky investment   a risky investment

To illustrate the procedure for estimating the risk premium, consider the case of the prime interest rate (the one-month rate on prime bank loans) compared to the one-month Treasury bills. Over the period from 1948 to 1989, the average prime return was 7.2 percent and the average one-month Treasury bill return was 5.0 percent. Therefore, the risk premium associated with prime lending compared to one-month Treasury bills is 2.2 percent. (This calculation ignores the fact that part of the difference in average return may be due to Treasury bills being exempt from state income tax.)

It is important to stress that the averaging procedures presented in this section work best for large samples. Because of the high variability of the returns on many types of securities, small samples can produce misleading conclusions. For instance, some analysts concluded that low-grade "junk" bonds offered large risk premiums on the basis of studies comparing the average returns on junk bonds to the average return on Treasury bonds from the period from 1982 to 1988. Unfortunately, that sample period proved to be too short because it did not include a significant economic downturn. When economic conditions deteriorated in 1989, defaults on junk bonds soared, and the estimated risk premium plummeted.

Putting the pieces together, Figure 7–1 shows how the interest rate on a hypothetical risky bond is determined. At the base is the average short-term, risk-free rate expected over the life of the bond (assumed to be 7 percent in the figure). To this is added a term premium (assumed to be 1.2 percent in the figure), a risk premium (assumed to be 1.7 percent in the figure), and a default premium (2.2 percent in the figure). Given these premiums, the total promised return on the security is 12.1 percent and the expected return is 9.9 percent. (For expositional simplicity, the premiums are added rather than compounded. Depending on how the premiums are defined, compounding may be more appropriate. The important thing is to be sure to apply the premiums in a fashion consistent with the way they were estimated.)

Corporate Bonds: Some Fundamentals

Like Treasury bonds, most corporate bonds are defined by four parameters: par value, coupon rate, maturity, and price. The first

FIGURE 7–1
The Building Blocks of the Promised Yield on a Hypothetical, Long-Term Risky Bond*

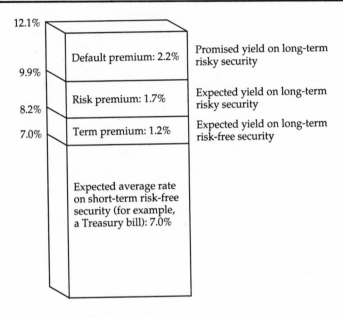

*The rates shown are also hypothetical.

three parameters are set by the issuing company and are stated in the bond indenture. The final parameter is determined by the market. The price adjusts until the yield on the bond is competitive with other bonds of similar risk available in the market.

Virtually all corporate bonds follow several standard conventions. First, the par value to be repaid at maturity is $1,000. Second, coupons are paid semiannually. As for Treasury bonds, the coupon payments equal the coupon rate times the par value divided by two. Third, bond prices are stated per hundred dollars of par value. Finally, dealers typically quote the bonds in terms of yield to maturity.

Promised yields, actual returns, and expected returns. The yield to maturity and the true annualized yield on a corporate bond are promised yields. They are yields that investors will receive if everything goes according to plan and the interest and principal are paid on schedule. Because default is always a possibility for corporate bonds, investors do not expect to earn the promised yield.

The internal rate of return that investors anticipate receiving is given by the expected return. The expected return will be less than the promised yield because investors will take into account the possibility that interest and principal payments may be delayed or omitted. Furthermore, the horizon over which the return is expected to be earned may differ from the maturity of the bond because of default or restructuring.

The promised yield and the expected internal rate of return are both ex ante measures, meaning that they are calculated before the bond matures or defaults. The actual return the investor earns cannot be calculated until the bond has matured, defaulted, or been called, so that all the cash payments are known. At that time, the actual return can be computed as the internal rate of return that discounts the stream of payments received to the purchase price of the bond. The actual return calculated in this fashion need not equal either the promised yield or the expected yield. For instance, a bond may have a promised yield of 15 percent and an expected yield of 12 percent, but the actual yield may be only 2 percent because of an early default.

Of the three measures, the expected return, stated as a true annualized rate, is the correct choice for estimating the cost of corporate debt. It takes into account the fact that the issuer of debt has the option to avoid, delay, or restructure obligations following a default. These options reduce the effective cost of corporate debt below the promised yield.

Estimating the expected return on corporate debt. The problem raised by risky debt is that only the promised yield is observable, but it is the expected return that is required to estimate the cost of debt. Although the expected return and the default premium sum to the promised yield, neither the expected return nor the default premium can be observed directly. For this reason, the expected return must be estimated indirectly.

As discussed above, the expected return on a risky bond equals the risk-free rate, given by the yield on a Treasury security of comparable maturity plus a risk premium. Because Treasury yields are readily available, estimating the expected return is equivalent to estimating the risk premium.

The most straightforward way to estimate the risk premium is to rely on bond ratings or effective bond ratings and to calculate historical averages. This assumes, of course, that bonds with similar ratings are equally risky. The risk premium is estimated for a given rating class by calculating the historical average difference between a sample of bonds with that rating and Treasury bonds with equal maturity. (Some appraisers prefer to match duration rather than maturity. For most bonds, the distinction is not critical. The possible exception, high-yield bonds, is discussed later in this chapter.)

Bond ratings are provided by both Standard & Poor's and Moody's as well as a number of smaller investment research firms. The rating classifications used by Standard & Poor's are AAA, AA, A, BBB, BB, B, CCC, CC, C and D. Moody's classifications are Aaa, Aa, A, Baa, Ba, B, Caa, Ca, C, D. Bonds with a rating of BBB (or Baa) and above are considered investment grade.[9]

To illustrate the procedure for estimating the expected return on a bond, assume, for the time being, that the bond is rated by either Moody's or Standard & Poor's. In that case, the estimation procedure involves two steps. First, the average risk premium over Treasury bonds is estimated for bonds with a rating equal to those of the appraisal target. For instance, if the bonds in question are rated B, the average risk premium is estimated by calculating the historical difference between returns on B-rated bonds and Treasury bonds with the same maturity. Second, the expected return on the bond in question is calculated by adding the estimated risk premium to the current true annualized yield observed on the lien date for a Treasury bond of the same maturity.

The risk premium for a given rating does not have to be reestimated de novo for every appraisal. A number of scholars, most notably Altman, have tabulated risk premiums on long-term

---

[9]For a more complete discussion of bond ratings, see S. A. Ross, R. W. Westerfield, and J. F. Jaffe, *Corporate Finance*, 2nd ed. (Homewood, Ill.: Richard D. Irwin, 1990).

TABLE 7–3
Return Spreads Earned by Corporate Bonds over Treasury Bonds*
(1978 to 1987)

Annualized Differentials in Basis Points						
AAA	AA	A	BBB	BB	B	CCC
52	83	117	180	288	176	206

*All of the averages are computed over the full 10-year period except for CCC bonds.
For CCC bonds, the average is calculated over the period from 1983 to 1987.
Source: E. I. Altman, "Measuring Corporate Bond Mortality and Performance," *Journal of Finance* 44 (September 1989), pp. 909–22.

corporate bonds as a function of the bonds' ratings.[10] Altman's findings, reported in Table 7–3, show that the historical risk premiums rise as bond ratings fall, but only to a point. The risk premiums reach a maximum at a rating of BB and then fall, despite the fact that the promised yields were much higher on the B and CCC bonds. This indicates that at a B rating and below, the higher promised yield reflects only an increase in the default premium and not a higher risk premium. However, this conclusion should be interpreted with caution due to the small size of Altman's sample of below BB grade debt.

As a specific example, suppose the appraiser needs to estimate the cost of BB rated debt with a 10-year maturity as of July 1, 1989. On that day, the true annualized yield on 10-year Treasury bonds was 8.27 percent. Adding the 288 basis point risk premium that Altman's study indicates is appropriate for BB bonds, the expected return and, therefore, the cost of capital for BB debt come to 11.15 percent.

If the appraiser decides to rely on studies such as Altman's, it is important that they be current. Not only do current studies typically employ larger samples, but in some cases, adding a few years of data can significantly affect the results. In the case of low-grade bonds, for instance, adding 1988, 1989, and 1990 to Alt-

---

[10]E. I. Altman, "Measuring Corporate Bond Mortality and Performance," *Journal of Finance* 44 (September 1989), pp. 909–22.

man's sample dramatically reduces the estimates of the risk premium because the junk bond market collapsed in 1989 and 1990.

In some cases, the appraiser may choose to use judgment to adjust the estimated risk premiums. For example, in Altman's sample, the historical risk premium of B and CCC debt is 100 basis points less than that of BB debt. This is inconsistent with economic logic, because lower-rated, higher-risk bonds should not offer smaller risk premiums. The anomaly is most likely due to measurement error caused by the small sample of below BB bonds.[11] Thus, the appraiser may choose to assume that below BB, the risk premium is constant.

For investment grade debt, appraisers often assume that the default premium is small and offset by the compounding effect so that the expected return equals the yield to maturity. This introduces only a minor measurement error. It also greatly simplifies the estimation problem because promised yields are observable directly. For example, appraisals of AT&T prepared by the company and by the state of California both used the average yield on AT&T's outstanding debt as an estimate of AT&T's cost of debt. Of course, the observed yield can be used only if the appraisal target's debt is marketable. An advantage of the risk premium approach is that it can be applied to nonmarketable debt as well as publicly traded debt provided that an effective rating can be estimated.

Nonrated debt. The deficiency of the risk premium approach is that it requires a rating for the appraisal target's debt. If the target's bonds are not rated, then an effective rating must be estimated. The most direct procedure for estimating the effective rating is to find a comparable company with rated debt. Presumably, the target's debt rating, if it were available, would equal that of the comparable company. In this context, it is critical that

---

[11]It is also possible that differences in duration between bonds of various ratings could explain part of the difference. As noted by M. E. Blume, D. B. Keim, and S. A. Patel, "Returns and Volatility of Low-Grade Bonds 1977–1989," *Journal of Finance* 46 (March 1990); pp. 49–74, lower-grade bonds tend to have higher coupons and more extensive call provisions, both of which reduce their duration.

companies considered to be comparable have similar capital structures, because the amount of leverage is an important determinant of the rating of a company's debt.

If a comparable company with rated debt cannot be found, then the appraiser must attempt to estimate the effective rating of the target's debt directly. As noted in Chapter 4, this can be done by developing a model that mimics the debt-rating process. As one example of how a model can be constructed, Altman developed a Z *score* that measures a firm's financial health and is highly correlated with bond ratings.[12] Following Altman, a Z score can be computed for both the appraisal target and for companies in the same line of business with various debt ratings. The target is presumed to have an effective rating equal to that of companies with similar Z scores.

More recently, Altman's approach has been elaborated, extended, and incorporated into software packages. These packages are designed to mimic the bond-rating process followed by Moody's and Standard & Poor's and to provide effective bond ratings. One of the best packages currently available is Debt Rater, which was developed by the Alcar group. The appraiser enters financial data into the package from the balance sheet and income statement for a period of years, and Debt Rater calculates the effective rating. Similar products are under development by several financial consulting firms and investment banks.

Dealing with short-term debt. Short-term debt introduces another difficulty. The problem is that the cost of debt should be measured over the duration of the firm's cash flows, but the interest rate on short-term debt is fixed only until maturity. Even if the debt is automatically rolled over at maturity, the interest rate is reset, so the cost of debt changes. The same problem arises in the case of long-term debt with interest rates that float over a short-term index. For instance, interest rates on bank loans are generally reset monthly at a margin over the prevailing prime rate. FEC's borrowing rate is prime plus ½ percent, reset monthly. Because short-term rates change frequently, the

---

[12]E. I. Altman, "Financial Ratios, Discriminant Analysis and the Prediction of Corporate Bankruptcy," *Journal of Finance* 43 (September 1978); pp. 589–605.

current short-term interest rate may differ from the expected average cost of short-term funds over the long run. This can be a serious problem if short-term interest rates are seen as being extraordinarily high or low on the lien date.

To illustrate the potential impact of this problem, consider the conditions that prevailed at the beginning of June 1981. At that time, the 1-month Treasury bill was 18 percent and the prime rate was over 20 percent, but the 30-year Treasury bond rate was only 13.6 percent. Long-term rates were low, relative to short-term rates, because investors expected inflation to fall in the future. An appraisal assuming that a company would have to pay then current short-term rates over the long run clearly would overstate the cost of debt and understate the value of the firm.

There are three basic ways to deal with this problem. The first is simply to substitute the rate on the company's long-term debt for the rate on its short-term debt. The rationale for this approach is that over the long run, the average cost of short-term borrowing will equal the cost of borrowing long term. This simple approach, however, has two drawbacks. First, it ignores the term premium. Second, it does not take into account the fact that the long-term and short-term debt may not be of equal credit risk.

The second approach, which takes into account the risk premium and the term premium, is based on Equations (7–7), (7–8a), and (7–9). Substituting Equations (7–7) and (7–9) into Equation (7–8a) gives:

Expected average return on a = Long-term risk-free
short-term risky security   interest rate
                                  − Term premium
                                  + Risk premium   (7–10)

Equation (7–10) states the average cost of short-term borrowing over the long run can be approximated by the current long-term Treasury rate minus the historical term premium plus the risk premium associated with the short-term borrowing. When applying Equation (7–10), there are several points to bear in mind.

- The maturity of the Treasury security used to measure the long-term risk-free rate should match the period over which the average short-term rate is required.

- The Treasury bill utilized in conjunction with the long-term Treasury bond to estimate the term premium should match the maturity, or the interest reset period, of the short-term security in question.
- The risk premium associated with the company's short-term debt must be measured relative to Treasury bills using historical data for the security in question, or a comparable security.

To illustrate the procedure, suppose that the appraiser is asked to estimate, as of June 2, 1992, the average prime rate over the next 20 years. As calculated earlier, the risk premium for prime lending compared to 1-month Treasury bills is 2.2 percent, and the term premium of 20-year Treasury bonds with respect to 1-month Treasury bills is 1.2 percent. On June 2, 1992, the true annualized yield on a 20-year Treasury bond was approximately 8.01 percent (From Table 7–1, the Treasury bond maturing in November 2012 had a yield to maturity of 7.86 percent, which translates into a true annualized yield of 8.01 percent using Equation 7–4a). Following the prescription given by Equation (7–10), a 120 basis point term premium is deducted to reflect the average return difference between long-term Treasury bonds and 1-month Treasury bills. Next, a 220 basis point risk premium is added to reflect the historical difference between the return on prime loans and the return on 1-month Treasury bills. The result is an expected average prime rate over the next 20 years of 9.01 percent.

The third approach is to take advantage of interest rate forecasts. Major economic forecasting firms such as Data Resources, Inc. (DRI), forecast key short-term interest rates such as the prime rate and the Treasury bill rate up to 20 years into the future. These forecasts can be utilized to estimate the long-run cost of short-term funds.

THE COST OF PREFERRED STOCK

Preferred stock is considered only briefly for two reasons. First, preferred stock issues are not a major financing source for most American corporations. Financial managers are averse to using preferred stock financing because it is comparable to debt, but preferred dividends, unlike interest payments, are not tax deductible. Second, the preferred stock that is used is far from homogeneous. Many preferred issues have complicated call and conversion options. Calculating the cost of capital for such securities requires the application of sophisticated option pricing models, which are discussed in Chapter 9.

The preferred stock considered here is standard perpetual preferred paying a fixed dividend. It is assumed that the preferred stock is neither callable nor convertible. If the price of the preferred stock is available, the cost of capital is equal to the yield on the preferred given by:

$$k_p = D/P \qquad\qquad (7\text{-}11)$$

where:

k_p = Cost of preferred stock
D = Promised dividend on the preferred
P = Market price of the preferred

The problem with Equation (7–11) is that for many appraisal targets, the market price of the preferred is not available. Under such circumstances, the next alternative is to calculate the yield on comparable preferred issues. Because of the fixed nature of the preferred dividend, it is not necessary that the comparable preferreds be issued by comparable companies; it is only necessary that the comparable preferred shares be of equal risk. If ratings are available, preferred shares with equal ratings typically are assumed to be of equal risk. For unrated preferred issues, judgment is required in assessing risk. Because preferred stock is not widely used, research on the rating of preferred stock is scarce, and software programs analogous to Debt Rater are largely nonexistent. One rule of thumb is handy in this context: If the appraiser is comfortable assuming that the risk of default on the preferred is low, then the cost of preferred and the before-tax cost of the lowest priority debt should be approximately equal.

THE COST OF EQUITY CAPITAL

Unlike the payments on bonds and preferred stock, dividends on common stock are not contractually set, but rise and fall with the fate of the issuer. This added uncertainty makes estimating the cost of equity capital more difficult than estimating the cost of debt or preferred stock. To add to the complexity, there is not one accepted procedure for estimating the cost of equity but rather two fundamentally different approaches. One approach, referred to as the discounted dividend or the discounted cash flow approach, is based on an extension of internal rate of return analysis used to estimate the cost of debt. (Discounted cash flow, in this context, should not be confused with the discounted cash flow valuation model. In this case, it is dividends, not cash flows, that are being discounted. Needless to say, the name *discounted cash flow* is misleading, so the term *dividend discount* is used instead.) The other approach is based on asset pricing models that provide explicit mathematical formulas for the trade-off between risk and expected return.

The Dividend Discount Model

With some modifications, the internal rate of return method used to calculate the true annualized return on bonds can be utilized to estimate the cost of equity. Whereas the price of a bond equals the present value of future interest and principal payments, the price of a share of common stock equals the present value of future dividend payments. However, there are two complications that arise when solving for the internal rate of return for common stock. First, because dividends are not contractually set, a forecast of future dividends is required. Second, common stock does not have a definite maturity, so the dividend stream extends into the indefinite future. Taking into account these two complications, the dividend discount model for common stock can be written as:

$$P = \frac{E(D_1)}{(1 + r)} + \frac{E(D_2)}{(1 + r)^2} + \frac{E(D_3)}{(1 + r)^3} + \ldots + \frac{E(D_n)}{(1 + r)^n} \quad (7\text{–}12)$$

where:

P = Market price of the stock
$E(D_n)$ = Expected dividend payout in year n
r = Cost of equity capital

Given the stock price and a forecast of future dividends, Equation (7–12) can be solved for r, the cost of equity capital.

The reliability of the discounted dividend model for estimating the cost of equity clearly depends on the accuracy of the dividend forecast. The most common procedure for forecasting future dividends is to develop explicit forecasts up to a given horizon and to assume that thereafter, dividends grow at a constant rate. One special case of this procedure, referred to as the constant growth model, is based on the assumption that dividends grow at a constant rate, g, right from the start. When dividends grow at a constant rate, Equation (7–12) simplifies to:

$$P = \frac{D_1}{(1 + r)} + \frac{D_1(1 + g)}{(1 + r)^2} + \frac{D_1(1 + g)^2}{(1 + r)^3} \qquad (7\text{–}13)$$

which reduces to:

$$P = \frac{D_1}{r - g} \qquad (7\text{–}14)$$

Solving Equation (7–14) for r gives:

$$r = \frac{D_1}{P} + g \qquad (7\text{–}15)$$

A simple example illustrates how the constant growth model works. On December 31, 1991, Pacific Gas & Electric's stock price was $25.375 and its quarterly dividend payment was $0.38, so that its annual dividend yield was about 6.0 percent. Assuming that dividends were expected to grow at an annual rate of 7 percent per year, the constant growth model gives a cost equity capital of 13 percent.

The constant growth model has the drawback that it can be applied only to mature companies whose dividends are expected to grow at a constant rate, such as electric utilities. For younger, more dynamic firms, the dividend growth rate is likely to be rapid at the start and then decline slowly toward a constant long-run level. When dividend growth is variable, there is no simple solution to Equation (7–12), and explicit dividend forecasts are required for each future year, at least up to the point where constant growth can be assumed to begin. This is illustrated by the case of Apple Computer. At the end of 1991, Apple's stock price was $43.00 and the company paid a quarterly dividend of $0.12, so that its annual dividend yield was 1.1 percent. To apply the dividend discount model, assume that it was forecast that this dividend would grow at 40 percent per year for the next five years, 25 percent per year for the following five years, and 15 percent per year for the five years after that, before settling down to a long-run growth rate of 7 percent. Given these assumptions, the entire dividend stream is specified, up to the time when steady growth begins. Once steady growth begins, the present value of the remaining payouts can be calculated by dividing the following year's dividend by $r - g$. This makes it possible to write a simple computer program to solve Equation (7–12) for r. In the case of Apple Computer the *quarterly* internal rate of return that results from solving Equation (7–12) is 4.0 percent. This quarterly rate is transformed into an annual rate using the compound interest formula:

$$\text{Annual rate} = (1 + \text{Quarterly rate})^4 - 1$$

giving an estimate of approximately 17 percent for Apple's cost of equity capital.

It is also possible to apply Equation (7–12) to companies that do not currently pay dividends. As long as the appraiser can forecast when the dividend stream will begin and predict how it will grow after it starts, Equation (7–12) can be solved for r. However, forecasting future dividends for companies that have never paid a dividend is a good deal more difficult than forecasting dividends for companies such as Pacific Gas & Electric that have a long history of paying predictable dividends.

In some situations, it may not be possible to forecast future dividends with sufficient confidence to apply the dividend growth model. For instance, the appraisal target may be a nondividend paying, privately held company that has no plans to go public or pay dividends. Alternatively, the target may be a subsidiary of a larger corporation. In situations such as these, there is still one alternative to abandoning the dividend discount model. The model can be applied to companies that are comparable to the appraisal target but pay more predictable dividends. For example, Union Pacific Railroad does not pay a dividend because it is part of Union Pacific Corporation. Although Union Pacific Corporation pays a dividend, the cost of capital derived from those dividends is the average cost of capital for the entire conglomerate, which includes subsidiaries in timber, mining, and construction. It would be inappropriate to assume, therefore, that the cost of capital for Union Pacific Railroad equals the cost of capital for Union Pacific Corporation. However, the appraiser might be able to find other comparable railroads to which the dividend discount model could be applied. Because the cost of equity capital is determined by the nature of the assets being financed, the cost of equity for Union Pacific Railroad should be approximately equal to the cost of equity for the comparable railroads.

There is one important complication to keep in mind when selecting comparable companies for application of the dividend discount model. As noted in Chapter 4, the cost of equity capital depends on the investment risk of the equity, which depends, in turn, on the company's capital structure. More highly levered companies will have riskier equity and a higher cost of equity capital. If the dividend discount model is to be applied to a "comparable" company, the appraiser must verify that the comparable company has a similar capital structure. If it does not, the cost of capital estimated for the comparable cannot be applied to the appraisal target without an adjustment to reflect the impact of leverage on risk. Unfortunately, such adjustments cannot be made in the context of the dividend discount model because the model does not explain how the cost of capital is related to risk. To make the adjustment, an asset pricing model that explicitly states how risk and return are related is required.

Asset Pricing Models

Unlike the dividend discount model, which provides an estimate of the cost of equity capital but does not explain what that estimate depends on, asset pricing models mathematically state the relation between investment risk and required return. This added power comes at a price. Asset pricing models are a good deal more complex than the dividend discount model. They are also more difficult to interpret and more awkward to apply. In addition, the accuracy of the models remains a subject of continuing debate.

The idea that risk and expected return are related depends on the assumption that investors are risk averse. To induce an investor to bear more risk, compensation must be offered in the form of an increment in expected return frequently referred to as a risk premium. Before introducing the asset pricing models, therefore, it is necessary to explore what is meant by risk aversion and explain how it produces risk premiums.

Risk aversion and risk premiums.   Risk aversion is based on a simple idea with a big name—the declining marginal utility of consumption. The declining marginal utility of consumption says, in basic terms, that the wealthier you are, the less you will value another dollar. The implications of this idea for investment behavior and risk taking are best illustrated by an example. Suppose you are offered a bet. A fair coin will be flipped: If it lands heads, you win $250,000; if it lands tails, you lose $250,000. Assuming you are one of the vast majority of people who would refuse to take this bet, ask yourself why. The answer given by economists is that the added happiness, or utility, associated with winning $250,000 is smaller than the sorrow, or disutility, associated with losing $250,000. Put another way, the added utility from consuming an added $250,000 worth of goods is less than the lost utility from having to forgo consumption of $250,000 worth of goods.

Due to the declining marginal utility of consumption, investors will not take risks unless a premium is offered. In the case of the coin flip, for example, what would the minimum payoff for a win have to be before you would take the bet and risk the $250,000 loss? $350,000? $500,000? If the answer is $500,000, then the expected profit from the bet is:

Expected profit = Probability of losing · $ lost
+ Probability of winning · $ won
= ½ · −$250,000 + ½ · $500,000
= $125,000

This minimum expected profit represents the premium required to induce you to bear the risk of making the bet. For this reason, it is referred to as a risk premium.

On reflection, there is something a little odd about the previous example. In a coin flip, there are two parties to the bet. If one party is to receive a risk premium, then the other party must pay the premium. But that makes life pretty dismal for the person paying the premium. Not only does he or she bear the risk of the bet, he or she also has to pay the risk premium. Why would risk averse investors ever pay a premium for bearing risk? The answer is, they never would. As will be shown shortly, premiums are paid only for bearing risks that cannot be avoided. The risk of coin flips can be avoided by "just saying no" and not betting. Thus, rather than paying a premium, risk averse investors will simply refrain from betting. That is why $250,000 bets on coin flips are rarely seen.

It may seem that the popularity of Las Vegas and Atlantic City contradicts the prediction that risk averse investors will "just say no" to gambles that do not offer a risk premium. There is, however, an important distinction between casino gambling and investing. In most cases, people risk only a small fraction of their wealth in the casino. They gamble because it's fun and exciting, not because they expect to make money. In fact, the expected losses can be thought of as the price of having fun. The cost of a Las Vegas show is the price of admission, the cost of the casino is the expected loss. But this analogy applies only to small-stakes gambling. Most people do not liquidate their pension funds and take the money to the casino. When the stakes are large, investors are almost universally risk averse.

Nonetheless, there are apparent exceptions. The Hunt brothers risked billions of dollars in silver gambles that could have been avoided by just saying no. How does the theory of risk aversion explain why some people make such huge bets? The answer is that not everyone agrees on the probabilities that define the risk. What appears risky to one investor may appear safe to another. Consider the coin flip example. At the outset, it was assumed that the coin was fair, so that the probability of it landing heads was $\frac{1}{2}$. But suppose that an investor believes that the coin is unbalanced, so that the probability of it landing heads is $\frac{3}{4}$. Under such circumstances, the investor will conclude that a bet on heads entails less risk and offers greater expected return than if the probability was $\frac{1}{2}$. Similarly, an investor who believes that the probability of the coin landing tails is $\frac{3}{4}$ would conclude that the risk of betting on tails is less risky and offers a greater expected return. If there are two such investors, then they are

likely to make a bet on the coin flip. As a further illustration, recall the discussion of football betting. For there to be an active
betting market, investors must have different beliefs about the
relative abilities of the competing teams and, therefore, different
assessments regarding the probability that one team will beat
the spread.

Reading through the opinions of the Hunt brothers indicates
why they invested so much in silver. They believed that inflation
in the United States and upheaval in the Middle East, combined
with increasing consumption and decreasing production of silver, would drive the price of the metal sky-high. For them, the
risk of a huge investment in silver appeared reasonable in light of
the potential rewards. The people who were selling silver, on the
other hand, felt that speculative buying by the Hunts had driven
prices to the point where they were likely to collapse. To the sellers,
shorting silver appeared to be a low-risk, high-reward activity.
Thus, both the buyers and the sellers in the silver market believed they were earning a risk premium because they disagreed
about the probability distribution for the future price for silver.

High-stakes gambling and a good deal of speculative investing
can be explained by the fact that different investors have different
opinions. It does not contradict the fundamental premise that investors, as a class, are risk averse and will require a premium to
bear risk that cannot be avoided.

If only risks that cannot be avoided are associated with risk
premiums, then it is critical to determine what risks can be
avoided. The risks associated with gambling are easy to avoid by
choosing not to gamble. Unfortunately, this avoidance procedure
only works for a narrow class of risks. The risks associated with
owning a home, investing in a business, or holding a retirement
portfolio cannot be avoided so easily. There is a way, however, to
reduce, if not eliminate, the risks associated with most investments. The solution is diversification. The way it works can be
illustrated by another example.

Imagine that you are the owner of a house worth $250,000.
Suppose the chance is $\frac{1}{1,000}$ that the house will be destroyed by a
fire, flood, or storm next year. This means that the expected loss
is given by:

Expected loss = Probability of Loss · $ lost
= $\frac{1}{1,000}$ · $250,000
= $250

If you are risk averse, you will be willing to pay more than $250 to purchase an insurance policy, because the utility that results from paying $250 for insurance and having a house with certainty exceeds the utility associated with saving the $250 insurance payment but facing $\frac{1}{1,000}$ chance of losing the house.

Suppose that a risk averse homeowner would be willing to pay as much as $1,000 for insurance. A $1,000 payment would include $250 to cover the expected loss and a $750 risk premium to induce the counterparty to bear the risk. Though the homeowner may be willing to pay, is it necessary to offer a $750 risk premium to induce an insurance company to accept the risk? In a competitive insurance market, the answer is no. Because insurance companies can eliminate the risk by diversifying, the cost of insurance will be bid down to $250. (More precisely, the cost of insurance would be bid down to $250 plus the incremental transaction costs of writing another insurance policy.) Insurance companies diversify the risk of the house being destroyed by pooling it with thousands of other houses. If the pool is large enough, and if there is no connection between a disaster befalling one house in the pool and a disaster befalling any other, the insurance company can be highly confident that almost exactly $\frac{1}{1,000}$ of the total value of the pool will be destroyed. Assuming that there is no collusion in the insurance industry, competition between insurance companies will drive prices down to the point where the premiums they receive from homeowners will cover only expected losses and the cost of operations, including a normal profit. For you as homeowner, this translates into an insurance payment of just over $250 per year.

The bottom line is that homeowners do not have to pay the insurance companies a risk premium for bearing the risk of loss because insurance companies can eliminate the risk by diversifying. This idea—that diversification can reduce or eliminate risk—is one of the foundations of modern finance. In 1990, Harry Markovitz and William Sharpe shared the Nobel prize for showing how risk, expected return, and diversification interact in the market for common stock. (Merton Miller also shared the prize, but he was cited for different contributions.) Their work developed into what is today called the *capital asset pricing model*, or *CAPM*. The CAPM states how risk and return will be traded off in a competitive capital market.

THE CAPITAL ASSET PRICING MODEL

What makes asset pricing models such the CAPM difficult to derive is that some risk, but not all risk, can be avoided by diversification. Consider, for instance, an investment in Apple Computer. The risks associated with this investment can be seen as arising from two sources. First, there are risks that are unique to Apple. Will Apple design competitive products? Will Apple's operating system be accepted by computer users? Second, there are risks that affect all common stocks. Will the economy enter a recession? Will war break out in the Middle East?

The risks that are unique to Apple can be eliminated by diversification. Investors who invest only in Apple will suffer significant losses if Apple's new products are a failure, but investors who hold Apple along with hundreds of other securities will hardly notice the impact on the value of their portfolios if Apple's new products fail. Conversely, marketwide risks cannot be eliminated by diversification. If the economy enters a recession and stock prices fall across the board, investors holding hundreds of securities fare no better than investors who put all their money in Apple Computer. For this reason, the unique risk associated with Apple is called *diversifiable risk*, because it can be eliminated by diversification, whereas marketwide risk, which is not affected by diversification, is called *nondiversifiable risk*.

To draw an analogy with homeowner's insurance, diversifiable risks are those like the risk of fire, for which the chance of one house burning is largely unrelated to the chance of other houses burning (except for other houses in the immediate neighborhood). Marketwide risks are like the risk of earthquakes. If an earthquake hits, all the homes in the region will be damaged. This risk cannot be reduced by diversification except by writing policies outside the region.

The capital asset pricing model, which is the model most widely used in appraisal practice, is based on the distinction between diversifiable and nondiversifiable risk. Developed simultaneously by John Linter, William Sharpe, and Jack Treynor, the CAPM states that the risk premium, defined to be the difference between the expected return on a security and the risk-free rate, is proportional to that security's nondiversifiable risk as measured by the security's beta. Mathematically, the CAPM is written as:

$$E(r_i) - r_f = B_i \cdot [E(r_m) - r_f] \tag{7-16}$$

where:

$E(r_i)$ = Expected return on the ith security
r_f = Risk-free rate
B_i = Beta of the ith security
$E(r_m)$ = Expected return on the market portfolio

Right away, the CAPM seems confusing. How is it possible to speak of *the* expected return on the ith security? As noted in the discussion regarding the Hunts' silver investments, expectations depend on who is doing the expecting. The answer is that it is possible to speak of *the* expected return because one assumption on which the CAPM is based is that all investors have identical expectations. From a practical standpoint, therefore, the expectation in Equation (7-16) should be thought of as the average or market expectation. Going back to Chapter 3, this average expectation is analogous to the average expectation reflected by the point spread in the football betting market.

The CAPM relies on several other simplifying assumptions in addition to identical expectations. It is also assumed that securities can be traded without cost, that there are no taxes, that all investors can borrow and lend at the risk-free rate, and that the returns on securities are normally (or lognormally) distributed.[13] Because none of these assumptions hold in actual capital

---

[13]For a derivation of the CAPM and a detailed discussion of the assumptions on which it relies, see W. F. Sharpe and G. A. Alexander, *Investments*, 4th ed. (Englewood Cliffs, N.J.: Prentice Hall, 1990).

markets, the CAPM is an approximate theory. Nonetheless, empirical studies have found it to be a reliable, though by no means perfect, model for estimating the expected return on securities.[14]

In Equation (7–16), the difference between the expected return on the ith security and the risk-free rate, $E(r_i) - r_f$, is the risk premium for that security. The risk premium measures the return the investor expects to earn, *on average over the long-run*, in excess of the return on a risk-free investment. The words *on average over the long-run* are important. If the investor were certain to earn a return in excess of the risk-free, the investment would not be risky. In that case, a risk premium would not be justified.

The CAPM states that the risk premium for a security equals the market risk premium times the security's risk as measured by beta. If the security has a beta of 1.0, then the risk premium for that security equals the market risk premium. (To see why the beta of the market portfolio must be 1.0, apply the CAPM to the market portfolio by substituting $r_i = r_m$ and $B_i = B_m$ into Equation (7–16).) If the security is high risk, meaning that its beta is greater than 1.0, then its risk premium exceeds the market risk premium. Low-risk securities with betas less than 1.0 command smaller than average risk premiums.

Some appraisers characterize the CAPM as simply a mathematical restatement of the old saw: To get a higher return, you must be willing to bear greater risk. This characterization is both unfair and misleading. It is possible to bear more risk and not receive higher expected returns if you fail to diversify. Returning to the Hunt brothers example, almost all the risk associated with holding silver futures contracts can be eliminated by diversification. Nonetheless, the Hunts chose not to diversify properly and instead plunged into silver. In the context of the CAPM, this unnecessary risk borne by those who fail to diversify properly is not

---

[14]For a review of early empirical tests of the CAPM, see E. F. Fama, *Foundations of Finance*, (New York: Basic Books, 1976). A more current review is contained in Fama, "Efficient Capital Markets: II," *Journal of Finance* 46 (December 1991); pp. 1025–75. It should be noted that the empirical validity of the CAPM remains the subject of active research. For instance, E. F. Fama and K. R. French, "The Cross-Section of Expected Stock Returns," *Journal of Finance* 46 (June 1992); pp. 427–65, question whether the CAPM accurately approximates the trade-off between risk and return in the capital market.

TABLE 7-4
Betas for Selected Common Stocks (1984–1989)

Stock	Beta
Exxon	0.57
AT&T	0.62
Bristol Myers Squibb	0.68
McDonald's	0.71
Capital Holding	0.81
Ford Motor Company	0.90
Digital Equipment	0.91
McGraw-Hill	1.21
Tandem Computer	1.52
S&P 500 Index	1.00

Note: The betas were provided by Merrill Lynch and appear in Richard Brealey and Stewart Myers, *Principles of Corporate Finance*, 4th ed. (New York: McGraw-Hill, 1991). The betas were calculated using five years of monthly return data and the S&P 500 Index as a proxy for the market portfolio.

rewarded with higher expected return. What is rewarded with higher expected return is bearing nondiversifiable risk. This insight is one of the two major contributions of the CAPM. The other is providing a quantitative measure of nondiversifiable (or systematic) risk—the security's beta. The CAPM not only states that bearing risk leads to greater return in the long run, it also says how to measure risk and provides a mathematical equation relating risk and expected return.

A security's beta can be thought of as analogous to a magnification factor. Securities with betas greater than 1.0 magnify market moves and, therefore, are riskier than investing in the market portfolio. Securities with betas less than 1.0 shrink market moves and, therefore, are less risky.

To provide perspective on the CAPM, Table 7–4 presents estimates of beta for some well-known common stocks. In the table, the beta for the S&P 500 index equals 1.0 because the S&P 500 is used as a proxy for the market portfolio. Notice that the betas of companies that produce staples such as food and oil products are much lower than the betas of companies that produce high-technology products such as computers. Because the demand for staples is relatively constant in both good and bad times, these securities are less sensitive to market conditions. High-technology companies, on the other hand, are very sensitive to the state of the economy. In addition, financial leverage affects beta. The more a company borrows, the greater its beta will be.

Applying the CAPM

From Equation (7–16), it is clear that three quantities are required to apply the CAPM: (1) the risk-free rate, (2) the security's beta, and (3) the risk premium on the market. Of the three quantities, the risk-free rate is observable, but there is a problem deciding which risk-free rate is appropriate. The security's beta and the risk premium on the market must both be estimated. As will be seen, there is a good deal of controversy regarding how each of these quantities should be estimated.

Choosing the risk-free rate. Though finance textbooks refer constantly to the risk-free rate on U.S. Treasury securities, there is no special risk-free rate. A look back at Table 7–1 reveals that there are over 100 U.S. Treasury securities with maturities ranging from 1 week to 30 years. Furthermore, while U.S. Treasury securities are free from default risk, they are still risky securities for investors whose planning horizon does not match the maturity of the security. For example, if an investor has a 1-year horizon, then investing in 30-year Treasury bonds is risky because the price of the bond at the end of the year is uncertain. Finally, even a zero coupon Treasury security with a maturity that matches the investor's horizon is risky in real terms because the purchasing power of the dollars the investor will receive at maturity are unknown. Thus, there is no unambiguous choice for the risk-free rate.

Given this dilemma, one possible criterion for selecting the risk-free rate is to determine which maturity is most consistent with the theoretical derivation of the CAPM. In its most general form, as derived by Robert Merton, the CAPM holds only moment to moment, so Merton's theory implies that a short-term risk-free rate should be used.[15] Unfortunately, the theory also assumes that there are no transaction costs, that all investors can borrow and lend at the risk-free rate, and that all investors have identical expectations and the same investment horizon. Because of these discrepancies between the assumptions of the model and the characteristics of actual capital markets, the choice of the risk-free rate should not be based on theoretical considerations alone.

The problem with using a short-term rate such as the one-month Treasury bill rate, is that it makes the cost of equity capital, and therefore the appraised value of the firm, unduly sensitive to fluctuations in short-term interest rates. Consider, for example, a firm that earns $120 per year in perpetuity. If the cost of capital is 12 percent, the value of the firm is $1,000. (The present value of an income stream of $C per year in perpetuity equals C/r, where r is the discount rate.) If the cost of capital declines to 10 percent because the risk-free rate falls 200 basis points, the value of the firm will jump 20 percent to $1,200. During the late 1970s and early 1980s, it was not uncommon for short-term interest rates to rise or fall 200 basis points in a week or two. Such fluctuations in short-term rates, however, were not accompanied by 20 percent swings in stock prices. This indicates that the interest rate investors use to calculate the cost of capital changes more slowly than the one-month Treasury bill rate, suggesting that a long-term Treasury rate may be a more appropriate choice.

To further investigate this issue, Figure 7–2 presents a graph of the yields on 1-month Treasury bills, 10-year Treasury bonds, and 30-year Treasury bonds over the period from January 1980 to December 1989. The figure reveals that in comparison with the plot for 1-month bill rates, the plots for 10-year bond yields and 30-year bond yields are relatively smooth. For instance, during the first half of 1980, the 1-month Treasury bill rate plummeted from 16 to 6.8 percent, a drop of 920 basis points. At the same time, the 10-year bond rate fell 280 basis points from 12.8 to 10 percent. The figure also reveals that there is virtually no difference between the yields on 10-year bonds and 30-year bonds

---

[15]R. Merton, "An Intertemporal Asset Pricing Model," *Econometrica* 41 (November 1973), pp. 867–87.

FIGURE 7-2
Yields on 1-month Treasury Bills, 10-Year Treasury Bonds, and 30-Year Treasury Bonds (1980–1989)

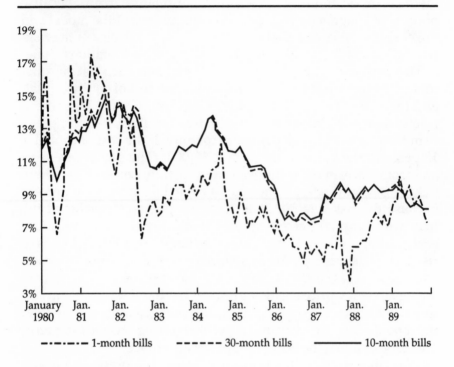

throughout the decade, despite large movements in the level of interest rates. Thus, for maturities greater than 10 years, the choice of the Treasury security used to estimate the long-term risk-free rate is largely irrelevant.

Using a short-term security to measure the risk-free rate also introduces an inconsistency into the appraisal process. The duration of short-term securities is a good deal less than the duration of the cash flows being discounted. Whereas 1-month Treasury bills have a duration of 1 month, the effective duration of common stock is on the order of 10 years or more, which is comparable to the duration of 30-year Treasury bonds.[16]

---

[16]Duration measures the average time an investment is outstanding. For zero coupon bonds such as Treasury bills, which provide only one payment at maturity, the du-

Some of the problems associated with using a short-term risk-free rate in the CAPM can be overcome by using a long-term Treasury rate instead. Long-term rates are less variable, and the duration of long-term bonds approximately matches the duration of the corporate cash flows that are being discounted. Therefore, the inflation forecast impounded in the long-term rate is comparable to the inflation forecast used when estimating corporate cash flows. The drawback is that the long-term Treasury bond rate includes a term premium that is not included in the CAPM.

This suggests that the best procedure is to use the expected long-run average of short-term Treasury bill rates. As noted earlier, this expected average can be calculated by starting with the long-term rate and netting out the term premium. More specifically, combining Equations (7–5a), (7–6), and (7–7) reveals that the long-term expected average of the short-term rate equals the long-term rate minus the term premium, or:

Expected long-run average   =   Yield on long-term, risk-free
of short-term, risk-free rate   bonds
                                    − Term premium

Using the procedure described previously, the term premium can be estimated and deducted from the yield on long-term Treasury bonds. For example, the expected average 1-month Treasury bill rate over the next 20 years can be estimated by subtracting 1.2 percent, the term premium estimated earlier, from the current true annualized yield on 20-year Treasury bonds.

Despite its theoretical appeal, the procedure of netting out the term premium is not widely employed in practice. It is more common to use a long-term Treasury bond (a maturity of between 10 and 30 years) to estimate the risk-free rate. However, this may be

---

ration equals maturity. For coupon paying bonds and dividend paying stocks, the duration is less than maturity because payments are made periodically prior to maturity. The duration of a 1-month Treasury bill is 1-month; the duration of a 10-year Treasury note with a 10 percent coupon and a 10 percent yield to maturity is 6.54 years; the duration of a 30-year Treasury bond with a 10 percent coupon and a 10 percent yield to maturity is 9.94 years; the duration of a stock that costs $100 and pays a fixed dividend of $10 into perpetuity is 10.50 years when the discount rate is 10 percent. For a detailed discussion of duration and derivations of the duration formulas, see Fabozzi and Fabozzi, *Bond Markets*.

due to the fact that most appraisers are unfamiliar with the literature on the term structure of interest rates. As understanding of the term structure becomes more widespread, the practice of netting out the term premium when applying the CAPM is likely to become more popular.

The risk premium on the market. The CAPM is a relative asset pricing model because it expresses the risk premium for an individual security in terms of the risk premium for the market, $E(r_m) - r_f$. The problem with relative models is that they answer one question by raising another. In the case of the CAPM, the added question is "What is the risk premium on the market?"

The market risk premium can be estimated by employing a variant of the averaging procedure that was developed to estimate the term premium. The estimate of the market risk premium equals the average difference between the return on a representative market index such as the S&P 500 and the return on the risk-free asset. When calculating the average, it is critical that the security used to measure the risk-free rate is also used to estimate the market risk premium. For example, if Treasury bills are chosen as the risk-free asset, the market risk premium should be estimated net of Treasury bill returns. If Treasury bonds are chosen as the risk-free asset, the market risk premium should be estimated net of Treasury bond returns.

Before an average can be calculated, the sample period must be determined. The longest period for which reliable stock price data are readily available is January 1926 to the present. But is it proper to average returns over the entire period? Stock returns were far more variable during the Great Depression than they are today, so perhaps the years from 1929 to 1939 should be excluded. Or perhaps periods during which the country was at war should be omitted.

The choice of the sample period would not be an issue if estimates of the market risk premium were similar over different periods of reasonable length, say 10 years or more. Unfortunately, this is not the case. Table 7–5 presents annual return data for the market risk premium calculated net of Treasury bill returns and long-term Treasury bond returns over the period from 1926 to 1989. The average market risk premium for each decade is also presented. (The decade of the 1920s contains only four years.)

The table clearly shows that estimates of the market risk premium are highly variable. On a year-to-year basis, they range from a low of −38 percent in 1931 to a high of 54 percent in 1933. (These figures refer to the market risk premium measured with respect to Treasury bond returns.) Even the 10-year averages vary markedly. The average risk premium was virtually zero in the 1930s but exceeded 20 percent in the 1950s.

Given the significant variation in the risk premium, altering the sample period when calculating the average is hazardous because it can greatly affect the estimate. To avoid data mining, a reasonable solution is to use the entire period from 1926 to the present, or as a substitute, the postwar period from 1945 to the present. Finer partitioning of the sample data, even if done with the best intentions, raises the specter of introducing bias.

The high variance of stock returns also raises a question regarding how the average premium is to be computed. To illustrate the issue, suppose that an investor earns returns of 10 percent, 20 percent, −25 percent, and 15 percent in four consecutive years. The familiar average, which is called the *arithmetic average* and which was presented in Table 7–5, is calculated by adding the four returns and dividing by four. The arithmetic average of the four returns is 5 percent, but this average has a curious deficiency: An investor who earns the arithmetic average each year makes more money than the investor who earns the sequence of annual returns used to compute the average. To illustrate, an investor who starts with $100 and earns 5 percent per year would have $121.55 after four years; however, an investor who earns 10 percent, then 20 percent, then −25 percent, and finally 15 percent—which averages to 5 percent—would have only $113.85 after four years.

The second average, called the *geometric average*, is designed to solve this problem. The geometric average return is the constant return an investor must earn every year to arrive at the same final value that would be produced by a sequence of variable returns. The geometric average is calculated using the formula:

Geometric average = (Final value/Initial value)$^{1/n}$ − 1

where n is the number of periods in the average. Applying the formula to the example:

Geometric average = $(113.85/100)^{1/4}$ − 1 = .0329, or 3.29%

TABLE 7–5
Average Risk Premiums on the Market

Year	Market Risk Premium over One-Month Treasury Bills	Market Risk Premium over Long-Term Treasury Bonds	Year	Market Risk Premium over One-month Treasury Bills	Market Risk Premium over Long-term Treasury Bonds
1926	8.34%	3.84%	1958	41.84%	49.48%
1927	34.35	28.54	1959	9.01	14.26
1928	40.38	43.53	1960	−2.21	−13.33
1929	−13.15	−11.83	1961	24.77	25.93
1930	−27.33	−29.55	1962	−11.45	−15.61
1931	−44.44	−38.03	1963	19.67	21.57
1932	−9.15	−25.04	1964	12.98	13.00
1933	53.67	54.04	1965	8.53	11.75
1934	−1.61	−11.45	1966	−14.80	−13.69
1935	47.52	42.66	1967	19.79	33.18
1936	33.73	26.42	1968	5.86	11.34
1937	−35.31	−35.24	1969	−15.06	−3.42
1938	31.18	25.63	1970	−2.49	−8.07
1939	−0.43	−6.37	1971	9.93	1.08
1940	−9.76	−15.87	1972	15.14	13.31
1941	−11.62	−12.51	1973	−21.60	−13.57
1942	20.05	17.11	1974	−34.47	−30.81
1943	25.56	23.84	1975	31.41	28.02
1944	19.40	16.91	1976	18.77	7.09
1945	36.09	25.68	1977	−12.31	−6.53
1946	−8.43	−7.98	1978	−0.63	7.75
1947	5.20	8.33	1979	8.04	19.63
1948	4.70	2.13	1980	21.15	36.37
1949	17.67	12.35	1981	−19.63	−6.77
1950	30.52	31.69	1982	10.88	−18.96
1951	22.53	27.96	1983	13.71	21.82
1952	16.70	17.19	1984	−3.51	−9.27
1953	−2.81	−4.61	1985	24.44	1.21
1954	51.76	45.44	1986	12.32	−5.98
1955	29.97	32.82	1987	−0.23	7.93
1956	4.09	12.14	1988	10.45	7.13
1957	−13.94	−18.26	1989	23.11	13.39

TABLE 7-5 (*continued*)

Average Premium over Treasury Bonds		Average Premium over Treasury Bills	
1920s	16.0%	1920s	17.5%
1930s	0.3	1930s	4.8
1940s	7.0	1940s	9.9
1950s	20.8	1950s	19.0
1960s	7.1	1960s	4.8
1970s	1.8	1970s	1.2
1980s	4.7	1980s	9.3
1926–1989	7.5	1926–1989	8.7

There are three properties of arithmetic and geometric averages that are worth noting. First, the geometric average is always less than or equal to the arithmetic average. (In the example, the geometric average is 3.29 percent compared to the arithmetic average of 5.0 percent). Second, the discrepancy between the arithmetic and the geometric average depends on the variability of the returns being averaged. The more variable the returns, the larger the discrepancy. Third, for a given sample period, the arithmetic average depends on the length of the observation interval, but the geometric average does not. The shorter the observation interval, the higher the arithmetic average. For instance, the arithmetic average of monthly S&P 500 returns over the period from 1926 to 1989 (calculated on an annualized basis) is higher than the arithmetic average of annual returns calculated over the same period.

Table 7–6 shows that with respect to the market risk premium, the difference between the arithmetic and the geometric average cannot be ignored. For the full period from 1926 to 1989, the arithmetic average return on the S&P 500 is 12.4 percent and the arithmetic average market risk premium (over long-term Treasury bonds) is 7.5 percent. In comparison, the geometric average return for the S&P 500 is 10.3 percent and the geometric average market risk premium is 5.3 percent. This difference in the market risk premium of 220 basis points translates into a 220 basis change in the cost of equity capital for firms with a beta of 1.0. Such a change will have a pronounced impact on the estimated value.

TABLE 7-6
Arithmetic and Geometric Average Returns

Historical Period	S&P 500 Return	Treasury Bill Return	Long-Term Treasury Bond Return	Market Risk Premium Net of Treasury Bills	Market Risk Premium Net of Treasury Bonds
Arithmetic Averages of Annual Returns					
Full period 1926–1989	12.39%	3.66%	4.88%	8.73%	7.51%
Prewar years 1926–1941	7.27%	1.25%	4.85%	6.02%	2.42%
Postwar years 1945–1963	16.22%	1.71%	2.16%	14.51%	14.06%
Modern period 1964–1989	11.63%	6.95%	7.13%	4.68%	4.50%
Geometric Averages of Annual Returns					
Full period 1926–1989	10.31%	3.60%	4.56%	6.53%	5.31%
Prewar years 1926–1941	2.99%	1.23%	4.73%	1.69%	–1.68%
Postwar years 1945–1963	13.01%	1.69%	1.47%	11.32%	11.53%
Modern period 1964–1989	9.79%	6.77%	6.42%	2.86%	2.78%

Which average should be used when calculating the market risk premium to be substituted into the capital asset pricing model? Because valuation is forward looking, the appropriate average is the one that most accurately approximates the expected future rate of return. As shown by Bodie, Kane, and Marcus, the best estimate of expected returns over a given future holding period is the arithmetic average of past returns over the same holding period.[17] For instance, if the valuation is based on annual cash flow forecasts, so that an annual discount rate is needed, then the market risk premium should be estimated by the arithmetic average of annual returns.

Some analysts feel that using a long-run average to estimate the risk premium is misleading because it gives insufficient weight to current conditions. Support for this view is provided by research by Fama and French, Lo and MacKinley, and Poterba and Summers indicating that expected returns on common stock, and therefore the market risk premium, vary over time.[18] There are two ways that variation in the risk premium can be taken into account. One approach is to build an explicit model of the market risk premium. Rather than simply averaging past values of the premium, a regression model is developed that relates the market risk premium to explanatory variables such as interest rates and dividend yields. Substituting current values of the explanatory variables into the regression model gives a predicted value for the current risk premium.

Unfortunately, there is not consensus, even among academic experts, regarding how these regression models should be specified or estimated. Furthermore, a poorly specified or improperly estimated model can produce a highly misleading risk premium.

---

[17]Z. Bodie, A. Kane, and A. J. Marcus, *Investments* (Homewood, Ill.: Richard D. Irwin, 1989).

[18]E. F. Fama and K. French, "Dividend Yields and Expected Stock Returns," *Journal of Financial Economics* 5 (November 1988), pp. 3–25; Fama and French, "Business Conditions and Expected Returns on Stocks and Bonds," *Journal of Financial Economics* 25 (November 1989), pp. 23–49; A. Lo and C. MacKinley, "Stock Market Prices Do Not Follow Random Walks: Evidence from a Simple Specification Test," *Review of Financial Studies*, Spring 1988, pp. 41–66; and J. Poterba and L. Summers, "Mean Reversion in Stock Prices: Evidence and Implications," *Journal of Financial Economics*, October 1988, pp. 27–59.

Given this uncertain state of affairs, appraisers who choose to develop their own models should do so with a good deal of caution. Of course, there is also the option of relying on models derived by others. Most major investment firms have developed models to estimate the market risk premium. If the appraiser has access to one of these models, it can be used to calculate the risk premium. However, it is dangerous for an appraiser to rely on the predictions of a model developed by someone else without first verifying its accuracy.

An alternative approach is to dispense with historical data and to rely on the dividend growth model. Due to diversification, dividends for market indexes such as the S&P 500 can be forecast more accurately than dividends for individual companies. In addition, many investment banks and brokerage houses make available their forecasts of future dividend growth rates for the S&P 500. For instance, at the end of 1990, Kidder Peabody Equity Research reported that the dividend yield on the S&P 500 was 3.7 percent and estimated that the dividends would grow at 8.75 percent over the long run. Substituting these numbers into the constant growth model, as given by Equation (7–15), produces an expected return on the market of 12.45 percent. Subtracting the true annualized yield on long-term Treasury bonds, which was 8.5 percent at the time, gives a market risk premium of 3.95 percent. Notice that this estimate is 355 basis points less than the historical average risk premium of 7.51 percent reported in Table 7–6. Such a discrepancy is not uncommon. In recent years, application of the dividend discount model has routinely yielded lower estimates of the market risk premium than the long-run historical average.

The discrepancy between the two approaches raises the difficult question of which should be selected. At this juncture, there is no clear answer. The dividend discount approach has the advantage that it is not based on the assumption that the market risk premium is constant. In light of the changes in the American economy and in American capital markets that have occurred in the last 65 years, this is a marked benefit. The drawback is that it is based on forecasts of future dividends. Consequently, the estimate of the premium depends on whose forecasts are selected. For this reason, suspicions may arise that a certain forecast was selected because it led to an estimate of the market risk premium supporting a conclusion that the appraiser had an incentive to draw. At a minimum, appraisers who choose to rely on the dividend discount approach should explain why they believe it produces a reasonable estimate of the market risk premium, particularly if that estimate is markedly different than long-run historical averages.

Estimating beta. A security's beta, the CAPM measure of nondiversifiable risk, is estimated by the slope coefficient in a regression of the security's return on the market return. Regression analysis is a statistical technique that fits a line to a series of points by minimizing the squared distances of the points from the line. In the case of the CAPM, the points are generated by pairs of returns: the excess return on the stock and the excess return on the market. The regression equation takes the following form:

$$r_{i,t} - r_{f,t} = B_i \cdot (r_{m,t} - r_{f,t}) + u_t \qquad (7\text{--}17)$$

where:

$r_{i,t}$ = Return on security i during period t
$r_{f,t}$ = Risk-free rate during period t
$r_{m,t}$ = Return on the market during period t
B_i = Beta coefficient to be estimated
u_t = Random error term

It is worth noting that $r_{f,t}$ is frequently omitted when estimating beta. This has virtually no impact on the results since variation in all possible measures of the risk-free rate is small compared to variation in equity returns.

If the appraisal target's equity is publicly traded, the appraiser has two choices for developing an estimate of beta. The first is to rely on published estimates. Betas are now available from a wide variety of sources. For instance, the *Value Line Investment Survey* reports beta estimates updated quarterly, and Merrill Lynch publishes a monthly *Security Risk Evaluation Report* that includes estimates of beta. Investment consulting firms such as Wilshire Associates and BARRA provide detailed information on betas for over 7,000 companies.

It is also possible to estimate beta directly, using regression analysis to calculate the relation between the return on the stock and the return on the market, as shown in Equation (7–17). Because modern computer spreadsheets such as Excel and 1-2-3 include macros for estimating regressions, beta can be estimated within a spreadsheet that contains the necessary stock return data.

Whether beta is estimated directly or the appraiser relies on commercial estimates of beta, there are five factors that affect the final result. If appraisers rely on commercial betas, they should be aware how the service providing the beta dealt with each of the factors. If appraisers choose to estimate beta directly, a decision must be made as to how each of the factors will be handled. The five factors that affect the estimate of beta are as follows:

- *The choice of the proxy for the market portfolio.* There is a wide variety of indexes that are used to measure the return on the market. Among them are the S&P 500, the Wilshire 5000, and the Center for Research in Security Prices (CRSP) value-weighted index. In most cases, the estimated beta is not particularly sensitive to the choice of the market index. However, the appraiser should be sure to select a widely diversified index that fairly reflects movements in the overall market. On this score, the Dow Jones 30 is a poor choice and is rarely used.

- *The observation interval.* The returns that go into the regression equation can be calculated over daily, weekly, or monthly intervals.

- *The sample period.* The length of the sample period is related to the observation interval. When daily observations are employed, the sample period can be as short as six months. When monthly observations are employed, the sample period must be at least two to three years in length. For example, Merrill Lynch uses five years of monthly returns and *Value Line* uses 260 weeks of weekly returns to estimate beta.

- *The estimation procedure.* The standard estimation procedure is ordinary least squares. However, when daily data are used, more complex adjustments may be required if the stock is thinly traded. For thinly traded stocks, Scholes-Williams estimators or Dimson estimators, which adjust for problems caused by thin trading, are often employed.[19]

---

[19]M. Scholes and J. Williams, "Estimating Betas from Non-Synchronous Data," *Journal of Financial Economics* 5 (December 1977) pp. 309–78.

• *The shrinkage factor.* No matter what procedure is used, beta is always estimated with error. Some analysts attempt to correct for this measurement error by shrinking the estimated beta toward 1.0, the average beta for all companies, or toward the industry average.[20]

Although a detailed discussion of how these five factors affect the estimation of beta is beyond the scope of this book, there are trade-offs caused by measurement error that are important to note. First, assuming that the true underlying beta remains constant, it can be estimated more accurately by using longer observation intervals and a long sample period such as the five years of monthly data employed by Merrill Lynch. The problem is that for some companies, particularly those in rapidly evolving industries such as computers and biotechnology, beta is unlikely to remain constant for five years. Thus, it is advisable to choose a shorter observation interval and a shorter sample period.

Second, the accuracy with which a company's beta is estimated may be improved by incorporating data for comparable companies. By calculating beta for other firms in the target's industry and then calculating a weighted average of the target's estimated beta and the industry average, measurement error can be reduced. In some cases, the market average rather than the industry average is used to calculate the final weighted average value of beta. For example, Merrill Lynch reports adjusted betas that equal two thirds times the estimated beta plus one third times the market beta of 1.0. It should be noted that one tricky issue in this context is selecting the weights. That decision depends on how confident the appraiser is in his or her estimate. The greater the confidence, the higher weight the estimate should be given.

Estimating betas for privately held companies. For privately held companies, the appraiser has no choice but to rely on betas estimated for comparable companies. When doing so, account must be taken of possible variation in capital structure. Because a firm's beta depends on its leverage, comparable firms

---

[20]M. E. Blume, "Betas and Their Regression Tendencies," *Journal of Finance* 3 (June 1975), pp. 785–96.

with different capital structures will have different betas. The basic formula relating the beta of a levered company with preferred stock and debt outstanding to an identical company that is all equity financed is given in the following equation:

$$B_{levered} = [1 + \text{Preferred/Equity}$$
$$+ (1 - T_c) \cdot \text{Debt/Equity}] \cdot B_{unlevered} \qquad (7\text{--}18)$$

In Equation (7–18), preferred/equity and debt/equity refer to the market value ratios of preferred stock to equity and debt to equity, and T_c is the corporate tax rate.

Based on Equation (7–18), the procedure for estimating the beta for a privately held company involves three steps. First, betas are estimated for a group of comparable companies. These betas, whether taken from published sources or estimated using regression analysis, are levered betas because they are derived from stock returns of the comparable companies. Second, the levered betas are converted to unlevered betas using equation (7–18) and data on the capital structures of the comparable firms. (The unlevered beta is the beta a firm would have if it were financed exclusively with equity. Unlevered betas are also referred to as asset betas because they measure the raw beta of a company's assets without the influence of financial leverage.) Assuming that the appraisal target and the comparable firms are truly comparable, the unlevered beta for the target company should be approximately equal to the average unlevered beta for the comparable firms. Third, Equation (7–18) is applied to convert the average unlevered beta for the comparable firms to a levered beta using the target's capital structure. This levered beta is then utilized to estimate the cost of equity capital for the target firm.

THE ARBITRAGE PRICING MODEL

The CAPM is not the only asset pricing model that is available to estimate the cost of equity capital. The most widely discussed alternative, at least in the academic literature, is the arbitrage pricing model, or APM. Although the APM has been the subject of intense academic research, it has yet to gain a significant following among practitioners. For this reason, only a sketch of the APM is provided here.

The APM is similar to the CAPM in that it is based on the idea that investors are rewarded for bearing systematic risk but not firm-specific risk. In the APM, however, systematic risk is identified not with the market but with a set of underlying economic factors. These economic factors represent the systematic economic forces that affect stock prices generally. Because the impact of these factors is economywide, the risk associated with each factor is systematic and cannot be eliminated by diversification.

Unfortunately, the APM does not identify the factors, it only posits their existence. It is left to empirical analysis to discern the identity of the factors. As a result, there is some disagreement regarding the choice of factors. A widely cited paper by Chen, Roll, and Ross identifies five factors: the monthly growth in industrial production, the change in expected inflation, the unanticipated inflation, the unanticipated change in the risk premium between risky bonds and Treasury bonds, and the unanticipated change in the yield spread between short-term Treasury bills and long-term Treasury bonds.[21] While these factors have been used in a number of studies of the APM, they are not universally accepted.

The equilibrium pricing relation that emerges from the APM is similar to the CAPM. A security's risk with respect to each factor is measured by the security's beta with respect to that factor. The expected return on a security equals its beta for each factor multiplied by the risk premium associated with that factor summed over all the factors, as shown in Equation (7–19) for a three-factor model:

$$E(r_i) - r_f = B_1 \cdot [E(f_1) - r_f]$$
$$+ B_2 \cdot [E(f_2) - r_f] + B_3 \cdot [E(f_3) - r_f] \qquad (7\text{–}19)$$

Two complications make the APM controversial and difficult to apply. First, as noted above, the factors are not theoretically identified and must be chosen on the basis of economic judgment and empirical analysis. This is an important practical issue because

[21]N. Chen, R. Roll, and S. A. Ross, "Economic Forces and the Stock Market," *Journal of Business* 59 (July 1986); pp. 383–404.

changing the factors will affect the estimated cost of capital. Second, the introduction of several factors multiplies the estimation problems. Betas and risk premiums must be estimated for several factors rather than for just the market portfolio. Furthermore, to estimate the factor risk premiums, it is first necessary to identify a set of "mimicking" portfolios whose returns are sensitive to only one factor. The risk premium associated with a specific factor is equal to the average return on that factor's mimicking portfolio net of the risk-free rate.

These complications have impeded widespread adoption of the APM in appraisal practice. Appraisers are apparently uncomfortable relying on a model that requires the application of sophisticated statistical procedures to a set of unidentified factors. In situations where the dividend discount model cannot be employed, the CAPM is generally the model of choice.

ESTIMATING THE CAPITAL STRUCTURE WEIGHTS

Given the costs of each type of financing, the last step in calculating the WACC is to estimate the weights w_d, w_p, and w_s that define the firm's capital structure. The appropriate weights to use are the firm's *long-run target weights stated in terms of market value*. These long-run target weights may differ from current market value weights. For instance, following a major debt issue, a company is likely to have a greater fraction of debt in its capital structure than it plans to maintain in the long run. Similarly, following a stock market crash, the equity weight may fall below a firm's long-run target. In addition, the target market value weights should not be confused with book value weights. In some situations, book value weights may approximate target market value weights, but this is not generally the case.

One simple and popular procedure for estimating the target weights is to assume that they equal the company's current market value weights. Unfortunately, this assumption involves a circularity. In most cases, a company is being appraised because the market value of its securities is unknown and, therefore, cannot be used to calculate the weights. If the market values are known, the firm can be appraised directly by applying the stock and debt approach without calculating the WACC. The circularity can be overcome in the case of debt and preferred stock by directly estimating the value of these securities, as described in Chapter 4. However, common stock is still a problem. The estimated value of the equity depends on the WACC, which, in turn, depends on the value of the equity.

In light of the circularity, an iterative procedure must be employed to solve simultaneously for the value of the equity and for the WACC. The iterative process begins with the selection of an initial estimate for the market value of the equity; the book value of the equity is a reasonable choice. Based on this initial estimate, the WACC is calculated. Using this WACC, the value of the firm is computed by discounting the forecast cash flows to present value. Subtracting the value of the debt and preferred stock produces a revised estimate of the value of the equity and a revised equity weight. This revised estimate is then used to calculate a new initial estimate of the equity weight. A workable procedure is to set the new equity weight to the original weight plus one half the difference between the revised weight and the original weight. Mathematically:

New weight = Original weight
         + .5 (Revised weight − Original weight)

Given the new weight, the WACC, the value of the firm, and the revised value of the equity are recalculated. The process is repeated until the change in the estimated value of the equity is less than some specified amount such as $1. At that point, the calculation terminates and the final iteration determines the WACC, the value of the firm, and the value of the equity.

It is also possible to avoid the circularity by estimating the long-run target weights directly. For example, the appraiser may assume that all the comparable firms have the same target capital structures. Given this assumption, the best estimate of the target capital structure is the average capital structure across the comparable firms. If the comparable firms are publicly traded, their market value weights can be calculated directly and averaged.

Alternatively, it is possible to ask management what its target capital structure is and use the indicated weights. Presumably, management should know the weights because it is management's job to determine them. This direct approach has two deficiencies. First, in some firms, managers may be responding to short-run financial problems rather than trying to determine the company's long-run financing mix. Second, managers have an incentive to provide financing weights to push the appraised value in the direction favored by management, so the weights provided may be biased. Consequently, the appraiser must take steps to assure him- or herself that the weights are provided in good faith.

Once the target weights have been estimated, they must be compared with the current market value weights. A comparison is required because financing costs are estimated under the *current* capital structure. If the appraiser concludes that the current capital structure and the target capital structure differ markedly, financing costs will have to be reestimated using the target capital structure. This is likely to be a difficult task because it involves hypothetical questions such as what would the borrowing cost be if the firm doubled its debt outstanding. Fortunately, this question rarely arises in practice. However, there are situations such as major restructurings where it becomes relevant. The appraiser is well advised to check for this possibility before estimating the WACC, in order to avoid unnecessary duplicative work.

CALCULATING THE COST OF CAPITAL FOR FORMS ENGINEERING

Forms Engineering is financed by a combination of bank debt, preferred stock, and common equity. To estimate FEC's WACC, costs and target weights must be estimated for each of these financing resources.

Interest on FEC's bank debt is charged at a rate of prime plus .5 percent. As of June 30, 1989, the prime rate was 11.07 percent, so that FEC's borrowing cost for the month of July 1989 would be 11.57 percent. In the months following July, the borrowing cost is unknown because it will fluctuate with changes in the prime rate. (Remember the valuation analysis is conducted as of July 1, 1989, using only information that was available at that time.) For this reason, the best estimate of FEC's cost of debt is the average prime rate over the long run plus 50 basis points. The procedure described earlier in the chapter is used to estimate the long-run average prime rate. On July 1, 1989, the true annualized yield on a 10-year Treasury bond was 8.27 percent. Subtracting a 1.2 percent term premium gives an expected long-run average one-month Treasury bill rate of 7.07 percent. Adding a 2.2 percent risk premium gives an expected long-run average prime rate of 9.27 percent. Finally, adding FEC's margin of 50 basis points, the cost of debt comes to 9.77 percent. Applying the assumed 40 percent tax rate, FEC's after-tax cost of debt is 5.86 percent.

The cost of FEC's preferred stock is difficult to estimate because the stock was issued to the founder as part of an estate planning program and has peculiar properties. Because those estate planning features are unique to FEC and are not commonly seen, they are not analyzed here. Instead, it is assumed that FEC's cost of preferred stock is equal to the before-tax cost of debt, and a rate of 9.77 percent is chosen.

The cost of equity capital for FEC is estimated by indirect application of the CAPM. Direct application is impossible because FEC's shares are not publicly traded. The calculation of beta for FEC, which is presented in Table 7–7, involves three steps. First, betas for the seven publicly traded comparable companies (American Business Products, Duplex Products, Ennis Business Forms, Moore Corporation, Reynolds and Reynolds Company, Standard Register, and Wallace Computer Services) are collected from *Value Line*. Second, these levered betas are converted to unlevered betas using Equation (7–18). When computing unlevered betas, a tax rate of 40 percent is assumed. The capital structure information necessary to calculate unlevered betas is also from *Value Line* and is shown in the second column of Table 7–7. Because none of the comparable companies have preferred stock outstanding, only the debt/equity ratio is reported. At the bottom of the final column, the average unlevered beta for the comparable companies of 0.86 is reported. Finally, data on FEC's capital structure, presented in the lower half of the table, are used to calculate FEC's levered beta. Because the market value of FEC's equity is much larger than its book value, the book value weights are inappropriate for calculating FEC's debt/equity and preferred/equity ratios. Unfortunately, market value weights are not available because the market value of FEC's equity is yet to be determined. Therefore, the beta calculation is based on management's estimates of the long-run target weights. As shown in the table, management expects the ratio of debt to equity to be about 0.25 in the long run, while the ratio of preferred stock to equity is expected to be about 0.12. These ratios translate into capital structure weights of approximately 73 percent equity, 18 percent debt, and 9 percent preferred. Based on these capital structure weights, Equation (7–18) implies that the levered beta for FEC is 1.10.

To apply the CAPM to calculate the cost of capital, it is also necessary to select a risk-free rate and to estimate the associated risk premium on the market. Because of its popularity in appraisal practice, the 10-year Treasury bond rate is chosen as a proxy for the risk-free rate. As of July 1, 1989, the effective annual yield on 10-year Treasury bonds was 8.27 percent. The market risk premium is assumed to equal its historical average of 7.5 percent measured with respect to long-term Treasury bonds. It is worth noting that this estimate is significantly higher than the premium calculated using the discounted cash flow approach applied to the S&P 500 in July 1989. At that time, the dividend yield on the S&P 500 was 4.1 percent, and a major investment house was forecasting a 9.2 percent rate of growth in dividends. Applying the constant growth model to these numbers gives an expected return on the market of 13.3 percent. In light of the 8.27 percent Treasury bond return, the implied risk premium on the market is only 5.03 percent, compared to the 7.5 percent premium employed here. On this score, the appraisal can be seen as producing a conservative value for FEC because using a lower risk premium would reduce the cost of equity capital and, thereby, increased the appraised value of FEC.

Substituting a beta of 1.10, a risk-free rate of 8.27 percent, and a market risk premium of 7.5 percent into the CAPM gives:

Cost of equity for FEC = 8.27% + 1.10 · 7.5% = 16.52%

Table 7–8 puts all the pieces together and calculates FEC's weighted average cost of capital using the target financing

TABLE 7-7
Calculating Beta for Forms Engineering

Comparable Firm Name	Debt to Equity Ratio	Tax Rate	Levered Beta	Unlevered Beta*
American Business Products	0.11	0.40	0.75	0.70
Duplex Products	0.19	0.40	0.85	0.76
Ennis Business Forms	0.12	0.40	1.00	0.93
Moore Corporation	0.08	0.40	0.90	0.86
Reynolds and Reynolds Co.	0.52	0.40	1.20	0.92
Standard Register Company	0.22	0.40	1.10	0.97
Wallace Computer Services	0.11	0.40	0.95	0.89
Average				0.86

Forms Engineering:

Book debt	$2,350,075
Book preferred	$1,055,580
Book equity	$2,773,000
Book D/E	0.85
Book P/E	0.38
Target D/E	0.25
Target P/E	0.12
t (tax rate)	40.0%

Calculating Forms Engineering beta from Equation (7–18)

Levered FEC beta = [1 + (Target P/E) + (1 − t)(Target D/E)] · (Unlevered average beta for industry) = *1.10*

*From Equation (7–18).

weights chosen by management. Notice that the target weight of equity is significantly greater than the book value weight. This reflects management's realization that the market value of equity is much greater than the book value. As shown in the table, the estimated WACC calculated using the target value weights is 13.98 percent.

It is possible that using target capital structure weights at this stage may introduce an inconsistency. Once the appraisal has been completed, the target weights used to estimate beta should be compared with weights calculated using appraised market values. If the two sets of weights differ significantly, the appraisal is

TABLE 7-8
Weighted Average Cost of Capital for FEC (July 1, 1989)

Debt			Notes to Calculations:
FEC short-term borrowing rate:			Prime + .5 percent.
Long-term T-bond as of July 1, 1989		8.27%	Annualized yield on a 10-year Treasury bond with a YTM of 8.1%.
Term premium		1.20%	Table 7-5. Difference between long-term bond average return and the Treasury bill average return (1926–1989).
Risk premium		2.20%	Difference between average one-month prime return over average one-month T-bill return (1948–1989).
Long-run average prime		9.27%	The long-term bond, 8.27% minus the term premium, added to the risk premium.
Before-tax cost of debt		9.77%	The long-run average prime rate plus .5 percentage point.
Aftertax cost of debt		5.86%	The before tax cost of debt: (1 − tax rate).
Preferred			
Cost of preferred equity		9.77%	Assumed to equal the before-tax cost of debt.

Equity

Historical market risk premium	7.50%		Table 7–6. Annual market return net of annual Treasury bond return (1926–1989).
Long-term T-bond yield	8.27%		Annualized yield on a 10-year Treasury bond. Table 7–7.
FEC leveraged beta	1.10		
Cost of equity capital	16.52%		Using the CAPM, which states: Cost of equity capital = Risk-free rate + beta · (Historical market risk premium).
Tax rate	40.00%		Estimated.

		Book Weight	*Target Weights*	*Iteration Weights**
WAAC				
Book debt	$2,350,075	38.04%	18.25%	15.87%
Book preferred	1,055,580	17.08%	8.76%	7.13%
Book equity	2,773,000	44.88%	72.99%	77.00%
Total book value	$6,178,655			
	WACC	11.31%	13.98%	14.35%

*Column results from Table 7-9c.

internally inconsistent. In such circumstances, the appraiser must go back and recompute beta using a revised set of target weights that are closer to the weights derived from the appraisal. This process is then repeated until the target weights and the weights calculated from the appraised values are approximately equal.

The final step is to discount the expected cash flows and the terminal value derived in Chapters 5 and 6 to present value. Rather than relying on the target capital structure weights again, an iterative procedure is used that takes into account the interrelation between the market value of the firm and the WACC. Because the value of the debt and the value of the preferred are assumed to be equal to their book values, the interrelation involves the WACC and the market value of the equity. A change in the WACC affects the market value of the equity, which alters the equity weight and thereby affects the WACC.

The iteration proceeds as follows. First, the market value of FEC's equity is initially set equal to its book value, and the capital structure weights are computed. (This starting point is arbitrary. As long as the iteration converges, any reasonable starting point can be selected.) Second, given the capital structure weights, the WACC is calculated and used to discount the forecast cash flows to present value. Third, the market value of the firm calculated from the discounting process is used to compute a revised value of the equity by subtracting the value of the debt and preferred stock. Based on this revised value, the initial assumption for the value of the equity is set equal to the original equity value plus one half of the difference between the original value and the revised value, and the program is rerun. This procedure is repeated until the change in the market value of the equity is less than $1.

The results of the iterative program are presented in Table 7–9. The table has three parts. Table 7–9a shows the initial conditions based on book value. Table 7–9b shows how the value and the WACC change after one iteration. For Table 7–9c, the iterative program takes the continuing value of $30 million, which was derived in Chapter 6, as given.

By the time the iteration is complete in Table 7–9c, the market value of FEC's equity has grown to $11.4 million, approximately $8.6 million greater than its book value of $2.8 million. The total value of the firm is $14.8 million, including debt of $2.3 million and preferred of $1.1 million.

The final WACC produced by the iteration is 14.35 percent, based on final capital structure weights of approximately 77 percent equity, 16 percent debt, and 7 percent preferred. These weights are close to the target value weights, and the final WACC is close to the WACC of 13.98 percent calculated using the target weights. Because the two sets of weights and the two WACC are approximately equal, there is no need to go back and recompute beta. Consequently, the final DCF value indicator for FEC is $14.8 million, and the final cost of capital is 14.35 percent.

CONCLUDING OBSERVATIONS

Given the complexity involved in estimating the cost of capital, it may appear that there would be wide variation in DCF appraisals due to divergent estimates of the WACC. Surprisingly, this is rarely the case. Differences in the appraised value due to divergent estimates of the WACC are typically small compared to variation in appraised values attributable to disparate cash flow forecasts.

There are several forces that keep estimates of the WACC from differing too much. First, estimates of the cost of debt are directly tied to observable market yields on the debt issued by the target company or on debt with a rating equivalent to the target company's debt. Second, estimates of the cost of preferred stock are typically based on observed yields for the target company or for companies that issue preferred stock of comparable risk. Third, the cost of equity capital also depends on market data, though not as directly. If the CAPM is employed, the cost of capital is tied to the risk-free rate (which depends on Treasury yield data), the market risk premium (which depends on historical return data), and the beta (which is estimated from market data). The dividend discount approach depends on the current market price of the security and the current dividend payout, although expectations of future dividend growth are not based on observable data. Finally, the capital structure weights depend on the financing weights employed by the target company and by comparable firms in the target's industry.

To illustrate how these factors constrain estimates of the cost of capital, suppose that two appraisers were asked to estimate the

TABLE 7-9a
The Discounted Cash Flow Value of FEC (Initial Conditions)

Initial Value	Amount	After-Tax Cost of Capital	Weight		Formula
Book (market) debt	$2,350,075	5.86%	38.04%	=	Book debt/Sum of debt, preferred, and market equity
Book (market) preferred	$1,055,580	9.77%	17.08%	=	Book preferred/Sum of debt, preferred, and market equity
Book equity	$2,773,000	16.52%	44.88%	=	Book equity/Sum of debt, preferred, and market equity
Market equity (initial)	$2,773,000		44.88%	=	Market equity/Sum of debt, preferred, and market equity
DCF equity value (final)	$14,515,655		Step 3 →	=	NPV cash flows less debt, less preferred
DCF firm value (final)	$17,921,310			=	Market equity (final) plus debt, plus preferred
WACC	11.31%				
Net present value of cash flows	$17,921,310				

(From Table 7-8.) — After-Tax Cost of Capital

Step 1 (Book equity / Market equity)
Step 2 (WACC / Net present value of cash flows)

	1990	1991	1992	1993	1994	1995	1996 Continuing Value
Cash flows	$1,206,570	$(1,882,858)	$1,634,772	$1,801,811	$1,999,643	$1,823,746	$2,416,952 $30,000,000

Procedure

Step 1: Set the market value (initial) of the equity equal to its book value.

Step 2: Use the initial WACC calculated (from Table 7–8) to discount the cash flow stream.

Step 3: In the cell entitled Market equity (final), calculate the estimated market equity value by taking the net present value of the cash flows and terminal value and subtracting the book debt value and the book preferred value.

TABLE 7-9b
The Discounted Cash Flow Value of FEC (after One Iteration)

Initial Value	Amount	After-Tax Cost of Capital	Weight	Formula
Book (market) debt	$ 2,350,075	5.86%	19.50%	= Book debt/Sum of debt, preferred, and market equity
Book (market) preferred	$ 1,055,580	9.77%	8.76%	= Book preferred/Sum of debt, preferred, and market equity
Book equity	$ 2,773,000	16.52%	44.88%	= Book equity/Sum of debt, preferred, and market equity
Market equity (initial) Step 4 →	$ 8,644,327	After one iteration.	71.74%	= Market equity/Sum of debt, preferred, and market equity
DCF equity value (final)	$11,867,521			= NPV cash flows less debt, less preferred
DCF firm value (final)	$15,273,167			= Market equity (final) plus debt, plus preferred
WACC	13.85%			
Net present value of cash flows	$15,273,847			

	1990	1991	1992	1993	1994	1995	1996	Continuing Value
Cash flows	$1,206,570	$(1,882,858)	$1,634,772	$1,801,811	$1,999,643	$1,823,746	$2,416,952	$30,000,000

Step 4: Keep replacing the market equity (initial) value with the newly calculated market equity (final) value until the difference between the two is less than $1. Notice how the WACC changes as a result of the changing equity weight.

TABLE 7–9c
The Discounted Cash Flow Value of FEC (after all iterations)

Initial Value	Amount	After-Tax Cost of Capital	Weight	Formula
Book (market) debt	$ 2,350,075	5.86%	15.87%	= Book debt / Sum of debt, preferred, and market equity
Book (market) preferred	$ 1,055,580	9.77%	7.13%	= Book preferred / Sum of debt, preferred, and market equity
Book equity	$ 2,773,000	16.52%	44.88%	= Book equity / Sum of debt, preferred, and market equity
Market equity (initial) [Final iteration →] $11,404,667			77.00%	= Market equity / Sum of debt, preferred and market equity
DCF equity value (final)	$11,404,667			= NPV cash flows less debt, less preferred
DCF firm value (final)	$14,810,322			= Market equity (final) plus debt, plus preferred
WACC	14.35%			
Net present value of cash flows	$14,810,322			

	1990	1991	1992	1993	1994	1995	1996	Continuing Value
Cash flows	$1,206,570	$(1,882,858)	$1,634,772	$1,801,811	$1,999,643	$1,823,746	$2,416,952	$30,000,000

Final iteration: Once the difference between the market equity (initial) value and the market equity (final) value is less than $1 and close to (or at) zero, the new estimate of the market equity is determined and the new resulting weight of this component on the company's cost of capital structure is obtained. This results in a new WACC.

cost of capital for Burlington Northern Railroad as of January 1, 1989. One appraiser (Mr. Low) is interested in choosing a low cost of capital to maximize appraised value, while the other (Mr. High) prefers a high cost of capital and a low value. Therefore, the range of their estimates should span reasonable estimates of the cost of capital for Burlington Northern Railroad, BNRR.

As of January 1, 1989, BNRR was financed with 36 percent debt and 64 percent equity measured in terms of market value. Recognizing that the cost of equity is greater than the cost of debt, Mr. High argues that BNRR's current capital structure weights are misleading because of a restructuring that occurred in 1988. He claims that long-run weights are 30 percent debt and 70 percent equity, the capital structure observed for selected comparable companies. Mr. Low, on the other hand, feels that BNRR's weights are appropriate.

BNRR's debt consists almost exclusively of corporate debentures and mortgage bonds issued to finance railroad equipment. Mr. High estimates the cost of debt to be 10.07 percent pre tax and 6.04 percent after tax based on the average ratings for Moody's Aa and Baa railroad bonds for January 1, 1989. Mr. Low, on the other hand, argues that investors do not expect to earn 10.07 percent because there is a chance of default. To adjust for this possibility, he deducts 25 basis points and concludes that the cost of debt is 9.82 percent pre tax and 5.89 percent after tax.

Both Mr. High and Mr. Low decide to use the CAPM to estimate the cost of capital. However, Mr. Low uses the 90-day Treasury bill rate of 8.49 percent to measure the risk-free rate, while Mr. High uses the long-term Treasury bond rate of 9.09 percent. Based on application of the dividend discount model, Mr. Low estimates the risk premium on the market to be 5.0 percent (measured relative to the Treasury bill rate). Mr. High assumes that the risk premium on the market equals its long-run historical average of 7.5 percent (measured relative to the Treasury bond rate). Finally, Mr. Low assumes that the beta of BNRR is 0.70, near the bottom of the range for railroads, while Mr. High uses a beta of 1.30, at the top of the range for railroads. Applying the CAPM, Mr. Low's estimate of the cost of equity capital comes to 11.93 percent, while Mr. High's comes to 18.84 percent.

Putting the pieces together, Mr. Low's estimate of the WACC, using his capital structure weights, is 9.76 percent. Mr. High, on the other hand, estimates the cost of capital to be 15.00 percent.

In practice, the range of WACC estimates is likely to be a good deal smaller than the range between Mr. Low and Mr. High. When BNRR was appraised for state tax purposes in 1989, a railroad appraiser (the equivalent of Mr. High) selected a WACC of 14.00 percent and a state appraiser (Mr. Low) used a rate of 12.00 percent. Of course, the range might have been wider if the company being appraised were a privately held software firm for which direct market data were not available. But even in that case, the combination of market data on comparable companies and the growing acceptance of the same basic theories among appraisers causes estimates of the cost of capital to converge.

In short, developments in finance theory and the increasingly widespread availability of market data are narrowing discrepancies in estimates of the cost of capital. Consequently, large differences in DCF appraisals can most often be traced to variation in the forecasts of future cash flow. Unlike the discount rate, which is derived by applying financial economic models to market data, forecasts of future cash flow depend on the appraiser's assessment of the future viability of the appraisal target and the demand for its product. Needless to say, opinions on the future success of a business can vary widely, particularly if the company has no track record. As the instant printing example presented in Chapter 5 illustrates, appraisals can vary by a factor of 10 or more due to divergent estimates of future cash flow.

Chapter Eight

Evaluating and Adjusting the Estimate of Value

The previous chapters have discussed a variety of approaches for estimating the value of a firm. Each of these approaches is likely to produce a different value indicator. The appraiser must determine, therefore, how the individual value indicators are to be aggregated into a final appraisal. Before the value indicators can be aggregated, however, there are two issues that must be considered. First, the appraiser must decide whether to adjust the individual value indicators to reflect a control premium or a minority discount. Second, the appraiser must determine whether a "marketability" adjustment is required.

This chapter begins with a discussion of the control premium or, viewed from the flip side, the minority discount. The next issue that is taken up is whether a discount should be applied if a company's securities are not readily marketable. It is possible that the two issues are interrelated. Such a relation would exist, for example, if investors were willing to accept a smaller discount on nonmarketable securities if they had control of the company. To date, however, the empirical studies of control premiums and marketability discounts have been conducted separately. Reliable information is not available about the relation, if any, between the two. For this reason, the question of whether there is a relation between the control premium and the marketability discount is beyond the scope of this book.

Once any necessary adjustments have been made, the final problem the appraiser faces is aggregating the individual value indicators into one estimate. In practice, some appraisers choose to aggregate by computing averages using predetermined weights. For instance, one utility appraiser derives a final value indicator by computing a weighted average in which the book value approach and discounted cash flow approach are given weights of 0.25, and the stock and debt approach is given a weight of 0.50. In addition, courts have adopted averaging formulas on occasion. It is argued here that formulaic averaging is misguided. Appraisal work is so idiosyncratic that a weighted average that works for one company is unlikely to be applicable to another. Therefore, weighting individual value indicators invariably involves case-specific judgment. As an aid in developing that judgment, some guidelines are provided, but they should not be interpreted as hard and fast rules.

VALUING CONTROL PREMIUMS AND MINORITY DISCOUNTS

There are a number of reasons why a controlling block of securities may be worth more on a pro rata basis than a minority position. Among the benefits of control are:

- The power to elect directors and appoint management.
- The power to determine cash payouts on common shares.
- The power to decide what investments are undertaken and how those investments are financed.
- The power to manage free cash flow and set perquisites.
- The freedom to choose when to sell or liquidate the company.

These control benefits may drive a wedge between the value of a controlling interest and a minority position. The problem facing the appraiser in dealing with the wedge is twofold. First, it must be determined whether a wedge exists. If there is evidence of a wedge, then its size must be estimated. Second, the appraiser has to decided whether to increase a value indicator to reflect a control premium or to reduce the value indicator to reflect a minority discount. That decision depends on the nature of the company being appraised and on the appraisal approach that was employed to arrive at the value indicator.

In appraisal practice, it is common to assume that control is valuable and that a wedge exists. Accordingly, many appraisers automatically move to the next step of estimating the magnitude of the wedge. The standard procedure for estimating the size of the wedge is to examine data on control transactions. For instance, Pratt reports that based on data provided by W. T. Grimm, the average premium paid in 134 control transactions during the period 1980 to 1987 was 41.5 percent.[1] Grimm calculates the premium as the percentage difference between the stock price of the target company five business days before the receipt of a bid and the price paid by the acquirer. Because takeover bids are often partially anticipated, the price of the target company's stock five business days before a bid may already reflect the possibility of a bid. To the extent that a bid is anticipated, Grimm's calculation understates the value of control. Nonetheless, the 41.5 percent premium calculated by Grimm is consistent with results obtained by investment banks that measure the premium as the percentage difference between the stock price six weeks before a bid was received and the price paid by the acquirer.

Academic studies have employed a different definition of the premium. The most commonly used estimate is the change in the stock price of the target, net of market related movements, during a specified period surrounding the first announcement of a takeover bid. For instance, one study examines the net change in the target's stock price from 20 trading days prior to the first bid until consummation of the transaction. Jensen and Ruback review a large number of these studies and report that average premiums are on the order of 20 percent for mergers and 30 percent for tender offers.[2]

Viewed from the other side, a premium of 41.5 percent translates into a discount of 29 percent $(1 - 1/(1 + .415))$ for shares that do not convey control compared with shares that do. This calculation makes it clear that the minority discount is just the mirror image of the control premium.

Although the procedure of examining past takeover transactions to estimate the value of control seems straightforward, it

---

[1]S. Pratt, *Valuing a Business*, (Homewood, Ill.; Business One Irwin, 1989); and W. T. Grimm, *Mergerstat Review*, (Chicago: W. T. Grimm, 1980–87.).

[2]M. C. Jensen and R. S. Ruback, "The Market for Corporate Control: The Scientific Evidence," *Journal of Financial Economics* 11 (April 1983), pp. 5–50.

involves a critical conceptual error. For many companies, the value of obtaining control may be negligible. A recent lawsuit between the estate of William Harrah and the Internal Revenue Service involving the valuation of Harrah's estate illustrates why this is true.

In 1979, Mr. Harrah died leaving in his estate 70 percent of the outstanding shares of Harrah's Corporation, a New York Stock Exchange–traded company. As of the lien date for estate tax purposes, the market price of Harrah's stock was $18. However, the IRS valued the estate's shares at $26.50 on the grounds that the estate held a controlling block of stock and that the average premium paid for control in corporate acquisitions and leveraged buyouts was 45 percent. To support this view, the IRS presented evidence from W. T. Grimm's *Mergerstat Review*, which showed that in the three years prior to the lien date, prices paid in successful tender offers and buyouts were 45 percent higher, on average, than market prices six weeks before the first announcement of the transactions.[3]

Like Pratt, the IRS assumed that the wedge between the value of a controlling position and the value of a minority interest could be measured by observing the premiums paid in corporate control transactions involving companies other than the target. The IRS's assumption presents a paradox. Suppose that a young entrepreneur, call him Bill Gates, starts a software company. After several successful years, he takes the company public and sells 30 percent of the stock to outside investors at $10 per share while retaining the other 70 percent. If the IRS argument is correct, his 70 percent block is immediately worth $14.50. This holds true not only for Mr. Gates but for any entrepreneur who holds a controlling block in a start-up company. As soon as the company goes public, the controlling block is worth 45 percent more than the minority shares. Does this happen in every case, or is there a flaw in the procedure for estimating the premium?

The defect lies in the estimation of the premium. The method used by Pratt and the IRS does not take into account the reason *why* premiums are paid in control transactions. Without knowing why premiums are paid, it is impossible to determine whether it

---

[3]W. T. Grimm, *Mergerstat Review*.

is reasonable to apply a premium (or the associated discount) to the appraisal target.

In this respect, both research in finance and common sense support the proposition that a buyer is willing to pay more than the market price for a controlling interest in a company only when the buyer believes that the future cash flow of the company, and thereby the value of the company, can be increased once it is under his or her control.[4] Thus, in situations where control transactions occur, it follows that the buyer expects to be able to enhance after-tax cash flow. It does not follow that potential buyers believe that a controlling block of *every* company is worth 45 percent more than the market price. More likely, the reverse is true. The fact that *most companies do not receive takeover bids* at premiums above the market price indicates investors believe that the shares of those companies are not worth significantly more than the market price. Otherwise, someone would make a bid. For this reason, it would be misleading to assume that the wedge between the value of control and the value of a minority interest in companies that are not takeover targets is 45 percent. In fact, the wedge would be zero for those companies that potential acquirers would not change in any way. At a minimum, there is no basis for concluding that the size of the wedge for a particular company equals the historical average of premiums paid in recent mergers and takeovers. Those transactions occurred because acquirers saw a potential for adding value that probably does not exist in the case of a typical company.

To determine the appropriate control premium (or minority discount) for a company that is not a takeover target, information on how a new owner might be able to add value to the firm is required. In this regard, recent research on the market for corporate control provides some helpful guidelines.[5] The research

---

[4]Of course, it is also possible that the acquirer simply misjudges the value of the assets and overpays. While this undoubtedly happens in a few cases, there is no evidence that it happens systematically. In fact, studies of the reaction of the stock prices of *acquiring* companies to corporate takeovers support the viewpoint that, on average, the acquirer pays a price equal to the value of the assets purchased. See, for example, P. Asquith, J. Brunner and D. J. Mullins, "The Gains to Bidding Firms from Mergers," *Journal of Financial Economics* 11 (April 1983), pp. 211–40.

[5]Papers on the subject include: M. Bradley, A. Desai, and E. H. Kim, "The Ratio-

studies suggest a variety of ways in which the transfer of control may lead to increased cash flow and enhanced value. They include:

1. *Synergy.* If the target firm has specialized resources that could be more profitably employed in combination with another firm, then the value of the firm as part of a larger organization should exceed its value on a stand-alone basis.

2. *Inefficient management.* If the firm's management is inefficient or incompetent, then replacing current management will increase cash flow and enhance value. Examples of inefficient management include excessive investment in projects that fail to earn their cost of capital, inability to cut costs and employment where necessary, and the unwillingness to shed inefficient bureaucracy.

3. *Excess perquisite consumption.* If managers consume excessive perquisites, then reducing the perquisites will increase cash flow. Though some perquisites are required to provide incentives, there are clear abuses. For example, Burrough and Helyar report that when Ross Johnson was chairman of RJR, he maintained 27 country club memberships and had a fleet of corporate jets at his beck and call, all at company expense.[6]

4. *Tax benefits.* If there are tax benefits that can be realized by a corporate control transaction, then a takeover will increase cash flows to shareholders at the expense of the government. For instance, a firm with several years of losses and no turnaround in sight may have to merge with a more profitable company to take advantage of the tax losses. In this situation, the control premium represents the cost of buying the tax loss.

---

nale behind Interfirm Tender Offers: Information or Synergy," *Journal of Financial Economics* 11 (April 1983), pp. 183–206; Bradley, Desai, and Kim, "Synergistic Gains from Corporate Acquisitions and Their Division between the Stockholders of Target and Acquiring Firms," *Journal of Financial Economics* 21 (May 1988), pp. 3–40; M. Jensen, "Agency Costs of Free Cash Flow, Corporate Finance, and Takeovers," *American Economic Review* 76 (May 1986), pp. 326–29; and S. Kaplan, "Management Buyouts: Evidence on Taxes as a Source of Value," *Journal of Finance* 44 (September 1989), pp. 611–32.

[6]B. Burrough and J. Helyar, *Barbarians at the Gate* (New York: Harper & Row, 1990).

If none of these factors are present, and if the appraiser can see no other reason why the transfer of control would lead to higher cash flow and greater value, then there is no reason to make a significant adjustment to a value indicator to take into account a control premium. Put another way, if the appraiser cannot identify what a buyer of the appraisal target would change to increase cash flow, then there is no reason to assume that a control premium exists.

Returning to the case of the Harrah estate, attorneys for the estate argued that Harrah's was one of the best-run gambling companies in the nation. Furthermore, management did not consume excessive perquisites, and there were no tax benefits or synergies associated with acquiring a gaming company. On this basis, the attorneys concluded, a controlling shareholder would be unable to increase cash flow above the level that Harrah was already providing its shareholders. Accordingly, there is no reason for a hypothetical buyer to pay more than the market price of Harrah's, and the control premium is zero. Although the Harrah case never went to trial, the IRS attorneys apparently found the argument convincing. The litigation was settled at a value of less than $19 per share.

One caveat should be added. Even if a controlling shareholder would not change anything today, he or she always has the option to exercise power. Such an option has value because it gives a controlling shareholder flexibility that minority shareholders lack. For instance, suppose that the current chairman, who is brilliantly running the company, suddenly has a heart attack and the two apparent heirs get into a vicious fight that is draining the firm. A controlling shareholder could step in and find replacements for both of them or sell the company, but minority shareholders would not be able to take either step.

Although options associated with control have value, the value of these options will be less than premiums offered in control transactions. Control transactions occur because there are benefits to be gleaned from buying the company *today*. Average premiums of 30 to 40 percent or more reflect the immediate benefits a buyer expects to realize. For well-managed companies that are not takeover targets, there are few immediate benefits. Furthermore, the value of any control options must be discounted to reflect both the possibility that they will never be used and the time between the current date and the time when the option may be exercised. This double discounting ensures that the value of the option to exercise control will not approach the premiums paid in takeovers.

Unfortunately, there is no straightforward procedure for estimating the value of the control option for companies that are not takeover targets. In fact, it is hard to imagine how any type of premium could be estimated for companies that never receive bids. Consequently, estimating the control premium remains a gray area where appraiser judgment, based on a detailed knowledge of the company, is required. Though the premiums will be less than those observed in corporate control transactions, how much less is an empirical question that depends on the nature of the firm being appraised. The key question is whether a controlling shareholder could create value that management is not currently providing for minority shareholders.

In closing, it should be noted that there is one situation in which a substantial control premium is justified despite the fact that the firm is not a takeover target. If management makes it clear that it has the power and will fight any takeover bid, then bidders may be deterred even when there are significant benefits associated with the transfer of control. Although management entrenchment is a possibility, it is not clear how an appraiser should handle it. If the appraiser decides to add a control premium because of entrenched management, the appraiser must be able to determine that management is entrenched and is not acting in shareholder interest. It is difficult to see how this could be done. Even if it is determined that management is entrenched, what should the size of the wedge be? To answer that question, the appraiser must estimate the benefits of replacing management. This is a nearly impossible task for an appraiser who is not a specialist in the business. In addition, the appraiser's conclusions are likely to be bitterly opposed by management.

Adding a Premium versus Subtracting a Discount

If the appraiser concludes that a wedge does exists between the value of a minority position and the value of a controlling block, the next step is deciding whether to add a control premium or deduct a minority discount from the value indicators produced by the various approaches. The decision depends on whether the value indicator, prior to the adjustment, is interpreted as an estimate of a controlling interest or a minority position in the firm. That, in turn, depends on the approach that was used to derive the value indicator.

In some cases, the decision is easy. For example, the value indicator produced by the stock and debt approach, which is based on the prices at which minority positions trade in the market, clearly reflects the value of a minority position. Similarly, the direct comparison approach will value a minority position if the comparables are appraised by the stock and debt approach. To value a controlling interest, an estimate of the control premium must be added. Conversely, if sales of entire companies are used to value the comparables, then the direct comparison approach will value a controlling interest. Consequently, a discount must be deducted to value a minority position.

The discounted cash flow approach is more ambiguous. On the one hand, it can be interpreted as valuing a controlling interest because the cash flows are forecast for the entire company. On the other hand, it can be argued that the forecast represents the cash flows current management is expected to produce. New management might be able to produce greater cash flows by taking advantage of the factors discussed earlier. In that case, it would be proper to add a control premium to the DCF value. Despite this ambiguity, DCF appraisals are most often interpreted as reflecting the value of a controlling interest in the firm.

The book value approach suffers from the same ambiguity. Because the balance sheet reflects the value of the entire firm, it is usually interpreted as representing a controlling interest. However, new management may choose to alter the balance sheet by selling assets or recapitalizing the firm, so it cannot automatically be assumed that the book value will remain unchanged.

Applying the control premium. Virtually all benefits associated with control accrue to common stockholders. Unless the company is in bankruptcy, holding a majority block of debt does not convey any added power because the rights of bondholders that are specified in the indenture are the same for all. Basically, the indenture delineates what the company must do to ensure that bondholders are paid their interest and principal and dictates what the bondholders can do if the payments are not received. Except in the case of bankruptcy negotiations, the powers of bondholders are limited to making certain that they are paid, not making operating decisions for the firm. In that respect, the interests of large bondholders and small bondholders are identical. In fact, a trustee is usually appointed that acts in the interest of all bondholders. The role of the trustee is to make sure that the interest and principal are collected in a timely fashion. For this reason, it is a mistake to estimate the wedge between the value of a minority and controlling position in a company's equity and apply that wedge to the entire value of the firm. The wedge should be applied only to the common stock.

To illustrate, suppose that on the basis of a DCF valuation an appraiser concludes that the value of the firm is $10 million equally divided between $5 million in debt and $5 million in equity. Assume, furthermore, that the appraiser feels that the value of the equity represents a controlling interest and that a 20 percent discount must be applied to value a minority position. The 20 percent discount should be applied exclusively to the equity, resulting in a value of $4 million. The value of the debt remains $5 million, so that the total firm value is $9 million. Applying the discount to the entire firm would give a value of $8 million, but discounting the entire firm implies that the value of the debt is also reduced by 20 percent. Because bondholders receive the same fixed payout, have little control as long as payment is received, and have equal rights if payment is not received, there is no reason to believe that small debt holdings are worth less, per bond, than large debt holdings. For this reason, it is improper to discount the debt by 20 percent.

In most cases, preferred stock can be treated like debt. Except in extraordinary circumstances, preferred shareholders do not have the power to set operating policy. Therefore, there are no significant rights that accrue to large holders of preferred stock that are not available to small holders. The exception is preferred stock with special voting rights. Warren Buffet often negotiates to buy such shares when he makes a major investment in a company. For such special preferred shares, the addition of a control premium may be appropriate.

In light of the preceding discussion, there are two ways to apply a control premium (or minority discount). One possibility is to apply the control premium to the equity alone, under the assumption that the premiums for debt and preferred stock are zero. The other way is to apply the premium to the total value of the firm. If the latter approach is chosen, and if the appraiser feels that the appropriate premium for debt and preferred is zero, then the equity premium must be prorated. For instance, if the equity control premium was estimated to be 20 percent and equity accounted for 50 percent of the total value of the firm, then the premium on a total firm basis would be 10 percent.

ADJUSTING FEC'S VALUE INDICATORS TO REFLECT CONTROL

In the case of FEC, the wedge is judged to be zero. FEC is a tightly run, well-managed firm. Consumption of perquisites is strictly controlled. Management is experienced and professional. The employees are highly motivated. There is no apparent change in operating policy or sales strategy that would increase cash flow. In addition, given the nature of the printing industry, with thousands of competitive firms, there are no clear synergies a buyer could exploit by acquiring FEC. Furthermore, an acquisition of FEC would not convey any special tax benefits. In short, there is no reason to believe that the cash flow produced by FEC could be increased by a change in management. Consequently, the value received by the minority shareholders, who benefit from management's current actions, is equal to that of a controlling shareholder. No minority discount or control premium is appropriate.

Nonetheless, Table 8–1, which is developed for FEC, illustrates how a control premium (or minority discount) would be applied if it were applicable. Because the book value approach and the discounted cash flow approach are assumed to value a controlling interest in the firm, a minority discount would be deducted to value small shareholdings. Conversely, the stock and debt approach and the direct comparison approach value minority holdings. Therefore, a control premium would have to be added to value a controlling block of shares.

TABLE 8-1

Calculating the Adjusted Value of Forms Engineering

	Adjusted Book Value Approach	Stock and Debt Approach	Direct Comparison Approach (using 5-year average)	Discounted Cash Flow Approach
Debt	$2,350,075	$2,350,075	$2,350,075	$2,350,075
Preferred stock	1,055,580	1,055,580	1,055,580	1,055,580
Equity	4,085,859	NA	12,632,000	12,687,696
Control premium adjustment to equity value (in %)	Control premium wedge is assumed to be zero	Control premium wedge is assumed to be zero	Control premium wedge is assumed to be zero	Control premium wedge is assumed to be zero
Marketability adjustment to equity value (in %)	25%	NA—but this would be zero if the equity were marketable	25%	25%
Adjusted equity value	3,064,394	NA	9,474,000	9,515,772
Total firm value	*$6,470,049*	*NA*	*$12,879,655*	*12,921,427*

VALUING NONMARKETABLE HOLDINGS

One of the themes stressed throughout this book is that spendable cash is the ultimate source of value to investors. Investors purchase securities in a company not because they want to own securities, but because they want to increase the spendable cash that they will have available in the future. If the securities an investor purchases are not publicly marketable, and thus cannot easily be resold, they will be worth less to the investor because they cannot be converted to cash quickly without accepting a significant discount in price. Assuming that the nonmarketable securities do not represent a controlling position, furthermore, the investor will have no discretion over when the securities are to be registered and thus become marketable.

Following Amihud and Mendelson, a marketable security can be thought of as equivalent to a nonmarketable security with an attached option that gives the holder the right to convert the security to cash at the market price.[7] Viewed in this light, the difference between the value of a marketable security and the value of an identical nonmarketable security is the value of the option to liquidate. The value of the option to liquidate is difficult to estimate because it differs across investors. Wealthy investors, who are not likely to need the cash and who are willing to hold for the long-term, will value the option to liquidate less highly than investors who may need their money at any moment. Presumably, the marketability discount that prevails in the marketplace reflects the value the marginal investor places on the option to liquidate. Unfortunately, there is no direct method for determining who is the marginal investor.

The value of the option to liquidate also depends on the characteristics of the security. Bonds offer a promised stream of interest and give bondholders the right to take partial control of the company or to force its liquidation if interest and principal payments are not made according to schedule. Thus, bondholders have access to a predictable stream of cash payments without selling the bonds. This mitigates the need to sell the securities to get

---

[7] Y. Amihud and H. Mendelson, "Liquidity and Asset Prices: Financial Management Implications," *Financial Management* 17 (Spring 1988); pp. 5–15.

cash and reduces the value that bondholders will place on the option to liquidate. For example, insurance companies often buy bonds with the intent of holding them to maturity because the interest the bonds provide matches payments the company expects to make. For such holders, the value of the option to liquidate is small. Equity holders, on the other hand, are paid only at management discretion. Holders of minority positions in nonmarketable equity have no control over when, or if, they will receive a return on their investment. This makes the option to liquidate particularly valuable to minority stockholders. Preferred shareholders fall in the middle ground. The preferred dividend assures holders of a cash payout under normal circumstances, but the payout can be suspended without forcing the company into bankruptcy and there is no assurance when the investor will be able to sell the preferred shares to get the principal back.

Given these distinctions between the classes of securities as well as the minor role played by preferred stock in most companies, a rule of thumb has arisen in appraisal practice. The rule is similar to that utilized in the case of the control premium. No marketability discount is applied to fixed income securities, including both debt and preferred stock, because of the rights these securities convey and the income streams they provide. Equity, on other hand, is assumed to be discounted if it is not marketable. Therefore, the discount on a firmwide basis equals the equity discount prorated by the fraction of equity in the firm's capital structure. Of course, this rule of thumb should not be applied in situations where there is clear evidence that the lack of marketability affects the value of a firm's fixed income securities.

The problem that remains is estimating the nonmarketability discount for equity securities. Three approaches have been employed in an attempt to solve this problem. The first approach is to calculate the observed discounts on transactions involving restricted shares of publicly traded companies. The second approach is to compare the prices at which shares in closely held companies traded prior to the firm going public, with the price set at the initial public offering or the price at which the security trades after the offering. The third approach is to calculate the costs of floating a public offering. It should be noted that this third approach assumes that the holder of the nonmarketable securities has sufficient control to initiate a public offering. The non-marketability discounts estimated by each of these approaches are considered in turn.

Estimates of the Restricted Share Discount

Because of the time and cost associated with registering securities with the Securities and Exchange Commission (SEC), publicly traded companies occasionally issue "letter stock" that is not registered and, therefore, cannot be publicly traded. Although letter stock cannot be traded on a public market, private transactions, which usually must be reported to the SEC, do occur. The restricted share discount can be estimated by comparing the prices at which letter stock trades with the prices at which comparable, registered shares trade in the public market.

One of the earliest and most widely cited studies of the discount on letter stock was conducted by the SEC.[8] Based on trades reported to the commission, the SEC estimated discounts for letter stock issued by companies that traded on the New York Stock Exchange, the American Stock Exchange, and in the over-the-counter (OTC) market. The commission found that the overall mean discount was approximately 25 percent, with higher discounts for smaller OTC companies.

One by-product of the SEC study was a new ruling that required investment companies registered under the Investment Company Act of 1940 to disclose the manner in which they valued restricted shares. This data made possible additional studies of the relation between the value of restricted and publicly traded shares.

In the years following the SEC study and the new SEC ruling, Gelman, Trout, Moroney, and Maher all published research on the pricing of restricted stock. In addition, private studies were conducted by Willamette Associates and Standard Research Consultants. Because all of these studies are reviewed in detail by

---

[8]"Discounts Involved in Purchases of Common Stock," *Institutional Investor Study Report of the Securities and Exchange Commission* (Washington, D.C.: U.S. Government Printing Office, 1971).

Pratt, only the conclusions are summarized here.[9] In each study, the prices paid for publicly traded shares were compared with the prices paid for letter stock at the same point in time. Despite the fact that the studies used different samples of transactions over various years ranging from 1960 to 1984 and under diverse market conditions, the results were remarkably consistent. Except for the Standard Research Consultants study, which reported a discount of 45 percent, all of the discounts were found to be between 31 and 36 percent.

In the most recent and comprehensive follow-up to the SEC study, Silber examined 310 private placements of unregistered stock between 1981 and 1988.[10] After eliminating issues that had warrants or other special provisions, he identified the private placements date for 69 companies through a computer search of public news releases. For each of these 69 companies, the price per share of the restricted stock was compared with the closing price (or the average of the closing bid and offer prices) for the company's publicly trading shares on the placement date. Silber reports that the average discount for this sample was 33.8 percent.

There are a number of reasons why the studies of letter stock may understate the discount that should be applied to nonmarketable common stock issued by privately held companies. First, restrictions on the transfer of letter stock are of limited duration—most lapse within 24 months. At that time, the holder can sell the shares in the public market. (Volume restrictions may still be imposed by SEC Rule 144). Second, by definition, letter stock is issued by companies that are already public. Therefore, when the restriction lapses, an initial public offering with the associated transaction costs and price concessions is not required because the letter stock is transformed automatically into publicly traded shares. For both these reasons, the discounts on letter stock issued by public companies are likely to be smaller than the discounts on nonmarketable shares issued by private companies. Therefore, the letter stock studies should be interpreted to imply that the discount for lack of marketability is at least in the range of 31 to 36 percent.

---

[9]S. Pratt, *Valuing a Business*. Pratt also provides complete references to all the studies.

[10]W. Silber, "Discounts on Restricted Stock: The Impact of Illiquidity on Stock Prices," *Financial Analysts Journal*, July–August 1991, pp. 60–64.

Estimates of the Private Share Discount

A more direct measure of the marketability discount is the difference between the price paid for shares in private transactions before a company goes public and the price at which such shares would have traded if the company were public. By definition, this discount cannot be observed directly. However, it is possible to observe the prices at which privately held shares traded prior to a public offering and compare them with the initial public offering (IPO) price. This was the approach taken by both John Emory and Willamette Associates.

Emory published two studies on the private share discount.[11] In both studies, the procedure was the same. A sample of companies was selected whose shares changed hands in private transactions five months or less prior to the company's initial public offering. The price in the private transaction was then compared to the IPO price. The first study covered the 1980 to 1981 period and included 13 companies. Emory found that the private transaction occurred at an average price 66 percent below the IPO price. The follow-up study examined 21 companies in the period 1985 to 1986 and found an average discount of 43 percent. In neither case, however, did Emory attempt to adjust for marketwide movements in stock prices between the date of the private transaction and the IPO date.

Emory argued that the discounts he found were likely to understate the marketability discount because the private transactors would have anticipated the public offering that was no more than five months down the road. In light of the forthcoming IPO, the discount stockholders would accept on their shares would be limited by the fact that they could wait and sell their shares after the public offering. There is, however, an offsetting bias that Emory overlooked. A company may plan an IPO and then choose not to go through with it because of negative developments. By including only successful IPOs in his sample, Emory has selected those companies for which the news between

---

[11]J. D. Emory, "The Value of Marketability as Illustrated in Initial Public Offerings of Common Stock—January 1980 through June 1981," *Business Valuation News*, June 1986, pp. 21–24; and Emory, "The Value of Marketability as Illustrated in Initial Public Offerings of Common Stock—January 1985 through June 1986," *Business Valuation News*, December 1986, pp. 12–14.

the private transaction date and the IPO date was sufficiently favorable that the deal could be consummated. For those companies, the stock price no doubt tended to rise, so that the estimated discount grew larger.

As reported by Pratt, Willamette Management Associates completed five studies on the prices of private stock transactions relative to subsequent IPO prices during the years 1975 to 1985.[12] The private transactions took place 1 to 36 months before an IPO. To control for movements in stock prices between the date of the private transactions and the IPO date, prices were adjusted using an industry index. For each private transaction, the discount was defined to be:

$$\text{Discount} = P_o - P_p\,(I_o/I_p)$$

where:

P_o = Price per share at the time of the public offering

P_p = Price per share in the private transaction

I_o = Industry index at the time of the public offering

I_p = Industry index at the time of the private transaction

Using this definition of the discount, the five Willamette studies found discounts ranging from 60 to 80 percent. The average discount for all five studies was approximately 68 percent. Because the Willamette studies included transactions up to 36 months before the IPO, the IPO anticipation problem that Emory felt would reduce the estimated discount is less severe. However, the information bias is probably more pronounced. Companies that did poorly in the 36 months following the private transactions would be likely to cancel their IPOs, while companies that did well would both see their value rise relative to other firms in the industry and would almost surely go through with the IPO.

In summary, the results of the studies of private transactions are quite dramatic. Taken as a whole, they suggest that the non-marketability discount is on the order of 50 percent or more.

---

[12]S. Pratt, *Valuing a Business*, pp. 251–55.

While the studies are not free of bias, the direction of the bias is unclear overall. Even if the information bias is larger than the IPO anticipation bias, so that the measured discount is overstated, it is hard to imagine that the net bias would explain more than a fraction of the estimated discount.

The Costs of Going Public

Controlling shareholders always have the option to overcome the nonmarketability problem by taking the company public. From their standpoint, therefore, the discount for lack of marketability should not exceed the flotation costs as a percent of the value of the equity. If the discount exceeds flotation costs, a controlling shareholder would chose to take the company public. Even if there is not a controlling shareholder, minority shareholders have an incentive to organize and to pressure management to take the company public when the discount significantly exceeds flotation costs. Consequently, another way to estimate the discount for lack of marketability is to calculate the costs of going public.

Flotation costs include underwriting fees, registration fees, legal fees, accounting fees, printing and engraving expenses, and listing fees. In addition to direct fees, underwriters sometimes receive warrants or other "sweeteners" as compensation in connection with the initial public offerings. (In this regard, one of the controversies surrounding Michael Milken and Drexel is that Milken often required issuers to provide warrants as sweeteners. In some cases, the warrants were then placed in Milken's private partnerships rather than being distributed to the buyers of the securities.) Because some of the expenses are fixed, flotation costs as a percent of firm value rise as the value of the firm falls.

A major study of flotation costs was published by the SEC in 1974.[13] The SEC examined almost 1,600 companies that sold new issues of common stock in the years 1971 and 1972. The results of that study are summarized in Table 8–2. As the table shows, flotation costs fall from about 24 percent of the value of the issue for

---

[13]Cost of Flotation of Registered Issues 1971–72 (Washington, D.C.: Securities and Exchange Commission, 1974).

firms that sell less than $500,000 to about 3 percent of the value of the issue for firms selling over $100 million. (Remember that these issue amounts are stated in terms of 1971 and 1972 dollars.)

The SEC study was updated by Smith, who examined 578 common stock issues during the period from 1971 to 1975.[14] The flotation costs reported by Smith are slightly less than those reported in the SEC study despite the fact that Smith includes the costs of warrants issued by the firm and provided to the underwriters as sweeteners in his estimate of expenses. Smith finds that most of the warrants were issued by small companies and that the value relinquished in this form was on the order of 5 percent of the value of the issue. In addition, Smith notes that the flotation cost estimates omit the opportunity cost of the issuing firm's employees' time. For small issues, this can amount to several percent of the value of the issue.

Despite minor differences, the flotation cost estimates reported by the SEC and by Smith indicate that the costs of going public range from about 20 to 25 percent of the value of the issue for small issues down to 3 to 5 percent of the value of the issue for large issues. The fact that these numbers are smaller than the discounts found in the studies of transactions involving restricted shares is a puzzle. If nonmarketable shares are worth as little as 50 percent of marketable shares, why do managers fail to remove the restrictions or take the company public? One possible explanation is that holders of restricted shares have no need to take the company public at that particular moment. The right to take a company public can be interpreted as an option. Going forward with an IPO is analogous to exercising the option. It is quite possible that the holders of restricted shares have no desire to exercise the option immediately. Such was the case for most of FEC's history. The company was controlled by a few large shareholders who had no desire to sell their shares and, therefore, saw no benefit from paying the flotation costs to take the company public.

It is also possible that management, by failing to take the company public, is not acting in the best interest of the shareholders. For instance, managers may choose to prevent the company from

---

[14]C. Smith, "Alternative Methods of Raising Capital: Rights versus Underwritten Offerings," *Journal of Financial Economics* 5 (December 1977), pp. 273–308.

TABLE 8–2
SEC and Smith Studies of Flotation Costs

Size of Issue (millions)	SEC Results			Smith Results		
	Underwriter Compensation (percent of proceeds)	Expenses (percent of proceeds)	Total Issuance Cost (percent of proceeds)	Underwriter Compensation (percent of proceeds)	Expenses (percent of proceeds)	Total Issuance Cost (percent of proceeds)
Under .5	13.2	10.4	23.6	7.0	6.8	13.8
.5 to .99	12.5	8.3	20.8	10.4	4.9	15.3
1.0 to 1.99	10.6	5.9	16.5	6.6	2.9	9.5
2.0 to 4.99	8.2	3.7	11.9	5.5	1.5	7.0
5.0 to 9.99	6.7	2.0	8.7	4.8	0.7	5.5
10.0 to 19.99	5.5	1.1	6.6	4.3	0.0	4.3
20.0 to 49.99	4.4	0.6	5.0	4.0	0.2	4.2
50.0 to 99.99	3.9	0.3	4.2	3.8	0.1	3.9
100.0 to 500.0	3.0	0.2	3.2			

going public in order to protect the power they have in a private firm. Public firms are subject to added scrutiny and regulation that serve to reduce managerial discretion. This is one reason why the marketability discount may be related to the minority discount. A controlling shareholder has the power to oust recalcitrant managers and ensure that the company goes public. Minority shareholders cannot take such action unless they are able to organize.

Finally, it may be the case that the studies of private transactions overstate the minority discount and, thereby, overstate the benefits of going public. For instance, the information bias may be larger than most researchers believe.

Given the state of current research, the safest conclusion to draw is that the appropriate marketability discount is on the order of magnitude of the cost of going public. It may be less if the appraisal target shareholders have no need to trade, but it may be greater if shareholders are anxious to trade and there are added impediments to an IPO, such as management entrenchment.

Applying the marketability discount. With the exception of the stock and debt approach, the marketability discount is applied to the value indicators produced by all the other appraisal approaches. A discount is inconsistent with the stock and debt approach because the approach is based on the assumption that the equity is marketable. The discount is clearly appropriate in the case of the direct comparison approach if the comparable companies are publicly traded and the subject company is not. In that situation, marketable shares are being directly compared to nonmarketable shares. With respect to the book value and discounted cash flow approaches, application of a discount is based on the assumption that both of the approaches estimate the value of marketable shares. Though this is common practice, there may be situations in which the appraiser does not agree. For instance, the discounted cash flow value of a commercial real estate holding company that owns income properties subject to secure long-term leases may not be subject to a discount despite the fact that the shares are not marketable because the shares are like bonds that provide a predictable income stream. Consequently, the value of the option to liquidate is small.

COURT RULINGS ON THE MARKETABILITY DISCOUNT

Courts of law have also struggled with the question of determining a marketability discount for closely held companies. The question of what discount to apply arises frequently in estate tax hearings involving private family firms. Pratt presents an excellent review of the court decisions in valuation cases involving marketability discounts.[15] He concludes that Courts have tended to recognize higher discounts for lack of marketability in recent years than they did earlier. Despite this trend, discounts for lack of marketability allowed in most court decisions are still at levels below those indicated by the empirical studies of the discount. The decisions are more in line with estimates of flotation costs.

It is also worth noting that the courts are quite rightly suspicious of the notion that there is a general marketability discount. The marketability discount depends on the type of security, the issuing firm, and perhaps the nature of the holders as well. For instance, shares of closely held companies that have no intention of going public command larger discounts, in the court's eye, than do restricted shares of public companies. In this sense, the marketability discount is like the control premium—not a general number but a characteristic such as a finger-print that differs from firm to firm and security to security. For the most part, courts seem to be aware of this, because judges have stated repeatedly that they attempt to weigh all of the facts related to the security and the company in question before deciding on the appropriate marketability discount. There is no typical discount that can be routinely applied.

Estimating the Marketability Discount for FEC

Because FEC's debt consists exclusively of bank loans that pay interest monthly and may be called if payments are not received, no marketability discount is applied to FEC's debt. This makes

---

[15]S. Pratt, *Valuing a Business*, pp. 257–62.

perfect sense because if FEC did not already have a loan outstanding, the bank would presumably be willing to lend funds
on the same terms. For simplicity, the FEC preferred stock, which
is unique to the company, also is assumed to be immune from a
discount for lack of marketability.

With respect to the equity, there is reason to believe flotation
costs provide the best indicator of the marketability discount for
FEC. One of the alternatives FEC's chairman was considering on
the lien date was taking the company public. Given the controlling position of the family shareholders, the chairman would
have met little opposition if this path were followed.

In light of the flotation cost studies, a marketability discount of
25 percent is chosen for FEC's equity. The relatively high discount
is selected for several reasons. First, the numbers in Table 8–2 are
in terms of early 1970 dollars. In 1970 dollars, the size of FEC's
issue would probably be in the $1 million to $4 million range, not
the $5 million to $9 million range. Costs for such small issues exceed 15 percent. Second, it may well be necessary for FEC to offer
warrants to market its shares. Third, management would have to
set aside the time to select an underwriter, collect the information necessary to price the issue, and negotiate with the underwriter. The opportunity cost of this time could be significant.

Table 8–1 shows how the marketability discount is applied
to the value indicators produced for FEC by each of the four valuation approaches. Because estimates of the value of the equity
are available, the 25 percent discount is applied directly to the
equity rather than applying a prorated discount to the value of
the firm. Notice that although a 25 percent discount is applied
to equity for the adjusted book value, direct comparison, and
DCF approaches, the dollar magnitude of the discount varies
from approach to approach. Because the adjusted book value of
equity is only $4.1 million, the discount is approximately $1 million. On the other hand, the direct comparison and DCF approaches value the equity at approximately $12.5, so that the
discount comes to over $3 million dollars. This brings the esti-
mated values closer together. After taking the marketability discount, the adjusted book value of FEC is $6.47 million, the direct
comparison value is $12.88 million, and the DCF value is $12.92
million.

AGGREGATING THE INDIVIDUAL ESTIMATES OF VALUE

Once the appraiser has estimated the value of the firm using the approaches presented in previous chapters and made necessary adjustments, the last hurdle is putting all the information into a final value indicator. One possible way to aggregate the individual indicators produced by each of the approaches is to calculate an average or weighted average. As noted in Chapter 4, this was the approach taken by the court in both *Central Trust* and *Bader*. The court calculated a weighted average of three direct comparison value indicators: one based on earnings per share, one based on dividend yield, and one based on book value. In both cases, the weights specified by the court were assumed to be applicable to any company to which the decision applied.

Some appraisers employ a similar procedure. They select a group of appraisal approaches and assign each a given weight in advance. The utility appraiser discussed at the beginning of the chapter provides an example.

Such predetermined weighting schemes have little to recommend them other than a quasi-scientific appearance. The problem is that an appraisal approach that provides useful information about the value of one company may provide almost no information about the value of another company. (In defense of the utility appraiser referred to previously, utilities are relatively homogeneous. Consequently, assuming that fixed weights can be applied to three appraisal approaches to reach a final value indicator is not necessarily a grievous error. Nonetheless, there is sufficient variation among utilities that the procedure is still questionable.) Part of the art of appraisal is developing the judgment to recognize situations in which one approach should be ignored entirely and another given significant weight. Because there are virtually an unlimited number of circumstances in which companies must be appraised, laying down in advance fixed rules that state how the competing approaches are to be weighted is impossible. Nonetheless, there are several guidelines an appraiser should keep in mind.

- As noted in Chapter 2, the book value approach to appraisal is likely to be of limited use. Except in unique situations where the earning power of a company is tied to its book value by regulation (as is the case with public utilities), book value and market value are not correlated in a reliable fashion. Therefore, book value approaches should typically be given little weight.

- A stock and debt value indicator, when it can be calculated, should generally be the given greatest weight. Unlike the other appraisal approaches, which are based on the forecasts and judgments of accountants and appraisers, the stock and debt value indicator reflects the market's assessment of the value of the company. For this reason, it is not excessive to give the stock and debt approach a weight of 100 percent if all the company's securities are publicly traded.

- As discussed in Chapter 4, the accuracy of the direct comparison approach depends on the ability of the appraiser to find truly comparable companies whose values are known or can be estimated accurately by other techniques. If the appraiser is confident that the comparables are similar to the appraisal target, and if the comparables are publicly traded so that they can be valued using the stock and debt approach, significant weight can be placed on the direct comparison approach. If the issue of comparability becomes murky, or if the comparables must be appraised by a less reliable technique, weight placed on the direct comparison approach should be reduced accordingly.

- The virtue of the discounted cash flow approach is that it can be applied in nearly any appraisal context. The drawback is that it depends on the appraiser's forecasts of future cash flows and estimates of the cost of capital. In situations where there is a long history on which to base cash flow forecasts and market data on which to base estimates of the cost of capital, a good deal of confidence can be placed in the DCF approach. However, the DCF approach is easily abused, particularly when applied to new companies or in novel situations. In such circumstances, value can be created out of thin air by optimistic forecasting. Therefore, the weight applied to a DCF forecast should be directly proportional to the confidence that can be placed in the cash flow forecasts. Unfortunately, it is sometimes difficult for an appraiser who developed the forecast to dispassionately assess the reliability of the cash flow forecasts. It should also be noted that it is often difficult to limit the weight placed on the DCF approach in the case of new ventures because the data necessary to apply other approaches are not available.

Though these general guidelines provide direction, they are not to be taken as marching orders. Any information that leads the appraiser to believe that one approach or another produces a more accurate estimate of value should be considered. Because each company has unique characteristics that affect its value and that may or may not be picked up by a particular valuation model, appraiser judgment is required to arrive at a final value indicator. Impeding that judgment by enforcing an averaging scheme that does not take into account the peculiarities of the individual case will general result in less accurate appraisals.

AGGREGATING THE VALUE INDICATORS FOR FEC

With respect to FEC, the stock and debt approach is not applicable because FEC's equity is not publicly traded. Of the three remaining approaches to valuation, only the direct comparison approach and the discounted cash flow approach produce reasonable values for FEC. The adjusted book value approach is significantly misleading because it fails to take account of FEC's organizational capital.

Both the direct comparison approach and the discounted cash flow approach have points in their favor. The main benefit of the direct comparison approach is that it does not require forecasts of future cash flows. This not only makes life easier for the appraiser, but also removes a source of potential bias. On the other hand, all of the comparables are significantly larger than FEC, and none of them focus on the direct mail business to the extent that FEC does. The discounted cash approach has the benefit that it does not rely, at least directly, on comparability. (It does rely on comparability to the extent that the direct comparison approach is used to estimate the terminal value. However, the importance of comparability in the DCF appraisal of FEC is reduced by discounting.) The estimated future cash flow reflects FEC's unique business mix. The drawback, of course, is that forecasting cash flow for a small company in a competitive business is always hazardous.

In light of the strengths and weaknesses of both the direct comparison approach and the DCF approach, an average of the two value indicators is not an unreasonable choice. Based on the results reported in Table 8–2, the decision to average does not make much difference for FEC because the two value indicators are nearly identical. However, the table is somewhat misleading in this respect because only the direct comparison value using five-year average data is reported. A look back at Table 4–4 reveals that the direct comparison values based on current data and on the trend line data are significantly lower. In addition, the apparent precision of the numbers reported in Table 8–1 should not be misinterpreted. Given the host of assumptions required in any appraisal, the best that can be hoped for is a range of value. With this in mind, a reasonable range for the total value of FEC is $12 to $13 million dollars. For a final value indicator, the midpoint of the range, $12.5 million, is as good a choice as any. If a final point estimate of value is provided, the appraiser should be careful not to convey a false sense of precision. The uncertainty associated with any valuation must be made clear to the client.

CONCLUDING OBSERVATIONS

There are no hard and fast rules for determining the extent that adjustments to appraised values, if any, are necessary to take into account control premiums and marketability discounts. The value of control depends on what current management is doing. If the firm is already being run efficiently and if there are no apparent synergies or tax savings, potential buyers are unlikely to pay a premium to acquire control. Similarly, the value of marketability depends on the nature of the company, on the type of securities issued, and on the holders of those securities. For these reasons, the adjustment decision must be made in light of the unique characteristics of the appraisal target and will inevitably involve an element of judgment. There are no generic control premiums or marketability discounts that can be automatically applied.

Judgment also must be employed when aggregating the individual value indicators to arrive at a final appraisal. Mechanical averaging rules are ill advised because approaches that yield meaningful value for some companies may be virtually worthless in other situations. The strengths and weaknesses of each approach have to be evaluated in the context of the particular appraisal.

Chapter Nine

Extensions of the Basic Valuation Models

There are three issues that were not addressed in the discussion of the basic valuation approaches, but that are becoming increasingly important in appraisal practice. The first is the valuation of international multibusiness firms. The four appraisal approaches presented in the preceding chapters were developed under the implicit assumption that the firm was in only one line of business and did business in only one country. In fact, most large firms incorporate many separate businesses and operate worldwide. For example, Monsanto Company in 1991 consisted of five separate business units: Monsanto Agricultural Company, Monsanto Chemical Company, Searle, The NutraSweet Company, and Fisher Controls International. Each of these units operated on a global scale.

A second problem, which was mentioned in passing in Chapter 7, is estimating the cost of capital for derivative securities such as options, warrants, and convertible bonds. With the growing sophistication of investment bankers and corporate finance officers, companies have been issuing derivative securities in greater volume. For example, options are frequently given to senior managers as part of their compensation package. Accordingly, appraisers need to understand the issues that arise when estimating the cost of capital for derivative securities.

The third problem that was not addressed is how to value managerial flexibility in the context of the discounted cash flow approach to appraisal. One of the often overlooked but not unimportant problems with the DCF approach is that it is based on cash flow forecasts, which fail to take into account the ability of management to react to changing economic circumstances. In some contexts, this failure to value managerial flexibility can lead to appraisals that significantly underestimate the value of the firm.

This chapter presents an overview of each of these three extensions to the basic appraisal models. The emphasis is on articulating the issues raised by each of the extensions rather than attempting to provide solutions. A broadbrush approach is chosen not only to simplify the presentation, but also because none of the three problems—valuing multibusiness firms, estimating the cost of capital for derivative securities, or valuing managerial flexibility—has been resolved fully. All three remain the subject of active research and lively debate.

VALUING MULTIBUSINESS FIRMS

The extent to which valuing multibusiness firms raises unique appraisal problems depends on the question the appraiser is trying to answer. If the goal of the appraisal is to estimate the aggregate value of the firm, then in some situations the multidivisional nature of a conglomerate enterprise can be ignored, and the appraiser can proceed as if the firm is in only one line of business. However, such aggregate valuation is often not possible, even when the appraiser is interested exclusively in the value of the total firm. When the appraiser needs to know the value of specific business units, then a disaggregated analysis is required by definition.

Before any of the four appraisal approaches can be applied to the subsidiary business units of a conglomerate firm, a number of issues must be addressed. First, the different lines of business must be defined. In defining business lines, the appraiser faces a trade-off. Because some of the inputs into appraisal models, such as the cost of capital and the market value to EBIDT ratio, vary across industries, the more finely business lines are defined, the more accurate the appraisal is likely to be. Unfortunately, the financial data necessary for appraisal analysis are often not available for narrowly defined business units. Furthermore, if the lines of business are too narrowly defined, the appraisal becomes unwieldy. For example, Monsanto provides complete financial data for each of its five subsidiary companies, but data on the individual businesses operated by each of those five subsidiary companies are not available. A reasonable definition of business lines, therefore, would be limited to the five subsidiary companies.

A second issue to be addressed is how to allocate cash flows among the various business lines. Allocation is complicated by the fact that subsidiary businesses within a conglomerate often have significant interaction. The appraiser must decide whether the *transfer prices* used to allocate resources internally reflect arm's length prices that the subsidiary would have to pay if it were an independent business. For example, Monsanto Agricultural Company buys chemicals from the Monsanto Chemical Company. Therefore, the prices charged for the chemicals affect the earnings and cash flow of both the agricultural company and the chemical company. It is possible that for internal business reasons, the price that Monsanto Agricultural pays for chemicals is greater than the arm's length price that Monsanto Chemical would charge an independent company. As a result, Monsanto Chemical's cash flow will be greater than if it were an independent firm and Monsanto Agricultural's will be less. Therefore, an appraisal that did not adjust for the artificial transfer price would overstate the value of the chemical company and understate the value of the agricultural company. The only way to eliminate this bias is to estimate an arm's length price for chemicals and to recalculate earnings and cash flow for both subsidiaries accordingly.

Finally, the appraiser must decide how to handle the problem of valuing the corporate headquarters. The simplest way to treat the headquarters is to allocate the costs and benefits associated with it to the individual business units. This avoids the problem of valuing the headquarters separately, because the value is automatically divided among the subsidiaries. Unfortunately, this approach also exacerbates the allocation problem. All the services provided by the headquarters, such as advertising, tax planning, financial analysis, accounting and legal support, as well as the cost of those services, such as executive and professional salaries, support staff compensation, and office rent, must be valued at effective market prices and apportioned among the subsidiaries.

The importance of each of the three issues—defining the sub-sidiary business units, allocating internal costs and benefits be-tween business units, and allocating the costs and benefits of the headquarters operation—depends on the appraisal approach em-ployed. To illustrate the major considerations, each of the four ap-praisal approaches is addressed in turn.

The Balance Sheet Approach

In its unadjusted form, the balance sheet approach can be applied to a division or an entire company as long as the necessary ac-counting information is available. Furthermore, if the goal of the appraisal is to value the total firm, the fact that the company is a conglomerate has no effect on the unadjusted balance sheet ap-proach. The analysis proceeds as described in Chapter 2.

When the balance sheet approach is applied to subsidiary busi-ness units, an allocation problem arises. The appraiser must de-termine whether balance sheet items should be altered to reflect interfirm transactions between business units and with corporate headquarters. For instance, an asset may be carried on one divi-sion's books at an artificially low price because it was purchased from another division. Unfortunately, there is no way to deter-mine whether an asset is carried at an artificial value simply by looking at the balance sheet. The appraiser must inquire as to who the asset was purchased from, what price was paid, and what the market price for such assets was at the time. Of course, making sure that an asset purchased from another subsidiary is properly accounted for does not mean that it is properly valued. As stressed in Chapter 2, historical book values for assets, even when properly recorded, typically do not equal current market values. This was the rationale for developing an adjusted balance sheet approach.

It is also important to note that from the standpoint of a sub-sidiary business unit, securities issued by the subsidiary and held by the parent are investor claims. When subtracting operat-ing liabilities from the net assets to calculate the value of the sub-sidiary, therefore, claims of the parent company should not be deducted.

Unlike the basic balance sheet approach, the adjusted balance sheet approach is difficult to apply to conglomerates on a firm-wide basis. Recall that balance sheet adjustments are designed to reflect factors such as inflation and obsolescence that drive a wedge between the market values of assets and their historical book values. The impact of such factors clearly depends on the nature of the assets and the business in which they are employed. For example, inflation adjustment is critical in the railroad business because railroad equipment is long-lived, while adjustment for obsolescence plays a key role in the computer business because of the rapid pace of technological change. If a multibusiness company owns both a computer firm and a railroad, it would be a mistake to apply one adjustment to all assets. The assets of the computer firm and the railroad should be segregated and adjusted separately.

The preceding example is not unique. In general, the only way to deal with the problems caused by different asset lives and different rates of obsolescence is to value a conglomerate firm on a business line by business line basis. This requires developing adjusted balance sheets for each subsidiary business unit.

Before attempting to construct individual balance sheets for each business unit, the appraiser should decide whether an adjusted balance sheet approach is likely to produce a valid value indicator. In Chapter 2, it was pointed out that with the possible exception of rate base–regulated companies, this is rarely the case. In most circumstances, therefore, the benefit to be derived from constructing adjusted balance sheets for each subsidiary is unlikely to justify the time and expense.

The Stock and Debt Approach

By definition, the stock and debt approach is applicable only to the parent company that issues securities. (If a subsidiary independently issues securities that are held by public investors as well as the parent, then the stock and debt approach can be applied to a subsidiary.) Therefore, it is applicable directly only when the appraiser is attempting to estimate the total value of a conglomerate firm. In such situations, the best value indicator is simply the sum of the market values of the company's outstanding securities, as explained in Chapter 3.

In situations where the appraiser is seeking to estimate the value of subsidiary business units, the stock and debt approach can still be employed as a consistency check. The sum of the appraised values of the subsidiaries, plus any value attributed to the headquarters, should equal the stock and debt value of the firm.

The Direct Comparison Approach

As explained in Chapter 4, the success of the direct comparison approach depends on comparability. This means that if a multibusiness firm is to be valued in the aggregate, the comparable firms must also be multibusiness firms with similar business profiles. Assuming such comparable firms can be found, the direct comparison approach can be applied without alteration. Unfortunately, conglomerate firms typically are composed of relatively unique mixes of businesses. This leaves the appraiser with the difficult task of deciding whether two conglomerates are similar enough to apply the direct comparison approach on a firmwide basis. If a clear decision cannot be made, the firm should be appraised on a business line by business line basis because comparability is much easier to assess at that level.

The great advantage of the direct comparison approach for appraising subsidiary business lines is that it reduces the valuation problem to the calculation and application of ratios. The problem is finding publicly traded firms that both can be valued using the stock and debt approach, and are exclusively in the same line of business as the subsidiary being appraised. In many cases, finding pure comparables is surprisingly difficult. For instance, Union Pacific Corporation's subsidiary, Union Pacific Railroad, is valued annually by tax appraisers in the states in which the railroad operates. If "pure" publicly traded railroads that were comparable to Union Pacific Railroad could be found, it would be easy to value the UPRR using a direct comparison. The problem is that essentially all the major railroads in the country are owned by conglomerates. Furthermore, the conglomerates that own the comparable railroads do not own the same mix of businesses as Union Pacific Corporation.

Assuming that publicly traded comparables can be found, the ratios calculated for those companies still should not be applied to the subsidiary business until the financial variables have been adjusted to take account of interfirm allocations. Once again, the problem is making sure that the allocations reflect arm's length prices. For example, if IBM were subsidizing its personal computer division by making memory chips available at below market cost, it would be misleading to apply market value to EBIDT ratios calculated for comparable personal computer makers to the EBIDT of IBM's personal computer division without taking into account the subsidy.

Once interfirm adjustments have been made, the direct comparison approach proceeds precisely as described in Chapter 4. As long as comparables for the subsidiary are available, the approach is applied exactly as if the subsidiary were an independent company.

The Discounted Cash Flow Approach

The DCF approach is sufficiently flexible that it can be applied to a conglomerate firm or to any of its subsidiaries. If the approach is applied to the aggregate firm, then cash flow must be forecast on a firmwide basis. The discount rate in that case is the average cost of funds for the firm as a whole. If the approach is applied to a subsidiary, then cash flow must be forecast for that subsidiary and discounted at that subsidiary's cost of capital.

To reflect the subsidiary's value as an independent business, the costs and benefits provided by headquarters and by other subsidiaries are netted out when forecasting cash flow. Once again, the allocations should be based on arm's length prices.

When applying the DCF approach to subsidiaries, the appraiser needs to bear in mind that each subsidiary business will have its own capital structure and cost of capital. As noted in Chapter 5, a common mistake is assuming that the cost of capital for a subsidiary equals the cost of capital for the parent firm. The best way to avoid this mistake is to think of a conglomerate as a portfolio of companies. Seen in this light, it becomes clear that the cost of capital for a conglomerate is the value weighted average of the costs of capital for each of the subsidiary businesses. Unfortunately, this implies that cost of capital for each of the subsidiary companies must be estimated as if the subsidiary were an independent company.

Unlike independent companies, the cost of capital for a subsidiary can rarely be estimated directly because most subsidiaries do not have publicly traded securities outstanding. They are, therefore, equivalent to privately held firms. As suggested in Chapter 7, the best way to estimate the cost of capital for privately held firms such as Forms Engineering is to find publicly traded firms that operate exclusively, or least primarily, in the same line of business. The cost of capital for these comparables can then be estimated using the standard techniques. As for FEC, the average cost of capital of the comparables, adjusted for leverage, is a reasonable estimate of the cost of capital of the subsidiary.

If comparable publicly traded firms cannot be found, then a less direct approach must be employed to estimate the cost of capital. For debt securities, this involves estimating the effective rating, as described in Chapter 7. For equity, a number of indirect procedures can be employed. If the subsidiary pays a dividend to the parent, the dividend discount model can be applied. Another possibility is estimating the effective beta for the subsidiary and applying the CAPM. By examining data on the betas of companies in similar industries as the target subsidiary, the appraiser can make an informed judgment regarding the subsidiary's beta. That judgment can be enhanced by discussing with management the risks of the business and the relation of those risks to economic activity. Before applying the CAPM to calculate the cost of equity, the beta of the subsidiary must be adjusted to reflect the subsidiary's use of leverage, as described in Chapter 7 for FEC.

When estimating beta for a subsidiary, the beta of the parent company may or may not provide useful information. The beta of a conglomerate equals the value weighted average of the betas of its subsidiaries. Therefore, if all the subsidiary businesses have similar betas, the parent firm's beta is a good proxy for all of them. However, if the betas of the subsidiaries vary markedly, the beta of the parent is unlikely to provide useful information about the beta of any individual subsidiary.

Like the financing costs, the capital structure weights used to calculate the WACC should be estimated as if the subsidiary were an independent company. The problem is that these capital structure weights may be a good deal different than the capital structure weights of the parent firm or the capital structure weights that headquarters imposes on the subsidiary. For example, a subsidiary may be financed 100 percent by loans from the parent, but this does not mean that the appropriate capital structure is 100 percent debt. Few independent companies in any industry are financed 100 percent with debt.

The solution, once more, is to find publicly traded companies that are comparable to the subsidiary and use their capital structures weights as an estimate of the capital structure weights of the subsidiary. If comparable firms are not available, then wider industry data, combined with appraiser judgment and management input, must be relied on, as with the estimate of beta.

Dealing with Multinational Firms

Valuing foreign subsidiaries raises two additional appraisal problems. The most obvious problem is that the financial flows of a foreign subsidiary are measured in terms of a foreign currency. Somehow, the value produced by those flows must be translated into U.S. dollars. The allocation problem is also exacerbated when a firm operates internationally. International companies have a host of political and tax incentives for moving costs and benefits from one locale to another.

If the subsidiary is located in a country with a developed capital market, the foreign exchange problem can be handled in a straightforward manner. The value of the subsidiary is estimated in terms of the local currency, using local currency accounting information, local currency cash flows, and a local currency discount rate. The estimated value is then translated into U.S. dollars at the spot exchange rate in existence on the lien date. (The spot exchange rate is the price of foreign exchange for immediate delivery. The price of foreign exchange for deferred delivery is referred to as the forward rate.) For instance, Apple Computer has a German subsidiary. If, on the basis of available German data, an appraiser estimates that the German subsidiary is worth 500 million deutsche marks on December 31, 1991, that value is translated at the spot exchange rate of $.64 per deutsche mark, which prevailed on December 31. The resulting value in terms of U.S. dollars is 320 million.

If the subsidiary is located in a country such as Peru that does not have a developed and free capital market, the analysis becomes more complicated. Without a developed and free capital market, it is no longer possible to estimate directly a local currency discount rate. Nonetheless, the appraiser may attempt to approximate the local currency discount rate and proceed as described above. Another alternative is to forecast cash flows the parent company expects to receive from the subsidiary each year in terms of local currency and then to translate these forecasts into U.S. dollars. This requires estimation of future exchange rates instead of a local currency discount rate. Because the foreign exchange market is often more developed than the local currency capital market, it may be possible to get data on forward foreign exchange rates in situations where data on local currency interest rates are not available. These forward rates represent the rates at which banks are currently willing to make a contract to exchange dollars for local currency at specified future dates. The U.S. dollar cash flow forecast is calculated by multiplying the local currency cash flow forecast by the forward exchange rate for that date. Once the cash flows have been translated into dollars, an American discount rate can be applied. It is by no means obvious, however, what American discount rate is appropriate. The correct discount rate must reflect the systematic risk of the dollar cash flows, including exchange risk and the risk that the money will not be received at all because of political problems in the foreign country or a deterioration in the relationship between the foreign country and the United States.

The guiding principle for allocating costs and benefits among the divisions of a multinational firm remains estimating the cash flows that would have occurred if all of the subsidiaries were independent firms. This is the same principle that national taxing authorities attempt to apply when determining whether a multinational firm is altering transfer prices in order to reduce taxes. For instance, a major international bank agreed to pay a settlement to the German government after it was charged with manipulating transfer prices so that profits disappeared in Germany (a high-tax country) and appeared in the Cayman Islands (a low-tax country).

Unfortunately, it is extraordinarily difficult to calculate arm's length prices for internationally traded goods. The IRS and other taxing authorities have been struggling for years to establish guidelines for determining arm's length transfer prices. Because it is unclear how an appraiser, with limited time and budget, could improve on the work of the taxing authorities, a reasonable rule of thumb is to reallocate cash flows between subsidiaries only when at least one country's government claims it is necessary to do so.

ESTIMATING THE COST OF CAPITAL FOR DERIVATIVE SECURITIES

Put simply, estimating the cost of capital for derivative securities is complicated. Application of sophisticated models such as the Black-Scholes option pricing model is required to estimate the cost of capital for even the simplest derivative securities.[1] Estimating the cost of capital for more realistic derivative securities such as convertible or callable bonds leads to equations of such complexity that they can only be solved by numerical techniques. Developing the computer programs to numerically solve the equations requires expertise in both mathematics and finance. Thus, an appraiser who finds that derivative securities account for a significant fraction of the target firm's capital structure should seek expert advice on estimating the cost of capital.

While sophisticated models and numerical techniques are useful tools for estimating the cost of capital for derivative securities, their power should not be overestimated. There are problems that the models hide from the unsuspecting. The most troubling problem is that cost of capital for derivative securities is not constant; instead, it depends, among other things, on the value of the company's equity. This leads to a complex interrelation between the cost of capital and the value of the firm.

To illustrate the problems caused by derivative securities, two specific examples are considered. The first example involves a hypothetical Microsoft warrant with characteristics that are chosen

---

[1]Fischer Black and Myron Scholes are credited with developing the first closed form solution to the problem of pricing derivative securities. The classic paper in which the model is developed is F. Black and M. Scholes, "The Pricing of Options and Corporate Liabilities," *Journal of Political Economy* 81 (June 1973), pp. 637–54.

so that the Black-Scholes option pricing model is applicable. The second examples involves an IBM convertible bond for which the cost of capital cannot be estimated without the application of numerical techniques.

The Microsoft Warrant Example

The lien date for this example is December 19, 1991. On that day, Microsoft stock was trading at $102.75. In his analysis of the cost of capital, the appraiser decided to use 10-year Treasury bonds to estimate the risk-free rate. On December 19, the true annualized yield on a 10-year Treasury bond was 7.25 percent. In addition, the appraiser decided to use 7.5 percent, the long-run historical average with respect to 10-year Treasury bonds, as a measure of the market risk premium. Finally, the appraiser estimated that Microsoft had a beta of 1.75. Given this information, the cost of equity capital for Microsoft was estimated to be 20.38 percent by applying the CAPM (Cost of capital = $7.25 + 1.75 \cdot 7.5 = 20.38\%$).

Suppose that, in addition to its other securities, Microsoft also has outstanding warrants. Warrants are long-lived options that give their holders the right to purchase the underlying stock. In the Microsoft hypothetical, the warrants give their holders the right to purchase Microsoft stock any time in the next three years at a price of $105 per share. As will be shown shortly, such warrants would have a market price of approximately $32.25. The price may seem extraordinarily high, because the warrants would be worthless if they had to be exercised immediately. Investors who exercised the warrants on the lien date would pay $105 for the stock, when it could be purchased in the marketplace for only $102.75. It is clear, therefore, that the value of the warrants is derived from the discretion and the leverage they provide. Holders of the warrants have the right, but not the obligation, to buy Microsoft at $105. If the stock soars, say to $200, by the expiration, holders will exercise the warrant and buy the stock at a bargain price of $105. If the stock fails to rise, they will let the warrant expire worthless. In that case, the investor loses only the amount paid for the warrant.

It is this contingent nature of options that makes their value dependent on the variability of the returns on the underlying stock. Because option holders benefit when the price of the underlying stock rises, but can let the option expire worthless when the stock price falls, they will pay more for options on highly variable stocks with the potential for dramatic upside moves. The Black-Scholes model, the original and best-known option pricing model, takes this into account by including the standard deviation of returns for the underlying stock as an input in the model.

The Black-Scholes formula for the price of options or warrants on nondividend paying stock is given by the following equation:

$$P = S \cdot N(d_1) - E \cdot N(d_2)e^{-rt} \qquad (9\text{--}1)$$

where:

d_1 = $[\ln(S/E) + (r + \sigma^2/2)t] / \sigma\sqrt{t}$
d_2 = $[\ln(S/E) + (r - \sigma^2/2)t] / \sigma\sqrt{t}$
P = Price of the option
S = Price of the underlying stock
E = Exercise price of the option
t = Time remaining before expiration (in years)
r = Continuously compounded risk-free rate of interest on a security that matures at the time the option expires
σ = Standard deviation of continuously compounded returns on the stock
$N(d)$ = Probability that a deviation of less than d will occur in a normal distribution with a mean of zero and a standard deviation of 1

Though the formula may appear daunting, computer programs that solve it are widely available. There are two points, however, that should be noted about the equation. First, it depends on the standard deviation of returns on the stock. Because this quantity is not observable directly, like all the other model inputs are, it must be estimated by computing historical returns and estimating their standard deviation. Second, the equation is stated in terms of continuously compounded returns, so care must be taken to express interest rates in the same form.[2]

---

[2]A discussion of continuous compounding can be found in any of the finance textbooks noted in Chapter 1.

In the case of Microsoft, the standard deviation of returns was estimated to be 35 percent per year. The other remaining input is the three-year risk-free rate. This rate is taken to be 7 percent per year compounded continuously. Substituting these numbers into the Black-Scholes formula gives a warrant price of $32.25.

The cost of capital for warrants can be estimated by applying the hedging argument used by Black and Scholes to develop their option pricing model. Black and Scholes showed that simple options such as the hypothetical Microsoft warrants can be replicated by borrowing just the right amount of money and mixing it with personal funds to purchase Microsoft stock. Unfortunately, the proper mix of personal investment and borrowing is a function of the price of the underlying stock and the warrant's remaining life, so that the mix has to be updated continuously to maintain the hedge. Nonetheless, at each point in time, the warrant can be thought of as being equivalent to leveraged ownership of the stock. It is possible, therefore, to calculate the beta of the warrant using the procedures similar to those developed in Chapter 7 for estimating the beta of leveraged securities.

Following this line of reasoning, Galai and Masulis showed that the beta of a warrant equals the following:[3]

Beta of warrant =

$$\frac{\text{(Beta of stock)(Delta of warrant)(Price of stock)}}{\text{Price of Warrant}} \qquad (9\text{-}2)$$

In Equation (9-2), delta is the hedge ratio derived from the Black-Scholes model. It is the number of shares of stock that the investors must purchase to replicate the warrant. For instance, if delta = 0.5, then to replicate a warrant, the investor must combine the purchase of ½ share of stock with the appropriate amount of borrowing. In the case of the Microsoft warrants, application of the Black-Scholes option pricing model gives a delta of 0.73.[4]

---

[3]D. Galai and R. Masulis, "The Option Pricing Model and the Risk Factor of Stock," *Journal of Financial Economics* 3 (March 1976), pp. 53–82.

[4]In the context of the Black-Scholes model, the hedge ratio is $N(d_1)$. Hedge ratios produced by more complicated option pricing models are presented by J. C. Cox and M. Rubinstein, *Option Markets*, (Englewood Cliffs, N.J.: Prentice Hall, 1985).

Substituting the data for the hypothetical Microsoft warrants into equation (9–1) yields:

$$\text{Beta of warrant} = \frac{(1.75)\ (0.73)\ (102.75)}{32.25} = 4.10$$

The beta of the warrant is more than twice that of the stock because of the implicit leverage provided by the warrant. Whereas it costs $102.75 to buy a share of stock, the equivalent of 0.73 shares of stock can be purchased for $32.25 by buying the warrant.

Applying the CAPM to a security with a beta of 4.10, the cost of capital for the warrant, as of December 19, 1991, is found to be 38.0 percent (7.25 + 4.10 · 7.5). The "as of" date is important. If the price of Microsoft stock rose to $125, then according to the Black-Scholes model, the price of the warrant would jump to $49.58 and the delta would increase to 0.825. Substituting these values into Equation (9–2), the warrant beta falls to 3.6 and the cost of capital drops accordingly. This illustrates the sensitivity of the cost of capital of derivative securities to changes in the value of the underlying security.

The problem with using the Black-Scholes model to estimate the cost of capital for derivative securities is that the model depends on a number of restrictive assumptions: markets are perfect, there are no taxes, the stock price follows a lognormal diffusion, the stock does not pay dividends, there is no reason to exercise the derivative prior to maturity, and investors are able to borrow and lend at a constant risk-free rate of interest. The hypothetical Microsoft was constructed so that these assumptions largely were satisfied. In most situations, however, one or more of the assumptions is not applicable. Unfortunately, as soon as the assumptions are relaxed, the pricing equations become so complex that closed form solutions cannot be derived. Nonetheless, approximate solutions can be calculated by applying the hedging argument and utilizing numerical techniques. The problem is analogous to that encountered by engineers. Closed form solutions can be derived only for simple problems like calculating the motion of colliding billiard balls. The equations for real-world problems, such as explaining the flow of air over an airplane wing, are so complicated that numerical approximations must be employed.[5]

Estimating the Cost of Convertible Debt

Convertible bonds are an example of securities that include options. A convertible bond is a bond that can be exchanged for a fixed number of shares of stock at certain times during its life. The option feature arises because of the discretion convertible bonds give their holders—the bonds may be exchanged for stock, but they do not have to be exchanged. For example, on December 1, 1991, IBM had outstanding a convertible bond that matured on May 15, 2004. The bond, which was rated AAA, paid a coupon of 7⅞ percent and was convertible at any time prior to maturity into 6.51 shares of IBM stock. The price of the bond on December 1, was 92½, and the yield to maturity at that price was 7.64 percent.

In the parlance of convertible securities, the IBM bond is said to have a conversion ratio of 6.51 and a conversion price of $156.50. The conversion price measures the amount of the bond's par value that must be given up to purchase one share of stock. As long as the stock price is below the conversion price and the dividend payout rate is below the interest rate on the bond, bondholders will never voluntarily convert. Furthermore, they will not necessarily convert as soon as the stock price rises above the conversion price for two reasons. First, they lose the interest on the bond. Second, they lose the right to convert. As long as they hold the bond, investors maintain the right to convert. Once they convert, that right is lost.

Given its high rating, if the bond were not convertible, its yield to maturity would be a reasonable estimate for its cost of capital. However, if the bond were converted, its cost of capital would be equal to that of IBM's equity. Assuming that IBM's equity has a beta of approximately 1.0, the risk premium on the market is 7.5 percent, and the risk-free rate is 7.2 percent, the cost of equity

---

[5]See John Hull, *Options, Futures, and other Derivative Securities*, (Englewood Cliffs, N.J.: Prentice Hall, 1989), for details on the numerical procedure used to value derivative securities and to estimate their cost of capital.

capital for IBM is 14.7 percent. The bond yield of 7.64 percent and cost of equity of 14.7 percent place bounds on the cost of capital for the convertible bond. The problem is determining where, within that range, the cost of capital lies during the period of time in which the bondholders have the right to convert, but have not yet done so.

From an option pricing perspective, a convertible bond that is not callable is a combination of a straight bond and a nondetachable warrant that gives the bondholder the right to buy the stock at the conversion price by turning over the bond. The warrant has the restriction that only the bond can be used to pay the exercise price of the warrant. To estimate the cost of capital for a convertible bond, therefore, an option pricing model is required to analyze the implicit warrant.

Interest rate derivative securities such as convertible bonds usually cannot be valued by applying the Black-Scholes model, or a simple variant of the model, for a number of reasons. First, the stochastic behavior of interest rates is difficult to specify. Furthermore, the evidence that is available on the behavior of interest rates is not consistent with the assumptions of the Black-Scholes model. Neither interest rates nor bond prices follow lognormal diffusions. Second, bond prices depend not only on the current short-term interest rate but on the entire term structure of interest rates. The Black-Scholes model assumes that there is one random variable. For example, in the case of the Microsoft warrants, the random variable was the Microsoft stock price. Third, the risk-free rate can hardly be assumed to remain constant in a bond pricing model because variation in interest rates is the prime reason that bond prices change.

The current solution to these problems is to use numerical techniques to value interest-sensitive derivative securities and to estimate their cost of capital. The first step in developing a numerical solution algorithm is to construct a stochastic model that approximates movements in interest rates. Simple models are based on the assumption that the entire term structure of interest rates depends only on variation in the short-term interest rate. More complex models allow for the term structure to depend on several "state" variables. Unfortunately, as of this writing, there is no strong consensus on the proper stochastic model for interest rates. Therefore, a conservative approach is to develop several models and to see how sensitive the conclusions are to the choice of model.

Once a stochastic model to approximate future movements in interest rates has been specified, future changes in interest rates are simulated by seeding the model with computer-generated random numbers. Based on these inputs, the computer generates one possible path for future interest rates. Assuming that actual interest rates follow this path, the values of interest rate–sensitive derivative claims are calculated. The process of generating a path for future interest rates is then repeated, and the value of the derivative securities is calculated. After the process has been repeated thousands of times, the average value of the derivative security across all the repetitions is calculated. This average is the numerical solution for the value of the derivative security.

Numerical simulations can also be used to estimate the cost of capital for the derivative securities. Returning to Equation (9–2), if the delta can be estimated, the cost of capital for the derivative security can be calculated. Because delta measures the gain or loss on the derivative security per dollar change in the value of the underlying equity, it can be estimated by changing the starting price of the stock slightly and recalculating the value of the derivative security. The ratio of the change in price of the derivative security to the change in the stock price, averaged over all the simulation runs, is an estimate of delta. Substituting that estimate of delta into Equation (9–2) yields an estimate of the beta of the derivative security to which the CAPM can be applied to calculate the cost of capital. In the case of the IBM convertibles, this procedure yields a cost of capital of 10.9 percent. A rough check reveals that this is a reasonable estimate because it falls between the cost of the convertible as debt (7.64 percent) and the cost of the convertible as equity (14.7 percent).

Convertibility features are not the only options that make the valuation of the interest rate–derivative securities complicated. For instance, many bonds are callable. A callable bond is a bond that can be repurchased at the issuing company's discretion at a fixed price during a predetermined period of time. It is not uncommon for bonds to be both callable and convertible. This makes it possible for the issuing company to force conversion by calling the bond. If the value of the shares into which a bond can be converted exceeds the price at which the issuing company can call the bond, then a call by the issuer will "force" investors to convert their bonds. Callable and callable-convertible bonds can also be valued using numerical techniques.

The fact that numerical techniques provide precise numbers for the cost of capital of derivative securities can produce a false sense of security. The output of a numerical model is only as accurate as the stochastic models on which the simulation is based. As noted above, there is a good deal of debate about the appropriate stochastic model to use to approximate future variation in interest rates. Changing from one stochastic model to another can have a marked impact on the estimated value of derivative securities and the associated cost of capital.

The sensitivity of estimates of the cost of capital to the assumed stochastic model puts appraisers in a difficult position. Most appraisers do not have the training necessary to evaluate the complicated financial models on which the numerical simulations are based. It is critical, therefore, that the help of disinterested experts be sought if derivative securities are a significant fraction of the firm's capital structure.

ESTIMATING THE VALUE OF MANAGERIAL FLEXIBILITY

The discounted cash flow approach to valuation is incomplete in that it fails to account for managerial flexibility. Recall how the DCF model works. Cash flow forecasts are constructed based on today's assessment of the company's future operations. Those projected cash flows are then discounted to present value. However, no account is taken of the fact that operating policy may be altered as conditions change and as managers become aware of new information. An example drawn from the path-breaking work of Brennan and Schwartz illustrates how valuable such flexibility can be.[6]

---

[6]M. J. Brennan and E. S. Schwartz, "Evaluating Natural Resource Investments," *Journal of Business* 58 (April 1985), pp. 135–57.

Imagine that the firm being appraised operates a gold mine. The future cash flows produced by the firm will depend on the future price of gold, the amount of gold found in the mine, and the cost of extraction. By developing forecasts for each of these variables, estimates of future cash flow can be constructed and discounted to present value. But this forecasting procedure ignores the flexibility that management has to respond to changing conditions. For instance, if the price of gold drops dramatically, the mine can be temporarily shut. On the other hand, production may be increased sharply following a revolution in mining technology that cuts the cost of extraction in half.

A simple numerical illustration provides further insight into how this flexibility increases the value of the mine. Suppose that the current price of gold is $400 per ounce and that it is known that there are 100,000 ounces of gold in the mine that can be removed next year at a cost of $380 per ounce. Assume, furthermore, that the price of gold next year will be either $300 with probability ½ or $500 with probability ½, so that the expected price of gold is $400, the same as today's price. Based on an expected price of gold of $400, the expected cash flow next year is $2 million ($20 dollars profit per ounce times 100,000 ounces). If the discount rate is 10 percent, the current value of the mine is $1.81 million. However, this DCF calculation ignores the fact that management has the option not to extract the gold next year if the price is not high enough. In fact, management would wait to see what the price of gold was before determining whether to extract it. If the price of gold turns out to be $300, the gold is left in the ground and the cash flow is zero. If the price of gold turns out to be $500, the gold is mined at a profit of $120 per ounce and the cash flow is $12 million. Accordingly, the value of the mine is:

Value of the mine = Present value of [½ · 0 (the gold is left
in the ground)
+ ½ · $120 · 100,000 (gold is mined)]
= PV($6 million) = $5.45 million

The DCF value ($1.81 million) understates the true value ($5.45 million) because it ignores management's option to leave the gold in the ground.

Although the gold mine example is oversimplified, options of a similar nature arise in the course of business at many companies.

Consider, for instance, an investment that involves developing and bringing to market new microcomputer software. The product development process takes three years and costs $10 million. Beginning in the fourth year, the project is expected to return $5 million a year for the next four years. If the discount rate is 10 percent, the present value of the cash inflows is $13.7 million, so the project appears to have a net present value of $3.7 million. But this calculation ignores management's option to stop work. One of the great risks of software development is that while a project is underway, a competitive product will be developed or market conditions will change, so that the product under development is rendered obsolete. The DCF analysis assumes that even when conditions change, the company plunges ahead with development as planned. The option pricing approach recognizes that management has the flexibility to terminate development as soon as it realizes that the product will not be competitive, thereby eliminating further costs.

Though managerial flexibility takes many forms, a number of situations have been identified in which the associated options are likely to be particularly valuable.[7] One is the option to accelerate or defer an investment. For instance, an oil company may have plans to begin construction of a new refinery in two years. However, if the price of oil jumps, construction can be accelerated, while if the price of oil plummets, construction can be deferred. These options to accelerate or defer the investment can add as much as 25 percent to the present value of the income stream expected from a refinery.

Related to the options to accelerate and defer are the options to expand and contract. In the oil refinery case, for instance, it may be possible to expand or contract the size of the plant in response to changes in the long-run outlook for the price of oil or other economic developments. An extreme example of the option to contract is to shut down the project entirely.

A third class of options arises because of project interdependence. Many projects are not independent, but instead consist of

---

[7]For a more detailed discussion of the value of managerial options and some example calculations, see L. Trigeorgis and S. P. Mason, "Valuing Managerial Flexibility," *Midland Corporate Finance Journal*, Spring 1987, pp. 14–21.

a series of links. For example, Brealey and Myers note that before a company can develop the Mark II computer, it must first develop and build the Mark I.[8] The knowledge and skill obtained in the production of the Mark I make it possible to develop the Mark II. In this context, investing in the Mark I project is analogous to purchasing an option on the Mark II project. Consequently, a company may choose to develop the Mark I, even though the Mark I project has a negative net present value considered in isolation, because undertaking the Mark I project gives the company the valuable option to develop the Mark II.

It is worth noting that the problem of undervaluing investment projects is likely to be particularly acute for strategic investments. Many strategic investments such as investments in R&D, brand names, distribution networks, or factory automation are but the first step in a chain of subsequent investment decisions. If the company takes the first step, it has the option to make a series of follow-on investments. If the company does not take the first step, the follow-on investments are lost. When valuing initial investments that are part of a potential chain, it is critical that the appraiser take into account the options they provide.

The examples illustrate that in many situations, managerial options will have significant value, but other than in the simplified gold mine example with a one-year horizon, they do not provide a method for valuing the options. In fact, valuing managerial options in a realistic setting is a daunting task. The best that can be hoped for is a reasonable approximation. The problem is complicated because accurate valuation of managerial options requires a complete description of all possible future events along with a depiction of how management would respond to each contingency. Figure 9–1 presents a more detailed example that illustrates the analytical approach.

The figure is based on a hypothetical overseas oil drilling project. The project has three steps: exploratory drilling, negotiation with the foreign government, and production and marketing. Each step is assumed to have two possible outcomes, one good and one bad. The exploratory drilling may find a large or

---

[8]R. Brealey and S. C. Myers, *Principles of Corporate Finance* (New York: McGraw-Hill, 1991), pp. 512–13.

FIGURE 9-1
The Oil Production Decision Tree without Options

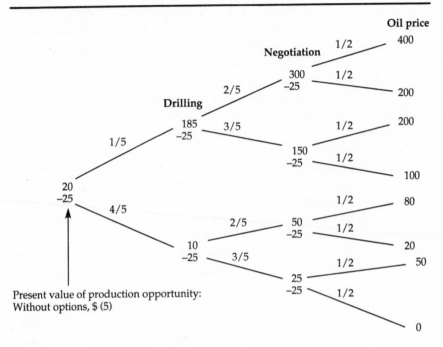

small field, the negotiations may be friendly or hostile, and the price of oil may be high or low when production occurs. A probability is assigned to each outcome given what has gone before. For example, the probability of finding a large field is ⅕, while the probability of finding a small field is ⅘. A final outcome is defined by an entire series of steps. The best final outcome is finding a large field, winning a favorable negotiation, and experiencing a high oil price during production and marketing. If that outcome occurs, the firm's revenue is $400 minus the drilling, negotiation, and production costs, each of which is assumed to be $25. Notice that once the outcome has been fully defined, the revenue is assumed to be known. Figure 9-1 shows the final revenues for all eight possible outcomes.

The DCF value of the project can be calculated by multiplying the net revenue associated with each outcome by the probability of that outcome and summing across all outcomes. For instance, the net revenue associated with the best outcome is $325 ($400 − $75) and the probability of that outcome is ⅟₂₅ (= ⅕ · ⅖ · ½), so that the best outcome contributes $13 (325 · ⅟₂₅) to the final present value. (When calculating the DCF value, time discounting is ignored for simplicity.) Computing the net revenue associated with each of the possible outcomes in this fashion and summing gives a total net present value of ($5), as shown in Table 9–1. Because the value is negative, the DCF approach implies that this project would be rejected.

The conclusion that an oil company would reject the drilling project is premised on the assumption that the company must make all the decisions at the start. That is, the company must say either yes, we are going through with the project, in which case they are committed to drilling, negotiating, producing, and marketing; or say no, in which case the entire project is dropped. In reality, a company can avoid this yes or no dichotomy by making decisions sequentially. The company can drill the well and then decide what to do based on the size of the field discovered. If a small field is found, the project can be terminated. Even if a large field is discovered, the company may choose not to go forth with production and marketing if the negotiations go poorly. To value options such as these, it is necessary to solve the decision tree backwards.

The backward solution proceeds as follows. Begin moving out the decision tree in Figure 9–1 from left to right until the last node on a branch is reached. For example, start with the top branch and follow it to the last node at which a large field has been discovered and negotiations have been favorable. At that juncture, there are only two remaining possibilities for cash flow, either $400 or $200, depending on whether the price of oil is high or low. Because each of these events has a probability of ½, the expected value at the node is $300 (½ · 400 + ½ · 200). Subtracting $25, which represents the cost of production and marketing, the value of the project given the positive results from the drilling and the favorable negotiations is found to be $275. Proceeding in this fashion, the expected value can be calculated for each of the nodes prior to the final outcome. For example, the value at the node where the drilling was favorable but the negotiations went poorly is $150 ($½ · 200 + ½ · 100) minus the $25 cost of

TABLE 9–1
Decision Tree Valuation Calculations

	Probabilities Associated with Each Event			Without Option Probabilities Associated with Group of Events	Revenues	Costs	Net Revenues	Contribution of Each Event to Total NPV
	Drilling	Negotiation	Oil Prices					
good, good, good	1/5	2/5	1/2	1/25	400	–75	325	13.00
good, good, bad	1/5	2/5	1/2	1/25	200	–75	125	5.00
good, bad, good	1/5	3/5	1/2	3/50	200	–75	125	7.50
good, bad, bad	1/5	3/5	1/2	3/50	100	–75	25	1.50
bad, good, good	4/5	2/5	1/2	4/25	80	–75	5	0.80
bad, good, bad	4/5	2/5	1/2	4/25	20	–75	–55	(8.80)
bad, bad, good	4/5	3/5	1/2	6/25	50	–75	–25	(6.00)
bad, bad, bad	4/5	3/5	1/2	6/25	0	–75	–75	(18.00)
				1.00				(5.00)

With Option

	Probabilities Associated with Each Event			Probabilities Associated with Group of Events	Revenues	Costs	Net Revenues	Contribution of Each Event to Total NPV
	Drilling	Negotiation	Oil Prices					
good, good, good	1/5	2/5	1/2	1/25	400	-75	325	13.00
good, good, bad	1/5	2/5	1/2	1/25	200	-75	125	5.00
good, bad, good	1/5	3/5	1/2	3/50	200	-75	125	7.50
good, bad, bad	1/5	3/5	1/2	3/50	100	-75	25	1.50
bad, good, good	4/5	2/5	1/2	4/25	0	-25	-25	(4.00)
bad, good, bad	4/5	2/5	1/2	4/25	0	-25	-25	(4.00)
bad, bad, good	4/5	3/5	1/2	6/25	0	-25	-25	(6.00)
bad, bad, bad	4/5	3/5	1/2	6/25	0	-25	-25	(6.00)
				1.00				7.00

production and marketing. Once the values have been calculated at each of the nodes one step before the end, it is possible to work back another step. This procedure is repeated until the beginning of the decision tree is reached. As shown in Figure 9–1, the backward solution yields the same value as calculating the expected cash flow directly, a negative $5.

The advantage of the backward calculation is that it makes it possible to take options into account. Once all the nodes have been filled in, those junctures at which the remaining expected value is less than zero can be identified. At that point, rational managers would let the option to proceed with the project expire by abandoning operations. In Figure 9–1, the value for proceeding once exploratory drilling indicates a small field is ($15). Therefore, zero should be substituted at this node and at all nodes to the right of it since the project would be terminated. Figure 9–2 reproduces Figure 9–1 with zero substituted at all nodes following a point at which management would choose to cancel the project. With the options included, Figure 9–2 and Table 9–1 show that the value of the project rises to $7. Because of the ability to terminate if exploratory drilling does not yield promising results, the project is worth undertaking. In fact, drilling the initial well can be thought of as buying an option to proceed with the project for $25. If the results are good, the option is exercised and the firm goes forward with the negotiations. If the results are negative, the option is allowed to expire and the project is terminated.

There is one other advantage to the option pricing approach that is not illustrated by the example because time is not explicitly considered. When a time element is added, it is also necessary to calculate a discount rate for each step of the tree. The DCF approach assumes that the discount rate is constant and equal to the WACC. However, the asymmetric nature of the payoffs introduced by the option to terminate the project means that the risk of the project is not constant. Using the option pricing approach, it is possible to take into account these changes in the discount rate. That analysis, however, is beyond the scope of this book.[9]

---

[9]For a further discussion, see Trigeorgis and Mason, *Valuing Managerial Flexibility,* or S. P. Mason and R. Merton, "The Role of Contingent Claims Analysis in Corporate Fi-

FIGURE 9–2
The Oil Production Decision Tree with Options

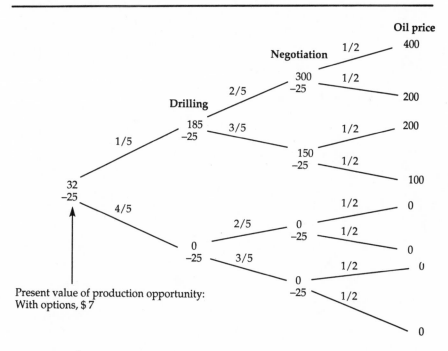

Do Appraisal Approaches Other than Discounted Cash Flow Take Managerial Flexibility into Account?

The foregoing demonstrates that the discounted cash flow approach fails to take into account investment options, but what about the other appraisal approaches? The book value approaches based on cost clearly ignore investment options because the cost of an asset does not take into account the options it may provide the owner. The liquidation value is less clear. If the company can sell its assets as part of an ongoing operation, then the buyer may be willing to pay for the options the assets convey. For example, if Campbell Soup sells its brand name along with its soup-

nance," in *Recent Advances in Corporate Finance*, ed. E. Altman and M. Subrahmanyam (Homewood, Ill.: Richard D. Irwin, 1985).

making facilities, the buyer would pay a price that reflects the options for profitable future investments conveyed by the brand name.

In an efficient market, the stock and debt approach will reflect the value of all managerial options. In valuing a company's securities, astute investors will take account of the options management has to respond to changing circumstances. Therefore, the appraiser does not have to adjust the stock and debt value to take into account managerial flexibility. This is another strength of the stock and debt approach.

The direct comparison approach should also take into account managerial flexibility as long as the comparable companies are valued by the stock and debt approach. Comparability, in this context, must be broadly defined, so that the comparable companies have similar flexibility in responding to changing conditions and possess similar investment options. In cases where the appraisal target is in an industry in which managerial options are likely to be important, such as natural resource exploitation, carefully choosing comparable companies that have comparable options is critical.

The fact that the stock and debt and direct comparison approaches typically take into account managerial flexibility and investment options while the standard discounted cash flow model does not is one reason why value indicators produced by the competing approaches may diverge. Holding all else equal, which of course cannot be done in practice, the difference between the stock and debt value of a company and the discounted cash flow value should be equal to the value of the investment options neglected by the DCF analysis.

Index

Also available from **IRWIN** *Professional Publishing...*

Valuing a Business
The Analysis and Appraisal of Closely Held Companies,
Second Edition

Shannon P. Pratt

More than 20,000 copies sold in the first edition. Includes step-by-step ways to compile the information you need for a final appraisal report.
ISBN: 1-55623-127-X

Workouts and Turnarounds
The Handbook of Restructuring and Investing in Distressed Companies

Edited by Dominic DiNapoli, Sanford C. Sigoloff, and Robert F. Cushman

Experts show you how to pick the right strategy, determine the tactics that work best, and choose the right people to drive the turnaround.
ISBN: 1-55623-335-3

The Art of M&A
A Merger/Acquisition/Buyout Guide

Stanley Foster Reed

Written by the very same people who are pinpointing the targets, structuring the financings, finding the money, negotiating the terms, writing the contracts, and, most important, closing the deals.
ISBN: 1-55623-113-X

Corporate Financial Analysis
Decisions in a Global Environment, Fourth Edition

Diana R. Harrington and Brent D. Wilson

Focusing on today's global business environment, the fourth edition of this hands-on management guide shows you how to evaluate the costs and benefits of financial decisions in the United States and abroad.
ISBN: 1-55623-900-9

Techniques of Financial Analysis,
Seventh Edition

Erich A. Helfert

This classic continues to serve as the clearest, most concise, and practical guide to the critical financial variables that must be weighed in decisions on investments, operations, and financing.
ISBN: 1-55623-388-4

Available at fine bookstores and libraries everywhere.